SO-AYD-168

AGRARIAN WOMEN

AGRARIAN

WIVES AND MOTHERS

STUDIES IN RURAL CULTURE • JACK TEMPLE KIRBY • EDITOR

WOMEN

IN RURAL NEBRASKA, 1880–1940 • *Deborah Fink*

THE UNIVERSITY OF NORTH CAROLINA PRESS • CHAPEL HILL • LONDON

© 1992 THE UNIVERSITY OF NORTH CAROLINA PRESS
ALL RIGHTS RESERVED
MANUFACTURED IN THE UNITED STATES OF AMERICA

The paper in this book meets the guidelines for permanence and durability of
the Committee on Production Guidelines for Book Longevity of the
Council on Library Resources.

96   95   94   93   92   5   4   3   2   1

Library of Congress Cataloging-in-Publication Data
Fink, Deborah, 1949–
      Agrarian women : wives and mothers in rural Nebraska, 1880–1940 /
by Deborah Fink.
          p.   cm.—(Studies in rural culture)
      Includes bibliographical references and index.
      ISBN 0-8078-2019-9 (alk. paper).—ISBN 0-8078-4364-4 (pbk. :
alk. paper)
          1. Rural women—Nebraska—History.   2. Farmers' wives—Nebraska—
History.   3. Nebraska—Rural conditions.   I. Title.   II. Series.
HQ1438.N2F56   1992
305.4'09782'091734—dc20   91-31410
                                                                                  CIP

The author is grateful for permission to reproduce passages from the following:

Diary of Hannah Priscilla Patterson Johnson.
Reprinted by permission of Helen B. Platt.

My Ántonia, by Willa Cather.
Copyright © 1918 by Willa Sibert Cather; copyright renewed 1946 by Willa Sibert
Cather. Copyright © 1926 by Willa Sibert Cather; copyright renewed 1954 by Edith
Lewis. Copyright © 1949 by Houghton Mifflin Co.; copyright renewed 1977 by
Bertha Handlan. Reprinted by permission of Houghton Mifflin Co.

The Nebraska Farmer, Editorial, 26 November 1932.
Reprinted by permission from The Nebraska Farmer.

A Prairie Doctor of the Eighties, by Francis A. Long.
Reprinted by permission of Huse Publishing Co.

Sandhill Sundays, by Mari Sandoz.
Copyright © 1963 by the University of Nebraska Press. Copyright © 1970 by the
Mari Sandoz Corporation. Reprinted by permission McIntosh and Otis, Inc.

To Kate Walters Hansen

Carole Henning Larson

Kathy Wilson Young

CONTENTS

ACKNOWLEDGMENTS

I am grateful to all the Nebraskans who cooperated by allowing interviews, giving me leads, and sharing their insights. Most must remain anonymous in order to protect the confidentiality of research subjects. One person from an institutional setting who was particularly helpful was Jean Dederman of Northeast Nebraska Technological College, who coordinates a program for homemakers returning to the labor force. Her interest in the project, her referrals, and her knowledge of the lives of rural women deepened the study.

The Rockefeller Foundation Rural Women and Feminist Issues Residency Program at the University of Iowa provided excellent space and support for the year I spent writing the book. Margery Wolf, the principal investigator for the program, offered good advice and encouragement. Jane Taylor Nelsen's careful reading and reflection on the Luna Kellie manuscript provided many insights. Cathy Lundoff, my research assistant, did library work, read drafts, and made comments. Among the other helpful commentators were Deborah Symonds, Linda Kerber, Malcolm Rohrbough, Katherine Jellison, Barbara Handy-Marchello, Rich Horwitz, Osha Davidson, and members of the feminist reading group.

Scholars outside of Iowa City have also shaped this book. Dorothy Schwieder of Iowa State University, with her broad knowledge of midwestern history, has offered helpful suggestions at all points. All of my work draws on the intellectual power of Carsten Hess, a Danish ethnologist whose writings and reflections on the cultural history of Denmark have opened my mind. Mikel Johnson and I have spent years talking out the issues in this book, and her insights and experiences have blended with mine. Paul Betz of the University of North Carolina Press has had faith in this manuscript and has worked perceptively and sensitively with me in its revision. Jack Kirby and two anonymous readers also critiqued the manuscript and influenced the final product. Pamela Upton, the project editor, worked skillfully to smooth out the wording and to convert the manuscript into a book.

The staffs of institutions where I used records, archives, and reference materials also contributed to my research. These included the Love and Thompson libraries at the University of Nebraska, the University of Iowa libraries, Parks Library at Iowa State University, the National Archives in Washington, D.C., the National Archives Repository in Kansas City, the Nebraska State Historical Archives in Lincoln, and the Boone County Courthouse in Albion, Nebraska. Donna Bailey, Carrie Louvar, Mara Soloway, and Maureen Taylor, office staff for the University of Iowa's women's studies and Rockefeller programs, extended much-appreciated help with typing, photocopying, and organizing.

My father and his wife, Donovon and Dorothy Walters, both lifetime residents of rural Nebraska, shared their diverse perspectives and enthusiasm for this project. My father encouraged my work and talked about his childhood. Although Dorothy's sense of women's lives has never been the same as mine, she has spent hours telling me stories of Boone County and her life. My mother, Susan Walters, has also told me many stories about rural Nebraska. Her experiences and her life choices were a major impetus in my desire to explore issues of women and family.

Three rural Nebraska women shaped my thinking at its roots. Kathy Wilson Young, my "best friend" from elementary years, was married and living on a Boone County farm with her husband and four children when I returned to do research. Her close nuclear family ties and her remarkable extended family have always fascinated me. Kathy's practical suggestions, continuing friendship, and infectious laughter oriented me while I was in Boone County. My sister, Kate Walters Hansen, has been a thoughtful observer of rural life. She shared her insights, introduced me to her friends, suggested texts, and told stories. Her knowledge of courthouse records and rural politics saved me time and mistakes. Carole Henning Larson, my college friend, was practicing law and living with her husband

and children in rural Saunders County as I was doing my work. Her needle-sharp intelligence and her refusal to separate this intelligence from her emotions have been touchstones for me for thirty years. Without implying that Kathy, Kate, and Carole will agree with everything I have written, I credit the ideas of these three women for every sentence.

A. M. Fink, George Fink, and Philip Fink have each contributed to this work. George, going above and beyond the call of duty, transcribed interview tapes for me. Philip, who throughout his life has taught me to have fun whatever I was doing, spent a summer with me while I wrote. He added his spirit to the project. A. M. drove back and forth between Nebraska and Iowa, spent a hot May day recording data from wills at the Boone County Courthouse, shared stories of his large family in rural South Dakota, read drafts, and postponed his own research travel to spend a year with me in Iowa City. His support and encouragement allowed the space I needed for this work to mature.

PREFACE

In the 1880s, an Illinois farmer who seemed to be in a rut had an exciting way out. In Nebraska, according to reports, were millions of acres of fertile, free land waiting to be farmed. There was no nobler calling than farming, no better way to bring up a family than on the Nebraska prairie. All it took was hard work. The land would provide ample wealth for the settlers and for uncounted generations of their descendants.

In 1883 Mary and Charles Lederer heeded the call and left the stifling tedium of their Illinois farm for Nebraska, where new opportunity awaited. Traveling with them to Nebraska were the four people they most wanted to know the prosperity and promise of a new life— their active, mischievous sons Louis, 8; Charles, 6; Noah, 4; and John, 1. After a number of months moving around and getting to know Nebraska, they got their farm. In 1885 they settled in Pierce County in east-central Nebraska. While Charles and the older boys broke the ground and tilled the fields, Mary set up housekeeping in a new sod house and tended to everyone. During the next ten years, she gave birth to five more children.

Mary Lederer, my great-grandmother, became a family legend as a pillar of strength. Although she and Charles never prospered as farmers, they raised their eight surviving children well. Mary midwifed childbirths and nursed sick neighbors; she sang hymns in the country church; she loved pretty things; and she never went to pieces. She worked. "For her untiring devotion, *God* gave her blissful resting," eulogized son Louis after her death in 1938 (Lederer 1944).

But what did Mary Lederer herself have to say about her life of devotion? Her husband, writing his memoirs in later life, declared that going to Nebraska was the kind of rash move that young people make before they know better. Mary wrote nothing. She had only minimal education and little chance to practice her basic reading and writing skills. When I asked my grandfather or my mother about her, I was usually answered with a parable stressing hard work, no complaining, sacrifice, and service. Everything seemed filtered and adjusted.

I have always wondered what Mary would say to me and other women of the third generation if we could sit down and tell each other what was on our minds. Was it her idea to come to Nebraska, or was it mostly her husband who wanted to come? What made her happy? What made her angry? What did she hope? What was she afraid of? What did she learn that we should know? What, in retrospect, would she change? Would she think we younger women had come a long way forward or backward?

This book is about Mary Lederer and the other rural women who lived in east-central Nebraska between 1880 and 1940. Among these women were three of my great-grandmothers, one grandmother, and many other relatives. I also grew up in rural Nebraska, although, having been born in 1944, I have known only an echo of the lives they lived.

Because the vast majority of these women lived and worked within their families, I have approached their lives through family roles. First and foremost they were wives and mothers. I had originally hoped to add a section on sisterhood—biological sisterhood and sisterly solidarity with other women and men—but mostly I couldn't find it. Households were likely to be nuclear, and too often the women had left their closest friends behind them as they moved from place to place. Whereas wealthier women could sometimes travel to keep in touch with each other, poorer women's leave-taking was apt to be for life. Many women like Mary Lederer, although not totally illiterate, were not fluent enough in reading and writing to keep up a correspondence that would evoke the distant person's presence.

Most of these women, like the women in my ancestral family, do not appear to have questioned the broad contours of their lives. They married (some of them unhappily), remained loyal and deferential to their husbands, and raised their children to reach beyond their roots to new successes. Some women—including some in my family—

disdained a political voice of their own and ridiculed suffragists. Looking for visible, decisive actions or words of resistance yields little. Their resistance, insofar as it existed, consisted of subtle acts of sabotage, of failure to find peace with their lives on the farms, in their ambitions for their children, and in what was called the "woman problem on the farm." In this book, I construct a context for these women's lives as wives and mothers, a set of conditions—political, economic, geographical, and cultural conditions—that makes sense of what the women did and did not do.

Although my research covered a wide area of east-central Nebraska, I have centered it on Boone County, the place I have always called my home, immediately south and west of where my ancestors settled in Nebraska. I left Boone County in 1961 when I graduated from high school. My parents also left after dissolving their household in the late 1960s. Before I returned to do this study, my closest ongoing family tie to the area had been through my sister, Kate Hansen, who married a farmer in 1973. Kate, her husband, and their three children lived just east of the Boone County line on a farm in Madison County. Largely through her, I had kept up on current gossip, community events, and farm politics in Nebraska.

The questions Kate and I raised together as we puzzled over the paradoxes of the rural women in our families form the core of this book. Agrarian ideology—the celebration of farming and farmers as the heart of American society—permeated the Hansen household, particularly in the context of farm crisis politics of the 1980s. Yet it meshed poorly with the lives of many rural women we knew. It left much of rural women's experience unexplored and seemed to prohibit the questions we needed to ask. Its intensity engulfed and silenced women's voices. What could women have to say that meant anything when measured against a farm crisis? And when, on the farm, was there *not* a crisis? Even though women did much of the work of farming, men seemed to be the real farmers—the ones who mattered. I came to believe that the crisis mentality and the grand political vision were part of a discourse that was foreign to most women.

Yet agrarian ideology was a powerful founding and sustaining principle in rural Nebraska. Many women readily observed that rural life was fundamentally better than urban life. They also voiced a contradictory view, although more tentatively and personally than they expressed the primary agrarian belief. The dominance of agrarian thinking about the past affected the way they remembered and told their stories. Those stories had layers of meaning, each in some sense true on its own terms but often contradicted or placed in a new light by a deeper understanding. An anecdote may clarify this. During my field research I interviewed Rachel, a woman born in 1910 who lived in the remains of what was once a small town in Boone County. I had known her only indirectly before, but she seemed pleased to meet me and talk about her memories, speaking softly and carefully about the old town, her family, and her friends.

In talking about change, Rachel detailed the dissolution of her town, the gradual abandonment of the businesses, and the people who had died or left. Now, she said, there were people living in some of the houses, but no one knew them and they were not part of community life. They weren't like the people who had been there before when there was really a town. One man who lived across the road was an alcoholic. In the early days, some men would go into bars, but no one would drink to cause trouble. In their town, people had lived together, helped each other, and had no trouble. They had had picnics, sleigh-ride parties, and ice cream socials to which everyone came. When Rachel's two children were old enough to start school, she had taken a job in one of the nearby businesses. Her children were independent and managed well. Unfortunately, she explained, her first husband had been in ill health and died young.

Toward the end of the interview the following exchange occurred:

Rachel: My first husband, he was not well. I always had to make the living. I did what I had to do. He was an alcoholic.
DF: And your family and friends helped you.
Rachel: Yes. I didn't like to take anything but what I needed. You know, when your husband's an alcoholic you need more. You don't know what to do. That's the biggest problem. What should you do?
DF: Did you have friends that you could talk these things over with?

Rachel: I didn't, because I thought it was my problem. I
didn't want to aggravate things, I guess.
DF: So this wasn't anything the town helped you with.
Rachel: There was nothing they could do. There was nothing wrong with the town.
DF: If he had had cancer it would have been different.
Rachel: Then they were real good. The second one [hus-
band] had cancer of the lungs. They said, "You'll find someone; you'll get married again." I said, "Why would I?" Of
course that's something I never did talk about. You didn't talk
about an alcoholic. I said, "One drank himself to death; the
next one smoked himself to death; probably the other one
would be running after women." I just thought that. So I said,
"No, never again." I'd enjoy other people, other families. So
my family isn't altogether . . . but nobody's is.

At one level, the small town formed a comforting community. They
were solicitous when Rachel's second husband died of cancer; at such
times rural communities brought food and provided company. When
Rachel said that there was no community problem with alcoholism in
the early days, she was probably truthfully reporting that alcoholism
was simply not a social reality. Community cohesiveness, based on
shared values, could not incorporate her husband's drinking. Rachel's
sister and parents, who lived in the town, must have been a help as
she struggled to raise two children, support a household, and cope
with an alcoholic husband, although she said that they did not provide childcare while she worked. Her family seems to have ignored
her husband's drinking. In fact, I may have been the first person with
whom she discussed the problem, even though everyone must have
known.

If the interview had ended fifteen minutes earlier, I would have
left with the image of a woman, twice married and widowed, with
warm family and community connections. What emerged at the end,
though, was not the standard pro-family statement but a quiet determination not to marry again. The nuclear family had not met Rachel's
needs, but little precedent existed for her to seek material or emotional support outside of that nuclear group. That her own life experi-

ence was not consistent with the rural ideal did not lead her to question the ideal but rather to suppress her words. She suggested that "nobody's" life quite matched the ideal, but the image of a close nuclear family and a comfortable social environment remained as a true representation of rural culture, if not rural society. In one sense the first part of her interview, in which she denied the presence of alcoholism in the earlier town, was a lie; at another level it represented a truth that became clear only in the context of a deeper understanding of her life than she had communicated at first. The layers of truth could entail diametrically opposite images of women's lives.

From having grown up in Boone County and from my fieldwork in rural Denmark and Iowa, I was aware of some potential problems in doing anthropological studies of rural society in Europe and America (Fink 1986, 10–17). What I had not faced before was the immensity of what I was asking of the women involved. I had thought that elderly women would appreciate an attentive listener who wanted to hear the stories of their pasts. This was true in some cases; for other women the past opened onto a sea of pain. Once I fully realized the impossibility of doing a direct interview with my own mother about her life within her nuclear family in the 1920s and 1930s, I could not escape the fact that for some women the past contained more pain than they wanted to process. At times I was appalled at my own cheekiness in asking these women to discuss their personal lives, but by then I had waded in and developed a commitment to the women and the work. I was not going to lay aside the project. And to proceed I had to continue to seek out women's stories and to build my analysis on the things they told me.

Many people, like Rachel, remembered the past selectively and screened out those things they could not accept as part of their lives. Thus, through their memories of the past, they constructed the histories they used to make their lives intelligible—to create their own self-images. What I was doing was probing these constructions and asking questions about how they were put together. Laura Ingalls Wilder, who wrote the popular "Little House" children's books about her rural childhood and marriage, described the selectiveness of her own memory of rural life: "We should be careful, don't you think, about the things we give ourselves to remember" (Wilder 1988b [1937], 180). Although her books painted lovely pictures of a contented rural life on the plains, she acknowledged that she had had to edit her memories: "All I have told is true but it is not the whole truth. There are some stories I wanted to tell but would not be responsible for putting in a book for children, even though I knew them as a child" (Wilder 1988a [1937?], 220). A woman telling her own story, as difficult as it might have been, had greater control in determining the events and the contours of the description than she did when I was asking questions about the unmentionable things that I wanted to know.

Midwestern writer Meridel Le Sueur (born in 1900) also knew the barriers that blocked women from telling their own stories. When she began to ask questions about her own family, her grandmother discouraged and resisted her probing. As Le Sueur remembered, "She hated my writing; she said, 'I spend my life concealing the terrible history of what happened to me and the terrible history of women. Now you are going to tell it!' And I was! She wouldn't tell you anything, and what happened to her was terrible. She was married into rape, she had five children, she hated their beginning and she hated their birth. . . . All those frontier towns were terrible towns of violence—violence against women" (quoted in Hoy 1987, 18). Many women, like Le Sueur's grandmother, did not want to relive experiences that were humiliating or heartbreaking.

My Nebraska fieldwork confirmed that women were less inclined than men to talk about the past. When I addressed mixed groups in rural areas about my work, most of those who volunteered their knowledge of rural women's lives were men. One warm May afternoon I lingered at a senior citizens' center after I had spoken about women's lives in the thirties. When I joined a table of men and women who were playing cards, a man asked me if I was a women's libber, to which I answered yes. He complained that everywhere he went women were screeching about equal rights. There were no equal rights in the thirties. Women just took care of their families, and they were too busy to talk about rights. Another man added, "It takes a heap o' livin' to make a house a home."

These men spoke first and most authoritatively, but the discussion sparked a different response from the women. Possibly because of the warmth of the day and the approaching summer, the women talked about weather: about how hot it was during the summers of the 1930s, about having to carry water in and out of the house, about not having good kitchen equipment, about cooking over corn cobs and wood fires with no air conditioning or fans. The only fan was a newspaper or dish towel that they would use to brush the numerous flies away while the men ate. They told how they would sleep on floors to try to keep cool. One woman remembered keeping a thousand chickens and dressing as many as eighty a day in the heat to sell. She did that only once. These women's memories, although they did not contradict the men's pronouncements, had a different tone and a different message. The women did not generalize about their experiences. They clearly recognized their own reality, but they were not willing to make general statements based on this reality. They seemed to accept the men's generalizations and to lay out their own experiences as exceptions to the rule.

The right to generalize is a privilege not universally granted, as is the right to be heard. Women's knowledge is more often coded in personal stories than in general principles. A primary tenet of feminist scholarship is the insistence on hearing women's voices whenever possible, instead of relying solely on the generalizations others (often men) have made about them. I have not discounted the words of any woman who spoke or wrote out of her own experience. Women's stories are a cornerstone of this study. I have used them, together with other sources, to build an understanding of women's lives.

As an anthropologist, I approached questions of agrarianism and rural Nebraska women's lives by first situating myself there and immersing myself in rural life. For part of the research I did off and on from 1986 through 1990, I stayed with my sister's family in rural Madison County, just east of Boone County. From February through June 1987 I rented an apartment in Albion, the county seat of Boone County. Going to Albion was going home, and I caught up with a number of lapsed acquaintances, talking to people at auctions, over coffee, at club meetings, in senior citizens' centers, in cafes, in grocery stores, in homes, and over breaks in my research into courthouse records. Of greatest importance was the information I obtained in interviews with thirty-six women and two men, most of which I taped and transcribed (see appendix).

Women's writings about their lives added to the data I gathered in the field. Family members and sometimes the women themselves gave me diaries, letters, and memoirs. Women's letters written to Eleanor Roosevelt and to President Roosevelt's cabinet members during the Great Depression, now deposited in the National Archives, included some from rural Nebraska. Memoirs written by rural women were deposited at the State Historical Archives in Lincoln. Published collections of writings by and about plains women provided valuable primary and secondary sources (Jensen 1981; Lee and Lewis 1979; Stauffer and Rosowski 1982; Riley 1988). Among the Nebraska women writers who published their reflections on rural life were Willa Cather, Mari Sandoz, Bess Streeter Aldrich, and Grace Snyder (through her daughter, Nellie Snyder Yost). Other rural women wrote letters and columns in the *Nebraska Farmer*. Like many others, I have learned much from reading Laura Ingalls Wilder's books about family life on the plains.

The collection and use of interview data are not without both practical and conceptual problems, and these problems extend to some degree to the use of other unpublished and published materials written by women. Anyone can misremember, especially after fifty or more years. Possibly the refusal of some people to be interviewed introduced a systematic bias.[1] The women who wrote letters, memoirs, and books were almost certainly more reflective and better educated than their neighbors. While I was fully aware of these potential pitfalls, the stories told by women themselves nevertheless guided my research.

Yet the women's stories are not the only truth. They may be interpreted in light of the facts outlined by other records, statistics, and writings. Wills, deeds, and court records provided documentation of women's property ownership, women's responsibility for mortgages, the assignment of property within families, separation and divorce statistics, child support and alimony, and incidents of violence against women. Demographic data in manuscript censuses, which are available to researchers for the 1910 census and earlier, include the residents of each household, as well as their nationalities, occupations, dates of marriage, dates of birth, and the childbirth record of each woman. The agricultural census of 1885, also in the public domain, includes details about farm operations and household composition at the point of the first significant population development in the county. Yearly school censuses list the names of every school-age child in every district; some of these school censuses include a full enumeration of each district household.

Beginning in 1930, the yearly Boone County Extension Service reports gave an overview of crop and livestock conditions, discussed drought and economic problems, and offered an indication of government involvement in rural family life. Further evidence of government intervention in rural families during the 1930s can be seen in Works Progress Administration papers and in the loan applications made to the Farm Security Administration, both deposited in the National Archives. Published decennial census reports and vital statistics reports are useful, as are local newspapers. Prominent business and professional men published accounts relating their perspectives on life in Boone County and the surrounding area in the early years of settlement (Long 1937; Barns 1970 [1930]; Turner 1903; Wells 1902). The recent *Boone County History*, a product of the Boone County Historical Society (1986), was also a helpful source.

Even though I have used some material that is open to the public, and though a determined detective could probably identify most of my informants, I have followed the anthropological ethics code of not revealing the names of my research subjects (Rynkiewich and Spradley 1976, 184). I have given my informants pseudonyms, and in places I have altered details in such a way as to disguise the identities of those involved. For people who have published their writings or deposited them in state archives, I have used actual names. I have also used some real names for those involved in events that occurred over a hundred years ago. Because this is in part a reflexive study, I have used my own name and real place names. References to my own relatives have involved carefully considered decisions, but I have not intended for most of those discussed in these pages to be personally identified.

Since beginning this study in 1986, I have presented different pieces of the research at professional meetings and in publications.

These have addressed issues of land ethics, women's moral capital, women's work, fertility, rural violence, agrarianism, and current farm politics (Fink 1987b, 1988, 1990, 1991; Fink and Johnson 1988; Fink and Carriquiry 1990; Schwieder and Fink 1988).

The first three chapters of this book lay the groundwork for my discussion of Boone County women as wives and mothers. Chapter 1 introduces the question of the position of farm women and grounds the inquiry in the particularity of eastern Nebraska in the late nineteenth century. Chapter 2 outlines the development of Jeffersonian agrarianism and the ways in which women were and were not included in the philosophical underpinnings of family farming. Chapter 3 places the settlement of Boone County in the context of agrarian development as a whole and details specific environmental and economic conditions that colored women's family lives. The next two chapters analyze the position of rural women as wives. Chapter 4 discusses the early period of settlement and Chapter 5 details the period from 1930 to 1940. Chapters 6 and 7 concern the experiences of women as mothers. In the final chapter, I offer an overview of agrarianism as a factor in the history of Boone County and thoughts on the construction of a more inclusive ideological grounding for rural development. The appendix explains my interview sample and interview protocol. Some readers may want to read this first.

Ames, Iowa
April 1991

1 RURAL WIVES AND MOTHERS

For him it is good. It is not for me.—*Tillie Olsen,*
"Tell Me a Riddle," 1981 [1961]

In 1919 U.S. agriculture was at the crest of the World War I economic
boom that followed over twenty years of remarkable growth. At the
height of this widespread prosperity, a national survey of farm wom-
en revealed that the majority lacked even the basic amenities that
would make their work easier. Farm women reported that their husbands were inclined to spend money on labor-saving machinery for
themselves but not on equipment that would save women's labor
(*Literary Digest* 1920, 58). Farm women's working conditions, the
report stated, would provoke a walkout among industrial workers,
but on the farm women worked for love and service rather than
material gain:

> [The survey] may give a somewhat exaggerated impression of
> hardship, unless one thinks of the motive back of the work of
> wife and mother and the compensations that come to every
> home maker in her round of activities for the happiness and
> comfort of her family. . . . The varied interests of the farm
> woman's life, her contact with growing things, her enjoyment
> of seasonal changes in nature and her freedom from noise,
> dust, and confusion is not to be lost sight of in comparing her

conditions and opportunities with those of home makers in
urban communities. (Ward 1920, 5)

The belief that farm people were happier, healthier, and more virtuous than city people was firmly entrenched in American culture.
Thomas Jefferson had expressed this agrarian idealism powerfully in
the early years of the Republic. Both in his writings and in his political life, Jefferson promoted an agrarian democracy based on independent family farms. He believed that the vigor of the country depended
on the well-being of its farmers, who would form a core of material
prosperity and moral strength that would be infused into society as a
whole. Jeffersonian agrarianism has persisted as a dominant theme in
political discourse in the United States; variations on the theme have
appeared in every subsequent historical period.

The 1920 survey report implicitly acknowledged that the poor
working environment women found on farms might contradict the
Jeffersonian vision of abundance naturally accruing to people of the
land. But the writer resolved the contradiction by stating that, for
the farm woman, life's riches were to be found in contact with nature
and freedom from the irritations that the city woman faced. Mediating the contradiction for the farm woman was her special position:
the unique love that a rural woman knew as wife and mother more
than compensated for her hardship.

This book, which explores rural women's lives as wives and
mothers in the context of a dominant agrarian ideology, argues
against the conclusions of that 1920 report, against the agrarian view
of rural society as a world apart, and against the belief that rural
women have been uniquely spared the problems that other women
have faced. Whereas agrarian ideology has proclaimed that women
were liberated rather than limited by their service within the family
farm, my analysis indicates that rural women lived the same basic
contradictions as nonrural women, although the circumstances of
rural life put a unique stamp on the form of these contradictions.
Indeed, the title of an article on the national survey, "Why Young
Women Are Leaving Our Farms" (Literary Digest 1920), indicated
that conclusions about the natural and spiritual compensations of
farm life for women were not as definitive as the researchers might

wish. Although the young women who were leaving the farms were presumably daughters rather than wives and mothers, their rejection of farm life did not bode well for the future of family farming. Not only were young women moving to the cities rather than marrying farmers, but women who lived on farms were encouraging their children to leave.

Journalists and reformers had recognized women's widespread dissatisfaction with farming as a problem for some time, and the 1919 survey addressed this persisting pocket of trouble without naming it. Even rural women who treasured the agrarian ideal and hoped for close, strong nuclear families often found that their own experiences as wives and mothers were troubling or violent. Many also resented the hard work and limited educations that their children faced. Residence on nuclear family farms frequently isolated women from the comfort and support of female kin and friends.

Although modern agrarians tend to dismiss incidents of breakdown and violence in rural homes as recent urban intrusions, I believe that rural women's difficulties have had a more fundamental basis in the structure of farming and rural communities. Removing the discussion of family issues from contemporary upheavals, I focus this study on the period from 1880 to 1940, the years preceding the massive social and technological changes that have occurred since World War II. These years encompass both the unsurpassed boom in American agriculture in the first twenty years of the century and the unsurpassed rural depression of the second twenty years.

In writing about agrarian ideology and agrarian texts, I do not attribute their power to a disembodied set of ideas. Agrarianism was tied to substantial military, economic, and political force. During the Civil War and numerous battles with Native Americans, the United States used its military might to help establish small, family-operated farms as its economic foundation. The division of public domain lands into household-based farming units made manifest the government's military and economic power to shape the lives of its citizens. The establishment of the infrastructure that enabled these farms to survive was a joint venture of government and private capital, as was the printing and distribution of texts that proclaimed the superiority of family farming. The development of the plains was framed in terms of the interests of the common citizen rather than of the political and economic elite, and this representation translated itself imperfectly into the settlers' reflections on their own lives.

Feminists who accept a version of the agrarian formula have looked to the frontier West as a place where women could shake free of the strictures placed on them by the laws and customs of the East. The Homestead Act of 1862 allowed single women, as heads of family, to acquire their own land. Married women, by this feminist agrarian reasoning, worked side by side with their husbands, doing economically necessary work and translating their economic centrality into enhanced power within the home.

Single women did homestead, particularly after the turn of the century. But this homesteading is not so much the story of how single women began to support themselves as farmers as it is a story of how single women began to further their fortunes through shrewd investments of time, labor, and money. When these women succeeded in proving up on their homesteads, they almost invariably sold them, often to make money that would improve their prospects for marriage. Although even a modest sum of cash could work to a woman's advantage in various ways, the one-time profit from the sale of a homestead did not afford a woman a lifetime of security in an economic system that rewarded her poorly in other contexts.

Sooner or later, most women married. Feminist agrarians have tended, with some reservations, to see the economic opportunity offered by homesteading as a base for women's enhanced position within marriage (Harris 1984, 48). In addition, a woman's substantial contribution to the operation of a family homestead may have heightened her power vis-à-vis her husband. In this model, we see the frontier woman as a prototype of the modern married career woman whose work has moved her toward equality with her husband within their marriage. This reading of history owes more, I believe, to the spirit of the present than to a true reconstruction of frontier women's lives. When I imagine asking my great-grandmother—who gave birth to nine children, kept eight of them alive, carried water, washed clothes on a washboard, and scratched the earth to put food on the table—if she found it liberating to tend livestock and do field work on the farm, I see her shaking her head at the abyss that separates her life from mine. She might have done more of that kind of work if she had not raised seven sons, but it would have been a burden and not an avenue of freedom for her. Doing farm work in itself did little to elevate a woman's position; whether she reaped a fair return for her work depended on the social relations that organized the production. Gender represented one dimension of these relations.

This study centers on women in a bounded geographical space, central Nebraska—and more specifically, Boone County, a totally rural county in east-central Nebraska. Boone County was settled during the last wave of farming expansion in U.S. history. European Americans reached Boone County in 1871 and proceeded to plow, fence, and build to reconstruct the farming communities they had known in the East and in the rural villages of northern Europe. Rather than gradually developing from its own resources, Boone County boomed with the influx of eastern capital. Its collateral was the promise of an abundant agriculture, a promise that could not be fulfilled.

Boone County lies on the western margin of the cornbelt, in the area of transition between the Prairie Plains to the east and the Great Plains to the west. The soils and climate of Boone County proved to be only marginally suited to the establishment of the cornbelt agriculture of the prairies that its developers envisioned.[1] Agrarian exhortations, exaggerated claims about agricultural potential, and the promise of free land attracted farmers to Boone County lands and nonfarm entrepreneurs to service the farmers; the majority of these people, or their descendants, eventually left in disappointment at the poor economic returns on their labor. As settlers left, newcomers would appear with fresh resources to invest in agricultural development. Sporadic periods of abundant agricultural production and large doses of optimism spurred continuous in-migration until the agricultural depression of the 1920s, when hard times began to siphon off the population faster than it could be replaced.

Before World War II, most Boone Countians lived on family farms, and nearly all family farm women gained access to farming as the wives of farmers and the mothers of children who constituted the backbone of the farm labor force.[2] Women expected to work hard to make Boone County their home. Because farmers faced the constant threat of utter failure and destitution, a woman's work in bearing and provisioning the rural labor force was critical to the survival of both her family and the public economy. Although Boone County was never as successful agriculturally as the rich cornbelt farming regions on the prairies of Iowa and Illinois, it was more prosperous than other such farming regions in the Dakotas and western Nebraska. The women of Boone County fit the agrarian mold as centrally as any. My exploration of these women's lives as wives and mothers in a specific rural setting helps to ground agrarian ideology in a concrete ✓ manifestation of rural culture.

Families were the building blocks of rural society. Women, who were foremost wives and mothers, participated in rural society in terms of their family roles. When, for example, a farm woman went to her neighbor's home to help her cook food for a threshing crew that included both of their husbands, they were forming a wider rural social network on the strength of their roles as farm wives. When a mother joined other mothers to provide food for a school party, they came together because of their shared motherhood.

So central has the family been to Western culture, particularly the rural culture at the core of the recent American and European past, that some historians and social scientists have assumed that the family is a natural and universal human institution that takes on diverse forms and functions in different eras. Anthropologists have recently disputed this point. In studying kinship and social structures cross-culturally, these scholars have seen universal definitions of family dissolve.[3] Neither does a fixed definition of family stand the test of Western history in other than a tautological sense.[4] The concept of family is historically specific rather than naturally determined. The position of mother, a family member, is a culturally defined configuration, as is the position of wife.

A precondition for the existence of family is private life, which presupposes spatial and emotional separation between a public world of business and government and a private world of caring and intimacy. In the United States, these contrasting public and private spaces took on a distinctive meaning in the period following the Revolutionary War, when industrialization, the development of market relations, and the strengthening of state power increasingly took men out of the household.[5] Men assumed new economic and political roles while women came to be identified with the separate moral world of the home. Developing beliefs about the character of relations within the domestic unit contrasted with beliefs about the enveloping public domain. In the domestic sphere, a person's worth was granted rather than being achieved as it was in the evolving capitalist work-place. In contrast to the public world, people shared within the home; no one person monopolized resources while others went hungry or cold. Within the family, people loved and worked together for the common good; outside they competed against each other. Even when faced with wide discrepancies between the ideal and the every-day reality within their homes, people continued to develop their image of the family as a refuge set apart from the ruthlessness and confusion of the outside world.

With men tending to the business of the world, women had a place of their own within the home, and white middle-class feminists in the nineteenth century generally supported the separation of male and female spheres. Farm women as well as nonfarm women had their domains. Farm women were sometimes able to convert their separate work into profitable enterprises and to turn their profits to their own advantage (Jensen 1986). Morally, the developing domestic sphere promised a great elevation in the roles of women as wives and mothers. By the early nineteenth century, the marital ideal was coming to be the "companionate" marriage, in which a wife and husband came together on the basis of mutual respect and devotion and made decisions by consensus (Lebsock 1984, 17–18). If women could not participate as men's equals in the political world outside the home, they could aspire to equality with their husbands within the conjugal home. The position of mother was also elevated in the construction of this domestic domain. What Mary Ryan (1982) called "the empire of the mother" assigned a powerful new status to the woman as mother. The saying "the hand that rocks the cradle rules the world" encapsulated women's dreams of power, which they could exercise as mothers by being faithful to the duties of bearing and rearing children.

The family thus evolved as an arena of escape. If a man did not

approve of social morality, he could create a different private morality. If he was ground down and humiliated at work, he could go home
to a place where he was honored and served. If a woman found
herself unable to earn a living, she could marry and share her husband's wealth. If she had no rights in the legal system, she could bear
children and create her own empire in the home. The ideology of
separate spheres shaped the way that people thought about their
lives. It made things tolerable that would otherwise have been intoler-
able and thus served to depoliticize a range of concerns relating to
justice and equity. The family and the public world gave meaning and
value to each other. They were "separate spheres" that were defined
and reinforced by their opposites and, in truth, were inseparable from
them. The family has served a political function, and the U.S. government has always had some form of family policy.

The family has been the basic building block of state power.
Writing about Revolutionary America, Linda Kerber (1980, 285) concluded that egalitarian society rested on a base of deference, which
women protected and nurtured from nonpolitical positions. Without
this undergirding social consensus of deference, the United States
would have risked a violent disintegration of its revolution, similar to
that which occurred in France. Family values were also at the fore-
front of designs to strengthen and expand the state by claiming the
coast-to-coast central section of the North American continent for
settlement and population in European American family farm units.

The racial and ethnic specificity with which the government related to families shaped the contours of power and the distribution of
wealth. The encouragement of family farm organization in the nineteenth century applied only to European American families.[6] The
men, women, and children who came to Boone County, Nebraska,
were members of the favored European American racial/ethnic
group; they were given the land, military protection, and economic
support needed to build their homes and establish control. Government investments in this group of people were supposed to succeed;
the settlers would return their wealth and strength to the country
that supported them. They were the people who would realize the
destiny of the United States. They had the advantage of being the
chosen people, those whose sacrifices and pain would forge an hon-

ored place in history for themselves and their descendants. If the agrarian ideal were meaningful and reflected reality among women anywhere, it should have been in Boone County.

Yet even within the dominant European American group, not everyone was positioned to benefit equally from government programs assisting development. Settlers brought different levels of capital resources with them. The cornbelt farming that Boone County settlers attempted in this incipient Great Plains region guaranteed that, with or without an even start, many losers would emerge within a short time. Boone County women observed a widening of class inequality that in itself ran counter to the egalitarian promise of agrarian democracy. Struggle and hardship did not always bring out noble qualities; class differences shaped lives in unanticipated ways. Although delineation of class lines in a rural community presents analytical problems, class as an ongoing process of deepening economic separation touched everyone in Boone County. Many women, especially, were in a contradictory position with respect to class. Some acquired a certain class status through their fathers or husbands, but they were limited in the ways that they could exercise this privilege. Women of the propertied class could not allocate resources in a manner that went against the class interests of their men. Men without property were less able to control the women in their families, although the greater gender equality within propertyless families tended to be an equality of powerlessness. For women, power dynamics within the family often contradicted rather than reinforced class position.

Agricultural policy generally has affected rural women only indirectly through its impact on the structure of agriculture rather than as policy directed specifically to them as women. Such legislation as the Homestead Act of 1862 shaped the size of farms and the pattern of farm ownership, but it did not specifically address women's position in farming. Although a particular idea about how women would have access to farms and what they would do on those farms was implicit in the way that homesteading was projected, the Homestead Act was not aimed at farm women. The laws limiting their political rights, the customs regarding the distribution of family assets, and women's difficulties in supporting themselves independently all determined their position on the farm more concretely than did laws specifically related to women, land, and farming.

The ideology of agrarianism underlay an undifferentiated farm policy that did not address the reality of gender or class inequalities. In redistributing resources without sensitivity to these inequalities, the government compounded them. Women's problems were not limited to narrowly defined agrarian concerns; they touched on broader issues of economic and social justice (Flora 1986, 1988).

The structure and organization of the nuclear family channeled the flow of goods and services in a manner that isolated and weakened rural women. This does not imply that rural women were primarily victims, that they were powerless, or that they had no resources. Elsewhere I have argued that rural women's roles as producers on the farm and in small businesses forged a powerful and liberating tradition of women as workers (Fink 1986). Joan Jensen's (1986) study of mid-Atlantic Quaker women bases the nineteenth-century women's rights movement in the measure of autonomy that women gained through farm production in the years between 1750 and 1850. The economic autonomy arising from women's participation in production has been a necessary ingredient in their gaining control of their lives, and rural women may rightly serve as models of industry and competence in this regard. Without detracting from the importance of women's full participation in production as a necessary precondition to full involvement in social life, my thesis is that this was not a sufficient condition. The organization of labor within the nuclear family undermined its liberating potential. The work of their wives and children often gave men time for civic involvements beyond the family; women were seldom able to draw on the labor of family members for a similar release. When European American women gained power through their farm production, they did so because particular geographic, economic, or social conditions allowed them to draw on resources from beyond the nuclear family. Agrarian thinking tempered the contradiction between the tangible work that farm women did and the nebulous returns realized from their labor.

2 AGRARIANISM AND WOMEN

> *We have now lands enough to employ an infinite*
> *number of people in their cultivation. Cultivators of*
> *the earth are the most valuable citizens. They are*
> *the most vigorous, the most independent, the most*
> *virtuous, and they are tied to their country, and*
> *wedded to its liberty and interests, by the most*
> *lasting bond.—Thomas Jefferson to John Jay, 1785*

U.S. farmers and rural people have been society's cultural ballast. A 1987 poll showed that people across the country believed that farmers were hard-working, self-reliant citizens who would keep the nation on an even keel. They saw bedrock goodness and neighborliness in rural community life. Even with little knowledge of farm economics, most people felt that the government should spend more money on family farmers (Anthan 1987). There has been a strong sense that what comes from the country comes from the soul and is profoundly right and redemptive. Saving the rural way of life, we feel, may benefit us all (Lappé 1989).

Agrarianism, the belief in the moral and economic primacy of farming over other industry, rests firmly at the base of the collective U.S. ideological framework. Reaching from the pre-Revolutionary period to the present, agrarianism has been first a founding vision and then a sustaining ideal of the good life. Politicians have returned to it time and again as a way of explaining political programs and rallying citizen support. The authority of the European American pioneers' claims to land rested on their proclaimed superiority as farmers. Motherhood and apple pie, symbols for which wars are fought, spring from an American identity grounded in pure, honest, rural values. Agrarian ideology has appealed to urban as well as rural people, to wealthy as well as poor, to liberals as well as conservatives.

Women have joined men in accepting and promoting the agrarian vision, although not in exactly the same way. Agrarianism is a gendered ideology in that it projects different ideals for men and women. Men and women have each appropriated the concept and expressed it in different terms and in different forums. Serving as an ideological charter for the white settlement of Nebraska, agrarianism was a filter through which white women interpreted their lives.

Statements on the essential nobility of husbandry and the superiority of farm life over that of cities first appeared in ancient writings. A long-standing undercurrent of European culture, this theme emerged powerfully in the writings of the eighteenth-century French physiocrats, who declared that farming was the primary source of wealth in society and that government furthered the general social well-being when it allowed farmers to assume their natural economic primacy. King George III ("Farmer George") of England and George Washington were among the well-placed persons who operated farms, formed agricultural societies, and studied agricultural science during this period when farming was "the reigning taste" (Griswold 1971, 41).

Popular American writers and artists who were connected to European culture also placed farming at the center of their images of the ideal society. Benjamin Franklin located his farming ideal in a rustic American setting. Writing from the 1750s onward, Franklin looked to rural people for the hard work, honesty, and thrift that he felt had been submerged in the artificiality of the growing cities. Believing that urban luxuries threatened to ruin America, he consoled himself with the idea that the soul of the country was in its farming population. St. John de Crèvecoeur was another American whose popular works celebrated the special virtues of rural life. Crèvecoeur, a Norman who settled and farmed in New York, wrote *Letters from an American Farmer*, which was widely read in the 1780s and 1790s. According to Crèvecoeur, American expansion would entail three major geographical divisions: a rough, uncivilized frontier region; a middle region of farms; and an older region of cities. The middle farming region was the best. Its people would be the happiest and most virtuous, and they would be the strength of the country. Such writers as Crèvecoeur and Franklin romanticized husbandry and portrayed rural people as simpler, more natural, more honest, more noble, happier, and more independent than those living in cities. The new country would be good because of its farmers (Smith 1950, 124–29; Hofstadter 1956).

In a series of essays written between 1803 and 1813, John Taylor of Caroline, a Virginia planter active in agricultural societies and politics, formulated a detailed argument for the development of the United States as an agrarian democracy. Opposing the establishment of a strong federal government, he believed that the social well-being of the country depended on agriculturalists' maintaining their pre-eminent position. Taylor opposed taxation, a paid army, and government-chartered banks. He believed that the federal government harmed agriculture and weakened the whole society when it taxed farmers and used the revenue to strengthen manufacturing industries and transportation. Urbanism and commercialism had been the downfall of Europe, and the United States should avoid this corruption. Farming people were by nature happy, benevolent, and independent. So naturally good was agriculture that on Judgment Day it would be "agricultural virtues" that would admit souls into heaven (Taylor 1977 [1818], 314). If it held true to its founding promise, U.S. society would be homogeneous and agrarian (Bradford 1977; Taylor 1977 [1818]; MacLeod 1980).

Taylor's style and tone distanced him from popular readers, and his espousal of the cause of planter aristocracy put him out of touch with much of the diverse U.S. society. His close association with Thomas Jefferson, however, gave his statements a wider hearing and more historical currency than they might otherwise have had. Jefferson, who formulated the classic American definitions of agrarianism, declared that he and Taylor were of one mind on fundamental principles (Jefferson 1816, 669; Griswold 1946, 659). According to one of Jefferson's biographers, John Taylor may have been even "more catalytic" than Jefferson in the formulation of Jeffersonian agrarian principles (Malone 1962, 19). Although Jefferson proved to be more pragmatic and more flexible than his fellow Virginian, it was many of Taylor's beliefs that he expressed in more lasting and politically effective forms.

Like Taylor, Jefferson believed in the moral superiority of farmers, writing, "Those who labor on the earth are the chosen people of God, if ever He has a chosen people, whose breasts He has made His peculiar deposit for substantial and genuine virtue" (Jefferson 1784, 280). Like Taylor, Jefferson accepted John Locke's labor theory of property, which held that men established their right to property ownership through investment of labor.[1] In Jefferson's view, the state served to protect private property, which in the United States was mainly farms. Jefferson, who had more tolerance for central government than Taylor, saw farmers as the most loyal supporters of this government.

Jefferson tried without success to enact a homestead law granting free land to farmers in his native Virginia. He dreamed of and planned for the future expansion of the United States across the North American continent, believing the availability of land for farming to be a solution to problems of overcrowding and poverty in the cities: "Whenever there are in any country uncultivated lands and unemployed poor, it is clear that the laws of property have been so far extended as to violate natural right. The earth is given as a common stock for men to labor and live on. . . . The small landholders are the most precious part of the state" (Jefferson 1785b, 390). As president, Jefferson negotiated the Louisiana Purchase, which added the rich farming lands in the middle of the continent to the nation, and he chartered the Lewis and Clark expedition that explored the new territory.

For Jefferson, the breadth and richness of the land made America both different from and better than Europe. The broad mass of people in the United States could be farmers. In the United States, no one needed to suffer poverty, because uncultivated land would always remain to be worked. The teeming population of unemployed men that swelled the countries of Europe produced nations of second-class citizens; in the new country men would have land. A nation of property-owning cultivators would be a land of independent, vigorous, and free individuals. Such men would be public-spirited citizens, the backbone of the state.

Jefferson's belief in the moral supremacy of the farmer and the farmer as the bulwark of the state came from experience and observation as well as from the ideas of his associates and from literary sources. The deep comfort and spiritual renewal he found in living on his own extensive agricultural property and his pleasure in the study of plant and animal science convinced him experientially that farming was the most noble occupation. His strongest political supporters, like Taylor, were also farmers. Historian Joyce Appleby (1984, 25–50) has found that the abundant agriculture of the middle Atlantic region did, in fact, undergird the prosperity of the United States as a whole in the early years of the nation. Farmers reaped rich harvests and profited from exports to Europe. With abundant lands and a strong market for agricultural products, it seemed as if a favorable balance of trade through agricultural exports would support an expanding economy forever. No apparent contradiction existed between individual economic expansion and economic democracy.

The population of the farming areas grew rapidly, and the strength of the Jeffersonian movement came from these expansive agricultural regions. Although Jefferson's own inability to maintain his desired standard of living and public service without recourse to the odious institution of slavery and massive landholdings contradicted his agrarian vision and the labor theory of value, an apparent affirmation of agrarianism was embodied in the large number of prosperous farmers whose enterprise enriched the nation and spawned the American dream of universal prosperity.

Jefferson's writings contained all of the essential ingredients of agrarianism: belief in the independence and virtue of the yeoman farmer; the concept of property as a natural right; a preference for land ownership without restrictions on its use or disposition; the use of land as a safety valve to ensure justice in the city; the conviction that any man could thrive on a farm through hard work; and the idea of farming as the primary source of wealth for society as a whole. Agrarian ideology was compelling and popular. However, its formulation and the specific political agendas emanating from it have varied greatly. National policy questions about westward expansion and the distribution of lands taken from indigenous inhabitants centered on the application of agrarian principles.

Contrary to the principles of Jeffersonian agrarianism, public land sales in the early nineteenth century transferred vast amounts of land in units that were too large and too costly to be purchased by citizen farmers. Politicians were the major beneficiaries of this land policy; they controlled many acres of land, which appreciated in value as they encouraged westward expansion. In opposition to these sales, "squatters" would simply settle on tracts of land, take up farming, and defy government regulations. Some formed claims clubs and resisted forfeiture of the land they had farmed. Preemption laws passed in 1830 and 1841 allowed these settlers to buy their land for $1.25 per acre, but $200 for a 160-acre farm was beyond the means of most would-be farmers at that time. Many farmers—such as Abraham Lincoln's father, who migrated from Virginia to Kentucky to Indiana to Illinois—found it to their advantage to move westward and take up new claims rather than putting down roots. Government surveys and grants to railroads also drew people westward. These measures enhanced land values and kept settlers connected to the institutions of the eastern seaboard (Opie 1987).

Much of the diverse political maneuvering that accompanied the settlement of the midwestern and plains states, although ostensibly related to the development of the farming frontier, actually concerned the institutions and interests of the East more than the circumstances that would face settlers in the western areas. Slavery and the tendency of slaveholders to expand and monopolize land ownership represented a threat to small owner-operated farms as well as to nonfarm businesses that had to compete with slave labor. The system of slavery stood in opposition to the Jeffersonian ideal of yeoman farming; but outside of the mild-weathered South, it was not profitable for business owners to clothe and house slaves. Southern politicians wanted government policies that favored a slave economy; northerners wanted policies based on free labor. The incompatible views caused political division between North and South that resulted in controversy over the status of western lands. Mid-nineteenth-century southern interests opposed the practice of foster-

ing independent yeoman farmers on western lands. Northern reformers saw these lands as a safety valve for oppressed urban workers;
northern businessmen saw expanding markets, raw materials, and
new businesses.

Politicians bickered over the path of the proposed transcontinen-
tal railroad. Northern politicians hoped that an eventual cross-
country route through Nebraska would establish northern cities as
major railroad nodes, whereas southerners favored a southern route
that would benefit southern cities. The National Reform movement
led by George Henry Evans, which represented northeastern workers,
organized support for legislation offering free land to farming settlers. Editor Horace Greeley, a follower of the National Reform movement, declared that no factory owner could overwork or underpay his
employees for long if they had the choice to claim their own land
(Olson 1966; Robbins 1935; Smith 1950).

The Civil War cleared the way for northern interests to proceed
with their plans. Three pieces of legislation passed in 1862 signaled
their determination to promote small-scale farming in the frontier
region. With one act, Congress created the U.S. Department of Agriculture. The functions of the department, as the commissioner of
agriculture stated in his first report, were to include answering questions related to agriculture, stimulating inquiry, and inviting discussion on agricultural topics; the hoped-for result was that free labor,
smaller homesteads, greater agricultural diversity, and higher skill
levels would replace the kind of agriculture that had developed under
slavery (Newton 1863). A second measure, the Morrill Act, endowed
in each state a land grant college for the purpose of teaching and
doing practical research on agriculture and the mechanical arts. The
third piece of legislation, the Homestead Act of 1862, promised 160
acres of free land to any head of family who would stake a claim, live
on it, make certain improvements, and farm it for five years. With
these acts, Congress committed itself to the nurturing of a small-
scale, household-based agriculture that would require broad education and public investment if it were to flourish and return export
profits and tax money to the East.

Northern labor reformers had campaigned vigorously for the
Homestead Act, and its passage was a partial victory for them—only

partial because the act did not include effective restrictions on land monopoly and speculation. But the reformers thought that, even without these restrictions, free land would be a major boon for the urban poor. As the Homestead Act passed, Horace Greeley wrote: "We may congratulate the country on the consummation of one of the most beneficent and vital reforms ever attempted in any age or clime—a reform calculated to diminish sensibly the number of paupers and idlers and increase the proportion of working, independent, self-subsisting farmers in the land evermore" (quoted in Robbins 1935, 41). Greeley had no doubt that farming was a venture in which any willing unemployed man could thrive. In the northeastern states, the popular emphasis of the Homestead Act was its potential for improving conditions in the cities. In contrast, the strongest appeal of the Homestead Act for western politicians was its promise of the establishment of an empire based on fee-simple land ownership, fee-simple ownership meaning that the owner held the land without condition or encumbrance (Smith 1950, 170).

Although both the northern labor reformers and the western land dealers held agrarian values, their realizations of these values conflicted. The differing interests supporting the Homestead Act account for some of the immediate contradictions in its implementation. The National Reform movement, which advocated land grants to settlers and opposed land monopolies and grants to nonsettlers, reasoned on Jeffersonian grounds that labor on the land constituted the only valid claim to a land title. A man purchased his land with his labor. National Reformers had called for a statutory limit to the amount of land any one person could hold; they had also wanted to make homesteads inalienable, so that a homesteader would forfeit his land when he no longer farmed it. Western politicians had not been inclined to limit individual economic prospects. Limitation of property rights contradicted the strong current of American feeling—deriving from an interpretation of Jefferson's writings on property rights—that supported unfettered private ownership and control of property. Accordingly, the proposed limitations on the exercise of property rights were left out of the Homestead Act when it was passed. Politicians asserted that large land grants to railroads would help develop needed transportation and would also constitute a secondary source of cheap land for settlers. Westerners were clearly looking to free lands as a means of vast economic opportunity. In this, they were fully in accord with Jefferson's vision of farming as the basis of the nation's wealth and political power.

From the first, speculators abused the Homestead Act by filing in absentia, by filing multiple entries, and by failing to farm the land being claimed. Few urban workers had the experience or inclination, let alone the capital, to settle on a homestead and farm for five years. Contrary to romantic beliefs, farming was neither uncomplicated nor natural in the sense of being an inborn ability that men exercised without training. Even as the Homestead Act enabled a number of settlers to acquire farms, its many abuses and failures accelerated the concentration of landholdings. Where the principle of establishing and nurturing small, owner-operated farms clashed with the practices of ambitious land speculators, individual greed held sway. Historian John Opie (1987, 69) concluded his discussion of the Homestead Act by stating: "Unlike the National Reformers, westerners did not treat the Homestead Act piously; they saw it as a golden opportunity to make a series of quick killings." Although Jefferson envisioned a virtually limitless supply of fertile land, succeeding agrarians had to make choices between unlimited individual wealth and wide distribution of land. They equivocated, but no legislature has ever enacted an effective check on private economic expansion in the United States. Rural politicians have been among the most vehement defenders of individual economic privilege.

If agrarianism promised property and civil rights to men, what did it hold for women? It is possible to read most of what Thomas Jefferson wrote about farmers and citizenship and assume that he might have been using "man" in a generic sense, or that agrarian ideology might logically be extended to include women as the political equals of men. This reading is wrong. Jefferson's sparse references to farm women and his other reflections on women's proper place in society made clear that women's inequality was integral to his ideal society. His agrarian vision hinged on the subordination of women. Women were not farmers, and they did not gain property ownership through their labor. African American women, as well as men, worked on Jefferson's land without the rights of citizens. Jefferson did not believe that white women should do farm work except when their husbands were unable to farm and they were facing poverty. White women were the daughters, wives, and mothers of men, and their fulfillment came from comforting and supporting men within the family.

In a letter expressing his views on women's education, Jefferson wrote: "The order and economy of a house are as honorable to the mistress as those of the farm to the master, and if either be neglected, ruin follows, and children destitute of means of living" (Jefferson 1818, 689). The house and the farm were two different spheres, and the man was to be master of the farm. If women farmed, who would do the indispensable but unremarkable work of the house? The proper role of a woman was to support and promote the industry of a man and thereby partake in some measure of the privilege that accrued through his achievement. When Jefferson wrote to his own daughter admonishing her to give more attention to her studies, he based his advice to her on her future needs as mistress of a family and companion to him in his old age rather than on her need for education in order to address political or social questions (Jefferson 1787b, 418).

Jefferson rejected even an informal, indirect role for women in men's affairs. As ambassador to France, he noted with distaste that French women were so bold as to put forth their opinions on the operation of politics and family business (Jefferson 1788, 922, 932). Writing from Paris, he compared American women favorably with their French counterparts:

> [O]ur good ladies have been too wise to wrinkle their foreheads with politics. They are contented to soothe & calm the minds of their husbands returning ruffled from political debate. . . . Recollect the women of this capital, some on foot, some on horses, & some in carriages hunting pleasure in the streets, in routs & assemblies, and forgetting that they have left it behind them in their nurseries; compare them with our own countrywomen occupied in the tender and tranquil amusements of domestic life, and confess that it is a comparison of Amazons and Angels. (Jefferson 1788, 922–23)

Writing his autobiography in the latter years of his life, Jefferson reflected on the French Revolution and concluded that there might have been bloodless acceptance of a constitutional monarchy had it not been for the perversity of the French queen and the failure of the king to adequately control her: "I have ever believed, that had there been no Queen, there would have been no revolution. No force would have been provoked, nor exercised. The King would have gone hand in hand with the wisdom of his sounder counsellors" (Jefferson 1829, 110). Jefferson himself would have placed the queen in a convent.

Jefferson's ideal held that, in contrast to French women, women of the United States would not be pushy; their softer demeanors and agreeable personalities would make men's lives more pleasant. Jefferson believed that the United States should be broadly democratic in its promotion of property ownership and civic involvement for the large number of yeoman farmers that formed the core of the citizenry. Undergirding this public life would be the women who soothed and calmed their men and took care of domestic affairs. This formulation was in harmony with the emerging separation of housework and industry in the United States and doubtless derived from Jefferson's observation of this separation (Cott 1977; Ryan 1981).

Jefferson's canonical citizen was a farmer, and his canonical family was a farm family. He saw the farm and the home as separate spheres, and his agrarian ideology rested on this separation. The citizen farmer would be supported and enabled through the services of a woman who tended to the home and did not venture into his domain. Jefferson was clear on this point, even though he did not write about it at length. Women's proper work did not require social contacts outside the home and could in fact be hindered by such distractions. Jefferson had observed and rejected the European settlement pattern of farming villages. Such a pattern encouraged too much interaction among households, including women in the separate households. This crowding would lead to vices; farmers in such villages would be "less happy and less virtuous" than they would be living independently (Jefferson 1787a, 135). Domestic life separated people and promoted the individualism that Jefferson prized. He expected civic involvement from citizen farmers; he expected women to stay at home. They should devote their energies to meeting the needs of men so that these men could in turn devote sufficient attention both to their own farms and to politics.

The spirit that women nurtured in the home was more critical in determining the character of U.S. politics than Jefferson's sparse references to it indicated. As historian Linda Kerber (1980, 285) concluded, the developing democracy among men of the Republic rested on the continuing deference of women, who served them faithfully and nurtured the moral consensus that held the country together. Without women in the background, men's starring roles would disintegrate. But even though women, within their own domains, distinctively colored U.S. society, they were peripheral in Jefferson's writings and in succeeding elaborations of the agrarian ideal.

Jeffersonian agrarianism, having laid the ideological base of the homestead movement, assumed a new form in the homespun rural protest movements espoused by plains farm settlers in the last decades of the nineteenth century. The settlers who had arrived to farm the western plains after the Civil War were overwhelmed by hardships. Even when they surmounted the natural barriers to farming on the plains, they faced defeat through their financial vulnerability. Farmers with little cash needed access to short-term credit; they depended on railroads to ship supplies in and farm produce out at reasonable rates; they depended on grain companies to pay them enough to stay in business. Merchants, railroads, loan brokers, and land speculators all seemed to be preying on the vulnerability of the farm settlers. Complaints abounded. In the years from 1870 to 1900 farmers protested by organizing successively the Patrons of Husbandry (Grange), the Farmers' Alliance, and finally the Populist party. These organizations were major grassroots networks formed to empower farmers and enable them to stand up to monied interests.

The Grange, the Alliance, and the Populist party all picked up on the strain of agrarian ideology that portrayed the farmer as the most fundamentally virtuous and deserving member of society, the source of the wealth that others enjoyed. A popular song from the Grange period, "The Farmer Is the Man," reflects these beliefs:

Oh, the farmer is the man who feeds them all,

. . . .

The farmer is the man, the farmer is the man,

. . . .

When the banker says he's broke & the merchant's up in
   smoke

They forget that it's the farmer feeds them all

It would put them to the test if the farmer took a rest

Then they'd know that it's the farmer feeds them all.

                (quoted in Blood-Patterson 1988, 51)

When farmers went broke, the new agrarian wisdom asserted, it was not just too bad—it was not just that the farmer, like many other workers, was being controlled and often destroyed by the idle rich— it was uniquely unfair because the farmer, more than any other worker, should be rewarded as the one from whom all other wealth derived. Seeking only to serve, the farmer unselfishly neglected his own interests until, pushed to the brink, he was forced to call a limit. As expressed by the controversial but extravagantly eloquent Nebraskan William Jennings Bryan: "Burn down your cities and leave our farms, and your cities will spring up again as if by magic; but destroy our farms and the grass will grow in the streets of every city in the country" (Bryan 1966 [1896], 210). The farmer was "the man."

Women were active in the grassroots protest organizations. The Grange included women in its discussion groups and tried to draw them into a wider organizational circle than they had experienced on the family farms. Women were also writers, organizers, and lecturers in the Farmers' Alliance, which advocated woman suffrage as part of its program. Historians have tended to view these women's work in farm groups as an unprecedented movement into the male political sphere (Jensen 1981, 144; Wagner 1984, 1988). Yet another analysis questions this. In spite of broad participation, women were nonetheless subordinate to men in the farm movements, and movement support for women's issues such as suffrage was ambivalent and perhaps opportunistic (Nelsen 1989, 31–35). Support for women's issues in the Alliance was always secondary to male Alliance leaders' social and political programs (Jeffrey 1975, 85).

Whatever liberatory progress may have been represented by women's inclusion in the farm protests of the late nineteenth century, nothing in the political rhetoric suggests that women used this involvement to challenge the basic position of women in the agrarian ideal. Women were allowed to speak on established positions, but they did not challenge the political dictum that placed "the man" at the center of injustices toward farmers. The role of the woman, even in her political participation, was devoted to establishing the rightful supremacy of the (male) farmer.[2] In 1892, when Alliance activist Annie Diggs wrote about women's participation in Alliance campaigns, she answered an implied criticism of women who strayed from the home by insisting that Alliance women were not politically active by choice; they were only protecting and caring for their homes by protesting poor markets for their husbands' produce. Farm women were so devoted to their homes that they were willing to speak out for them politically. Diggs (1892, 165) reassured her readers that, for Alliance women, all women's issues, including suffrage and prohibition, paled before the overriding moral question of how to save the farm.

Rural grassroots protest dissolved around the turn of the century. The farm economy was improving, siphoning off some of the discontent. Disagreements within the movements also left some people disenchanted and unwilling to make the economic and personal sacrifices necessary for continuing agitation. Dissension crystallized over the question of fusion between the Democratic and the Populist parties. William Jennings Bryan united the two parties in his presidential bid in 1896, a move that splintered the grassroots support for populism in Nebraska. When he lost the election, the Populist movement, having reached its height without gaining any concrete results, was over.

The Progressive period of 1900–1920, a time of broad-ranging social reforms, produced a new, city-based movement for rural reform. Twentieth-century reformers, besides being more closely connected to the centers of power, were better educated and more politically astute than the Populists had been. They rejected the unsophisticated Populist leadership but implicitly adopted much of the Populist agenda. These reformers fully believed and expounded at length the Jeffersonian creed that the farmers were better and nobler than urban dwellers and that the well-being of the country as a whole rested on its rural population. The problem was that the twentieth-century reformers did not like what they actually saw in the countryside—particularly the Populists. They feared rural agitation, the possibility of rural disintegration, and most of all the ongoing flight of people from the countryside. The United States was becoming an urban nation, and who was going to produce the food for city people and provide the exports vital to the national economy? In their efforts to shore up the rural base, Progressive reformers succeeded in enacting most of the Populists' proposals, including railroad regulation, the income tax, an expanded currency and credit structure, direct election of senators, and the initiative and referendum (Hofstadter 1955, 94–130).

The Country Life movement was formed to stem rural disintegration by directly uplifting and improving the lives of rural people. In 1907 President Theodore Roosevelt, once a farmer and rancher himself, formed the Country Life Commission, naming seven urban-based agricultural professionals to address rural problems. Their charge was to survey the quality of rural life and to make recommendations on how the government might ameliorate rural conditions. The commission's report, which appeared two years later, enumerated problems of rural poverty, social disorganization, poor schools, poor roads, poor nutrition and health, soil depletion, and lack of responsible rural leadership. It recommended that the government make a concerted effort to build up rural society by offering training to make farmers more productive and economically efficient and by guiding and strengthening rural organizations (Bailey et al. 1909; Bowers 1974; Danbom 1979).

The Country Life Commission report did not ignore farm women. The commissioners found, in fact, that the problems of rural life weighed more heavily on the farm woman than on the man, because her well-being derived from that of the "farmer himself." The commissioners believed that the solution to women's problems lay not in structural change that would reposition the farm woman within rural society or enhance her status in the home, but in a general elevation of the standard of life on the farms (Bailey et al. 1909, 47). The rising tide would lift the farm woman as well as the farm man. President Roosevelt, in his preface to the commission report, emphasized that he was concerned with the problems of the rural woman only in terms of her position as wife and mother: "If the woman shirks her duty as housewife, as home keeper, as the mother whose prime function it is to bear and rear a sufficient number of healthy children, then she is not entitled to our regard" (Roosevelt 1909, 9). Any changes that affected the farm woman must come within the family framework that had historically defined rural women's horizons.

But by this time feminists were ready to make a response challenging this accepted order. Charlotte Perkins Gilman (1909), an urban feminist, stepped forward to ask a question that had apparently escaped President Roosevelt and the Country Life commissioners: "Why are there no women on the president's commission?" If one accepted the well-being of the farm population as the touchstone for the well-being of the rest of the country, she reasoned, then the conditions of farm women were part of this total well-being and not a mere adjunct to the quality of farming men's lives. Farmers, Gilman said, could not speak for farm women; male Country Life commissioners could not prescribe the remedies for women's problems.

The editors of *Good Housekeeping* magazine, in which Gilman published her criticism, endorsed her suggestion and initiated their own national inquiry, which reached 675,000 farm families. In cooperation with four eastern farm publications, the *Good Housekeeping* inquiry solicited women's answers to questions about what they needed for their own happiness, for the development of their home life, and for their children (*Good Housekeeping* 1909, 122).[3] This inquiry prodded the government to be more attentive to women's voices, and in 1913 the U.S. Department of Agriculture initiated its own survey of farm women, albeit on a more modest scale than *Good Housekeeping* had attempted. In a letter sent to 55,000 wives of official crop correspondents of the department, the secretary of agriculture asked the women to express freely any thoughts they had on how the U.S. government could be of service to farm women (USDA 1915).

This survey, together with the Country Life Commission report, laid the groundwork for the U.S. Department of Agriculture Extension Service, established by the Smith-Lever Act of 1914. Reflecting a division of labor predicated on a male farmer married to a housekeeping wife who raised children to be future farmers and farmers' wives, the Extension Service divided its programs into agricultural education for the farmers, home economics for the wives of farmers, and youth programs in agriculture and home economics for farm boys and girls. Although this plan fitted neither the actual division of labor on farms nor the subsequent on-the-ground use of the programs, the farm/male, home/female division was government policy.

The Department of Agriculture increased more than thirtyfold from 1890 to 1920 (Hofstadter 1955, 118). Through the Extension Service, government employees organized the major rural secular associations and shaped their expressions of agrarian ideology.

The work of the twentieth-century urban reformers of rural life rested on agrarian premises similar to those of the Populist agitators. Whereas the Populists believed that nonfarming middlemen were extracting the farmers' lifeblood, however, the new reformers saw the evil cities as a unified entity extracting the lifeblood of the countryside. To rally the vigor of the countryside was to strengthen natural immunities and save society from the disease of the city. Joseph Ross, a sociologist who studied the West and rural life, wrote in 1909: "The problem of the city has thus far failed to be even approximately solved. But in the face of increasing perplexities caused by the difficulties of municipal administration, by the weakening of churches and religious influences, by the sundering of social ties and the destruction of family and neighborhood restraints, the chief reliance of all serious thinkers has been upon the virile American of our rural communities" (Ross 1909, 391).

Country Life Commission chairman Liberty Hyde Bailey, dean of the New York College of Agriculture at Cornell University, expressed a similar agrarian fundamentalism in medical metaphor: "The city sits like a parasite, running out its roots into the open country and draining it of its substance. The city takes everything to itself— materials, money, men—and gives back only what it does not want; it does not reconstruct or even maintain its contributory country"

(Bailey 1911, 20). The farmer's home was the center of the nation's morality, the social foundation, the source of all wealth; the city was its polar opposite. Presumably, these twentieth-century reformers were making a supreme sacrifice by living in cities and overseeing rural change. The farming population, properly organized, would save the nation from the blight of urban greed, crime, and filth. Only rural people could do it.

In the twentieth century, the farm that was organized around the labor and economic support of a nuclear family came to be called a "family farm." This usage, which appeared in the early years of the century, became common in the late 1930s, when such industrialists as Henry Ford were proposing capitalist farm production systems.[4] Family farms contrasted with both large-scale capitalist farms and socialist collectives. Family farm terminology captured an agrarian feeling by identifying the farm with a family unit, which in turn evoked men's responsibility and women's moral presence. The family as a unit for organizing production invoked kinder, more coopera- tive, more altruistic characteristics than could be found either in the evil corporations controlling production in the cities or the evil gov- ernment controlling production on socialist collectives. The connec- tion of family and farm even today continues the association of farm- ing with a way of life that is superior to that of nonfarmers. As they were on nineteenth-century homesteads, family farm women are wives and mothers who support their husbands and raise their chil- dren to do farm work.

Politicians and social reformers appropriated and manipulated Jeffersonian agrarianism for a variety of ends ranging from personal aggrandizement to Populist protest to social stabilization. The ideo- logical context in which Boone County citizens existed in the period from 1880 to 1940 was that of agrarian values. Disputes arose over the application of agrarian principles, but no public voice, either locally or nationally, questioned the bedrock agrarian truths.

This agrarian vision demanded a subordinate woman, usually concealed and peripheral. Women might be mentioned in one para- graph or as an afterthought within a larger treatise on farming. They were necessary appendages to male farmers, just as statements about women were appendages to the primary subject of agrarian writing. Women stirred inside the agrarian system and urban reformers took note of the hardships farm women faced. Yet no one publicly questioned the assumption that farm women would interpret their lives in terms of their duties as wives and mothers in service to the overarching good of the farm.

Celebration of the agrarian ideal encouraged women to seek fulfillment in lives that matched the agrarian prescription. By this reasoning, rural women did not face the evils that city women did, and the remedies for their dissatisfaction would be found in better and truer agrarian expressions, not in questioning male dominance.

3 THE LAND, THE PEOPLE

I had the feeling that the world was left behind, that we had got over the edge of it. . . . Between that earth and that sky I felt erased, blotted out. I did not say my prayers that night: here, I felt, what would be would be.—Willa Cather, My Ántonia, *1918*

The land—vast acres of rippling grasses waiting, needing, calling to be worked. A male settler described the land of central Nebraska as a woman who hungered for the firm step of her owner and master, who yearned to yield her prodigal production to the loving husbandman (Smith 1939). But the master of the land brought with him another woman, his wife, who could not evoke the same metaphors to voice her part in claiming the western land.[1]

With some exceptions, women approached farming beyond the Missouri River apprehensively. Like Willa Cather's narrator, Luna Kellie, who settled with her husband and small son in central Nebraska in 1876, felt that the Nebraska grassland was the end of the world (Kellie 1926, 8). Faye Lewis (1971), whose family left Iowa to farm in South Dakota in 1909, recalled that her mother dreaded the move. She feared rattlesnakes and fires and hated to think of death and burial in a place with no trees, no flowers, no shrubs. Grace Snyder, whose family moved to a farm in central Nebraska in 1885 when she was three, said of her mother: "She had grown up among the green fields and woods of Missouri, where she lived in a big white house. . . . I know she must have been nearly crushed by the unexpected bigness of the prairie, the blue of the sky, our rough, home-made furniture, and the almost total lack of neighbors" (Snyder

1963, 16). Women who had migrated to the prairie-plains transition region as daughters or who were born to settler families sometimes told of exciting and romantic adventures they had as girls in the new land. But their mothers had grownup worries and vastly greater responsibilities in providing food, clothing, education, and health care for the household (Lewis 1971, 14; Sanford 1959, 33). Most women were reluctant pioneers.[2]

What was it about crossing the Missouri River that was so intimidating? Newcomers to central Nebraska noticed the lack of trees at once. Only about 3 percent of Nebraska was naturally forested, and these trees grew mostly on the banks of rivers and streams (Olson 1966, 14). Treeless lands stretched mile after mile, offering nothing but sky and grass for orientation. Luna Kellie (1926, 92) wrote that her eyes "hungered" for trees in Nebraska. She described trees as she would people, noting in particular the one cottonwood tree that was on their property when they came and the many different trees that they planted. With trees, she said, the children could have a swing and shade to play in; children "needed" a swing and shade in order to be children. Trees anchored people to the landscape and marked one place as distinct from another; a woman felt a nagging uneasiness without trees. In explaining her mother's misgivings about South Dakota, Faye Lewis (1971, 33) wrote that the "vast unshelteredness" troubled her mother, because there was nothing to make a shadow.

The scarcity of trees meant that lumber, which had to be imported, was too expensive for most settlers to use for houses. Instead, they dug into the sides of hills, if there were any, leveled the dirt for floors, and used cut chunks of sod to make the walls and roofs of dugouts or free-standing sod houses—soddies, as they were called. Those who had lived in frame houses before coming to Nebraska thought sod houses were primitive. One Kansas woman, on seeing her family's sod house for the first time, succumbed to a fit of weeping, the only time she ever allowed herself such indulgence, as her daughter recalled (Stratton 1981, 55). A Nebraska woman put it simply: "I cannot say I like a sod house." The dirt floor was always dirty, and rain would seep through the walls and roof, ruining carpets and furniture (*Nebraska Farmer* 1896, 313). During hard rains, sod house dwellers took shelter under umbrellas or furniture. Bedbugs, rodents, and snakes also found their way through the walls and roofs; they were irritating pests as well as health menaces (Smets 1957, 32). Dust constantly sifted off the dirt walls and worked up off the dirt floor, blanketing the house and making cleanliness impossible. The one comfort of soddies was their pleasant coolness in summer heat.[3]

Many pioneers told stories of how the walls or ceilings of their sod houses disintegrated, throwing the household into chaos. My great-grandparents, who had just built a sod house, had their entire roof lifted off in a wind and rain storm in 1885. The family—four sons ages three to ten, my great-grandmother (pregnant with twins), and my great-grandfather—hid in a cave for the night. Every household item was soaked or blown away. The next morning, the ten-year-old rode to the nearest neighbors for a dry match with which to start a fire to cook breakfast and dry their belongings so that they could rebuild. Luna Kellie told of barely getting her baby, husband, brother, and herself outside before their sod roof suddenly collapsed in the middle of the night. After that incident, she feared and hated sod houses, although she later had to move into another one (Kellie 1926, 57, 90). Some women and men lived in soddies for over fifty years and recalled them nostalgically; most did not. Loved or unloved, soddies were the most common form of Nebraska home for European Americans during the nineteenth century.

East of the Missouri River, trees had provided fuel as well as building material. Nebraska settlers had to adjust to not having the firewood that they had always considered a fact of life. Coal, like wood, was expensive. Central Nebraskans twisted or trampled straw and grass for fuel. They also burned corncobs; if the price of corn was too low, they burned corn as well. Some collected cattle chips to burn. All of these fuels burned quickly, so that heating fires required constant feeding in winter; at night they went out, leaving the houses cold. A Boone County woman recalled that her husband would buy a bag of coal to keep their house warm for a few days whenever she had a baby in the winter, but most of the time they survived with minimal heat.

Although they worked hard, the women who kept house in soddies derived little sense of pride from their work. My mother once described my grandfather's birth in a sod house and his farm childhood by asking me to imagine living in a place without beauty, without diversion, without light, with only work to fill out each day. It could be monotonous for a woman to do the daily cooking and washing of dishes for farm workers, to constantly have babies who kept her inside or close to the soddy, and to have no relief. In Nebraska, women encountered a bleakness that they had not known before.

In addition to the lack of trees, settlers also coped with extreme weather in Nebraska. The scarcity of water worried farmers acutely. The average yearly precipitation is nearly even from mid-Iowa eastward to the Atlantic coast; it diminishes rapidly from the Missouri River to the Rocky Mountains (Baltensperger 1985, 3–4). The average yearly precipitation at the center of Boone County is twenty-five inches, which means that Boone County, like most of Nebraska, is basically too dry for successful row-crop farming, at least using the farming practices of the East. But "average" has little meaning in Nebraska, where the climate seems always to seek the outer limits. Precipitation varies by as much as 50 percent from the average in any given year. In early years, when it varied upward, crops tended to thrive; when it varied downward, the mood was gloomy and apprehensive. Rain became an obsession with farmers: they reckoned it by the hundredths of an inch; they watched the enormous sky and learned to read the different cloud textures and colors; they learned to smell a coming rain and to feel it in the wind; they believed strange stories about how to make it rain.

If not enough precipitation came or if the timing or form of the precipitation was wrong, farmers would have no feed for their livestock and no crop to sell. On the other hand, too much rain in the spring could delay planting and diminish production, yet the seeds needed water as soon as they were in the ground. Farmers worked frantically to get the planting done if they smelled a rain coming or saw rain clouds in the sky. If the rain was too heavy—and this happened from time to time—it might wash out newly sown seed, drown seedlings, or carry topsoil away and leave a hard crust. In the midst of a good growing season, a hailstorm might shred gardens, corn, and wheat in a few minutes. August, when it tended not to rain,

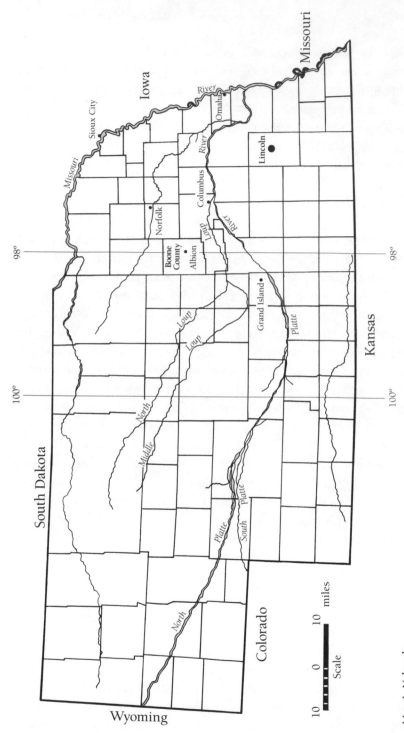

Map 1. Nebraska

was always a critical month. Sometimes hot, dry August winds would sweep up over the land, sucking moisture from the crops and leaving them dead. Grasshoppers, which thrived in dry weather, would eat anything that remained. Even when total yearly precipitation should have been adequate, poor timing and excess evaporation might kill the crops; then again, even when the total precipitation was less than average, one or two timely rains might save everything. In Nebraska you never knew (Baltensperger 1985).

When precipitation fell right, as it tended to in the early 1880s, 1910s, and 1940s, farmers did well; when the rains failed, as they did most dramatically in the 1890s and 1930s, the farmers' best efforts counted for nothing. Many lost their homes, left in discouragement, or sank into poverty and stayed only because they had nowhere else to go (Baltensperger 1985; Boone County Extension Service 1939).

Then there was the wind. People coming from regions of trees and hills had never known winds like Nebraska winds. Luna Kellie (1926, 7) said that, when she first came, the constant wind made her feel that she never wanted to go outside; it was a misery. Some winds, like spiralling tornadoes or the gale that blew off my great-grandparents' roof, damaged property and killed people as well as livestock. With no large trees or outbuildings to act as breaks, wind could destroy women's gardens and tree seedlings. Wind mixed with snow produced blinding and disorienting blizzards that froze both livestock and humans. When drought left the plowed fields bare, the winds would whip up the soil, making black blizzards that choked animals and humans and left fences, equipment, gardens, and buildings buried in drifts of dirt. Aside from the central sandhill region, Nebraska soils were well suited to growing corn and other grains, given enough moisture, but the winds blew tons of topsoil from exposed fields, destroying their natural fertility.

Winds also fanned the grass fires that started in dry weather and spread "like wildfire" across the thick, matted vegetation covering the plains. Before European settlement of Nebraska, such fires had regularly swept across the grasslands, burning off encroaching tree seedlings and renewing the soil and grasses. As farmers settled, their homes and fields initially were dispersed across large, wild grassland ranges, which could easily be set on fire either by lightning or by human carelessness. Fires burned haystacks, barns, and houses. Every settler's story included at least one harrowing tale of fighting a wind-driven fire to save a farm, of children trapped and killed in a fire, or of a narrow escape. In dry seasons, firefighters battled plains fires with little or no water (Pyne 1982, 84–99).

Walter Prescott Webb (1931, 9), writing about the Great Plains, said that civilization east of the Mississippi stood on three legs: land, water, and timber. On the Great Plains, two of those legs—water and timber—were missing, and only land remained. The missing legs gave plains life a distinct character, as people adapted to a stark and insistent environment. Carrying eastern patterns of life to the margin of the cornbelt stretched these patterns to their limits—and sometimes past their limits. Boone County was not quite the Great Plains; it was not quite the cornbelt. Its settlers, not least the women, moved onto a land they could not trust.

But European Americans were neither the first inhabitants nor the first farmers on the plains. Native peoples had been there for thousands of years. In 1800 the Arapaho, Cheyenne, Sioux, Pawnee, Ponca, Omaha, and Oto peoples were all living in Nebraska (Olson 1966, 21). The Pawnee, Ponca, and Omaha nations claimed parts of Boone County, having adapted to the environment by combining farming with extensive hunting. The nomadic Sioux appeared later, as the Pawnee and Omaha were weakened through their contacts with whites. The Pawnee, who built circular earthlodges on the banks of streams, located their permanent villages beside rivers and creeks in the region immediately south of Boone County. Pawnee women raised corn, beans, squash, and pumpkins on the flood-bottom soils next to the water. By both hunting and farming, they created a stable subsistence base. Although none of the historical Native American nations is recognized as having ancient roots in what is now Boone County, the Pawnee appear to have had the most valid recent claims to that land (Baltensperger 1985; Holder 1970; Olson 1966; White 1983).

The original peoples might have kept the land if European Americans had heeded early warnings against white settlement in Nebraska. In the eighteenth century, the French and Spanish had "owned" the land without establishing settlements. The United States acquired Nebraska from France as part of the Louisiana Purchase in 1803. An early U.S. explorer, Major Stephen Long, returning in 1820 from a trek along the Platte River to the Rocky Mountains, declared that the land was a desert and that it should remain forever "the unmolested haunt of the native hunter, the bison, and the jackall" (quoted in Olson 1966, 3). As late as 1879, a Department of the Interior "Report on the Lands of the Arid Region of the United States" by John Wesley Powell stated that the land west of the 100th meridian was unfit for agriculture and that the area east of it, which received less than twenty-eight inches of rain annually, would be only marginally suited to agriculture. One way or the other, this covered most of Nebraska.

Until 1854, when Nebraska became a territory, European Americans used the land only as a transit route and for trading outposts. In addition to the sectional conflict that had stalled the country's western development, the western plains nations had defended their land by force. But the drive to control the width of North America, to realize manifest destiny, drove the U.S. government persistently into the center of the continent. Conflicts with the powerful Sioux in the northwestern part of the state and disease epidemics introduced by Europeans drastically reduced the Pawnee and Omaha populations and made them increasingly vulnerable to incursions of both white and Sioux. This weakness came at the very time that whites were ready to move. The Omaha ceded their Boone County territory to the U.S. government in 1854. The Pawnee—weakened by war, deepening poverty, and U.S. interference in tribal government—gave up their Boone County lands in 1857. Nance County, immediately south of Boone, was a Pawnee reservation until 1875, when harassment from both whites and Sioux convinced the few remaining Pawnee to relocate in Oklahoma (Olson 1966; White 1983).

The United States had to work to get whites into Nebraska as well as to get native peoples out. In the process, Nebraska's image changed from that of a desert to a garden. Once it had been established that Nebraska was tillable, agrarian ideology would bolster a persuasive argument for abrogating treaties and displacing original nations. In petitioning the U.S. Congress for the extinction of the original hold-ers' land rights, the Nebraska legislature drafted the following statement:

> Whereas, the Indians now on special reservations in Nebraska hold and occupy valuable and important tracts of land, which while occupied will not be developed and improved; and Whereas the demand for lands which will be improved and made useful, are such that these Indian lands should no longer be held, but should be allowed to pass into the hands of enterprising and industrious citizens; . . .
>
> [W]e urge upon our delegation in Congress to secure the removal of all Indians now on special reservations in Nebraska to other . . . localities, where their presence will not retard settlements by the whites. (*Laws of Nebraska*, 1870–71, quoted in Sheldon 1936, 10–11)

If Nebraska was farming country, it was for white farmers only.

Science and business joined forces to change the public image of Nebraska. Samuel Aughey, a University of Nebraska geography professor, advanced a timely and optimistic theory that cultivation of the soil would produce a more humid environment, which in turn would increase the rainfall. Railroads picked up the slogan "rain follows the plow" and used it in their literature promoting settlement in Nebraska. Railroad promotional pamphlets, called "boomers," circulated widely, picturing Nebraska as a place of abundant rainfall and superior agricultural potential (Baltensperger 1985, 58). The *Nebraska Farmer* solicited and printed testimonials to Nebraska's superiority as a farm state; according to these, Nebraska had thousands of the most beautiful farms anywhere, with no weeds, just thick shocks of wheat and big cornstalks with fat ears of corn (Smith 1892, 523).

If the government land was free, what was there to lose? The first white settlers reached Boone County in 1871, but only a hardy few came before the railroad. In 1880 the Union Pacific completed a railroad line coming up the Beaver Valley and linking the county seat to Columbus, a commercial center forty-five miles to the southeast. Rounding out this rosy picture, the early 1880s brought good rains and good crop yields, lending credence to the belief that if settlers

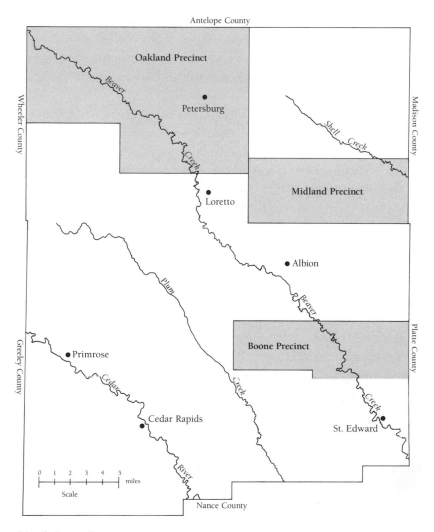

Map 2. Boone County

only had faith and committed themselves to farming, the plains would open to them and embrace them. Suddenly the population boomed. Eastern investors were eager to put their money into rural development in Nebraska (Baltensperger 1985; Barns 1970 [1930]; Olson 1966).

Boone County settlers, like most others in eastern Nebraska, initiated the same mixed grain and livestock farming that prevailed in the prairie states. Sales of corn, cattle, and hogs constituted the primary source of farm income; farm life centered around this production. Many farmers also milked one or two cows and kept a flock of chickens to provide dairy products, eggs, and meat for the household table and a less seasonal, secondary source of income. Almost every farm family hoped to raise potatoes, vegetables, and fruit for its own use and for occasional sales. In addition, scattered farm dwellers had small production enterprises consisting of orchards, bees, ducks, geese, or sheep.

Albion, the seat of Boone County, was far enough from existing commercial centers to develop its own clientele. It became a secondary civic and commercial hub for surrounding farms. A steam flour-and-feed mill, two newspapers, a livestock sales barn, a grain elevator, hotels, saloons, and numerous clothing, food, jewelry, and drug stores appeared in Albion to draw the trade of the growing farm population that surrounded the town. Farmers recorded land transactions at the courthouse, consulted lawyers, and negotiated with insurance companies and loan brokers in Albion. An opera house, the Carnegie Library, elementary and high schools, and several churches answered cultural and spiritual needs. By 1900, although it had less than 1,400 residents, Albion had become the metropolitan center of Boone County (see table 3-1). Outside of Albion, nine other smaller towns developed as minor trade and service sites and fourteen country post offices were established (Barns 1970 [1930]; Mundschenk 1986).

Midwesterners predominated in Boone County's settler population. As was true of the farming frontier in general, those in the vanguard of settlement were native-born, coming from New England, the middle Atlantic states, and states contiguous to the frontier (Eblen 1965, 412). More Boone County settlers were born in Iowa

Table 3-1. Population of Boone County and Albion, Nebraska, 1880–1940

Year	Boone Co.	Albion
1880	4,170	330
1890	8,683	926
1900	11,689	1,369
1910	13,145	1,584
1920	14,146	2,000*
1930	14,738	2,172
1940	12,127	2,268

Source: U.S. censuses.

*Estimated.

than in any other state. Different sets of my great-grandparents, typical of many Nebraska settlers born in eastern states or European countries, had sojourned in the midwestern states of Ohio, Illinois, and Minnesota before settling in Nebraska. Only 15 percent of the 1900 population was foreign-born, and these persons were overwhelmingly from the northern European countries that had dominated the early settlement of the Atlantic states (see table 3-2). No Poles, Italians, Spaniards, Asians, or Middle Easterners settled in Boone County. The 1900 census listed two African Americans and no Native Americans in the Boone County population (Census 1901, 547). Although some Germans and Norwegians clustered in ethnic neighborhoods during the first years, most foreign-born settlers were spread throughout the county. As in Nebraska as a whole, the dominant ethnic character in Boone County was northern European American (Baltensperger 1985, 70).

Farmers formed the backbone of the settlement of eastern Nebraska. Many of these men were Union veterans who had fought not so much against the principle of slavery as for the cause of free labor and the small white farmer. Farmers were seeking fertile land, but they had other economic motives on the side or in the background.

Land speculation was endemic throughout American frontier history. Before the development of the stock market, real estate was the

Table 3-2. Birthplaces of Foreign-born Boone County
Residents, 1900

Country of Birth	No.
Australia	4
Austria	21
Belgium	15
Canada	89
Denmark	63
England	125
France	2
Germany	502
Holland	2
Hungary	1
Ireland	154
Luxembourg	2
Norway	363
Russia	57
Scotland	9
Sweden	349
Switzerland	16
Wales	3
Unknown, born at sea	7

Source: Census 1901, 768.

principal form of investment in the United States, and eastern speculators invested heavily in Nebraska lands. Local agents worked for
them and reaped their own profits from the trade in land. Farmers
themselves could not be neatly separated from speculators, because
they also dealt in land and realized unearned gains from the growing
land market. A farmer might work to make a living, but he or she was
also conscious of the speculative potential of the land. Many of these
farmers had come from Iowa, where land speculation was more ram-
pant than in any other state. Speculation was in the marrow of the
U.S. economy, and Nebraska farmers, even—or especially—in their
poverty, were not isolated from the encompassing system (Bal-

tensperger 1985, 48; Fite 1985; Opie 1987, 58; Swierenga 1968; Worster 1979).

The free land offered by the Homestead Act did not put an end to speculation; it merely provided new avenues. The speculative designs of homesteaders became ever more transparent and acceptable as European settlers pushed west onto land that could never be profitably worked in 160-acre farms.[4] The Kinkaid Act of 1904 allowed homesteads in units of 640 acres in thirty-seven counties of western Nebraska, but these farms never became economically viable even at 640 acres. Eastern Nebraska proved to encompass the last lands on which settlers had even the semblance of a fair shot at proving up and farming on 160-acre farms.

Speculation, though present in Boone County and throughout eastern Nebraska, rested on the value of land as farmed by small-scale farmers. Most Boone County settlers had been farmers before they came to Nebraska. Many hoped to make their living on Boone County farms and, if lucky, realize enough profit to retire in a Boone County town. This may have involved speculation, but the settlers' dreams were not complicated or unreasonable.

As on the cornbelt farms to the east, Boone County farmhouses were separated, each sitting on a farm operated by an independent $\rangle$ household. Men were responsible for field crops and large livestock; women helped the men and were themselves responsible for poultry, butter making, and gardening. Except for the raising and butchering of hogs or steers, women did the work of provisioning the household with meat, potatoes, eggs, vegetables, milk, butter, and fruit. To get flour, which they used to make the staple bread and noodles, they either had farm wheat ground commercially or they purchased milled flour. Cornmeal for making cornbread was also ground commercially or purchased. They bought sugar, spices, and salt to preserve their food and enhance its flavor. Women paid for these food items—and for coffee, cloth, and clothing—from the proceeds of egg and butter sales. Men's income bought livestock, seeds, fencing, and farm equipment and paid the taxes. Any surplus income from these sales was apt to be invested in land or equipment. Even though they produced most of their own needs, the settlers' lifeways connected them by a vital umbilicus to the economy of the eastern cities.

From the beginning, the Nebraska farm economy fluctuated: it rose, dropped, wavered, or boomed in no particular order or symmetry. Rains were plentiful in the 1880s, and the fertile, untilled soil revealed its full promise in these first years. The rains failed in the mid-1890s, and this failure came on top of the panic of 1893, which sank the whole country into a depression. Many farmers were ruined. The buoyant optimism of the early years ebbed, and various charities engaged in piecemeal efforts to collect food, clothing, and shoes for people who were isolated and desperate. In 1895 a farm woman wrote to the *Nebraska Farmer* that she lived in the most miserable place imaginable: "Misery likes company and it surely has plenty of it this year" (Kearney 1895, 152). Others were less glib: suicides increased and the state insane asylum in Norfolk received new guests.

The rains returned at the end of the 1890s, but by then settlers had learned how untrustworthy the Nebraska climate was, mostly due to the unreliable rains. Plowing—the remedy advocated by Professor Aughey—and a host of other gadgets and tricks all failed to affect the climate. Although Boone County settlers attempted to reproduce the rural communities they had known in the prairie farming states to the east, Nebraska did not provide them with the necessary resource base. The climatic severity and the unreliability of farming made it impossible for a large population in rural Nebraska to enjoy the same living standards as the propertied middle class in the eastern states. The climate and soil of Boone County proved disastrous for most of those who attempted to farm on the model established in the humid cornbelt. In marketing their produce, these settlers were competing with the farmers of Iowa and Illinois, who had a better climate, more farm capital, stronger infrastructure, and closer markets. When Nebraska farmers did produce good crops, they might be faced with low prices and increased pressure on land resources. Farmers deserted Boone County continuously from the first years of settlement, and the outflow increased in the 1890s. But succeeding waves of newcomers ensured population growth for the first forty years of white settlement.

Census schedules from 1900 and 1910 indicate the brief tenure of

Table 3-3. Number, Tenure, and Persistence of Farms in Boone and
Oakland Precincts, Boone County, 1900 and 1910

	No. of Farms in 1900	No. Persisting to 1910	Percentage of Farms Persisting
Boone Precinct			
Owned	54	15	28
Mortgaged	32	8	25
Rented	31	5	16
Total	85	20	24
Oakland Precinct			
Owned*	114	39	34
Mortgaged	74	28	39
Rented*	60	16	27
Total	185	62	34

Source: U.S. census schedules.

*Incomplete or illegible data in census schedule on farm tenure.

most farming settlers even after the disaster of the 1890s was past.[5] In
Oakland Precinct in the northwestern quadrant of the county, most
of the land was poorly suited to farming and gradually became part of
large ranches, although the initial settlers were small farmers. Boone
Precinct, with its fertile southeastern bottomland along Beaver Creek,
had some of the best farmland in the county. Of the farming households listed in 1900 in Boone and Oakland precincts, only 30 percent
appeared on the 1910 census forms. Table 3-3 provides an overview
of the owned, mortgaged, and rented farms in each precinct and the
persistence rate of each. Rental farms, which existed in substantial
numbers even in the early years of settlement, showed even less
stability than owner-occupied farms, but the persistence rate for each
category was well under 50 percent. Boone Precinct, with its richer
land and earlier settlement, was less residentially stable than the
incipient sandhills of Oakland Precinct, suggesting that such financial considerations as rents and interest rates were more telling than
the relative quantity of production in the two areas.

Residential instability notwithstanding, the period between 1900 and 1920 represents the high-water mark for the Nebraska agricultural economy in terms of good production and good farm prices. The years from 1910 to 1914 have been called the golden age of American agriculture, and World War I heightened the boom. Boone County farmland values (exclusive of buildings) rose from an average of $18.13 per acre in 1900, to $61.33 in 1910, to $143.22 in 1920 (Census 1913b, 30; 1922b, 690). Some farmers thrived under the high demand for farm products. New farmers came to take over the farms of those who left, and the number of farms grew.[6]

Following the heady farm economy of the World War I period, farm prices fell flat, ushering in an agricultural depression that preceded the general 1930s depression by nearly ten years. Farmers who had bought land in the time of high land prices were unable to make their mortgage payments unless they had a layer of financial protection. One-quarter of Nebraska's farms failed between 1921 and 1923. Farmland prices dropped an average of 37 percent from 1920 to 1925 (Census 1932a, 1218). Banks were unable to recover the value of mortgages they had made, and 650 closed their doors during the 1920s (Creigh 1977, 185). After 1920 Boone County's out-migration exceeded in-migration; from 1920 to 1930 there was a net out-migration of 1,951 persons—12 percent of the 1920 population (Census 1932b, 615; 1922a, 595).[7]

Then the Great Depression hit, and in the middle of that another drought came, matching that of the 1890s. Drought, dust storms, grasshoppers, no money—the combination threatened the survival of rural Nebraska. Boone County's ten towns became six, and the farm population hemorrhaged: during the 1930s there was a net out-migration loss of 29 percent (Census 1932b, 615; 1943, 608).

Not everyone in Boone County prospered equally during the booms; not everyone suffered equally during the depressions. Class differences divided the population. Jefferson's agrarian ideal envisioned a middle-class society, an economic democracy where every man was his own master because every man owned land and the tools of his trade. An infinite supply of fertile, well-watered land was a key element in Jefferson's social theory, in which differences of wealth would not lead to class conflict. National Reformers, who saw the western lands as a safety valve for eastern cities, believed that those who went west to free land would not become subordinate to other property owners. They themselves would own their own means. In the grassroots protest movements of the late nineteenth century, impoverished farmers expressed their rage at the capitalists whose exploitation had betrayed the agrarian promise.

The Country Life movement put a different slant on the class position of farmers. The chairman of the Country Life Commission, Liberty Hyde Bailey (1911, 16), asserted that the "agricultural class" formed a natural balance between the "so-called laboring class" and the "corporate and monopolized interests." One way in which rural life was superior to urban life was in the absence of class conflict. Rural society consisted simply of an agricultural class, and this class-less class would point the way toward a society at peace with itself. Farmers would act independently because they owned their own farms and worked for themselves. To the Country Lifers, farmers were the only class that represented individualism, and the only danger in organizing them was that it might compromise this individualism: "Fortunately, the holding of title to land and the separateness of farm habitations prevent solidification [of class consciousness]" (Bailey 1915, 137).

Many people in Boone County have, at one level, shared the view of a classless rural community. The belief that rural settlers had equal opportunities has run strong in the past; I heard it repeatedly when I was in Boone County in the 1980s. Those who prospered were self-made, the implication being that the failures were also self-made. Said one farm woman, born in 1917, "I can't think of anyone we thought was worse off than anyone else." From women who had continued to live on farms up to the 1980s, I heard over and over, "Everyone was in the same boat," or similar remarks. Insofar as agrarian thinking applied to their experience, "everyone" had a farm, a few cows, and chickens; "everyone" struggled and survived.

Yet, in contrast to the people who said simply that everyone was "in the same boat," there were those who made clear that some people were poorer than others. Most of these were the poor themselves, who could view the economic structure from below and know that they were not economically equal to others. One woman, born in 1927, expressed her poverty as she knew it: "I always felt inferior, I guess, because the other kids had nicer homes and nicer clothes." A farm woman who took the census in her neighborhood saw the inside of this woman's house for the first time in 1940, although she had lived nearby since her marriage in 1929 and had visited other neighbors. Implicitly acknowledging a barrier between her household and the other family's, she said: "That was my first experience with them. It was the filthiest place I've ever been in. I shouldn't even tell you. . . . I don't know how to explain it. They were backward in some ways. . . . They didn't have too much of a social life. They didn't mix with people. People kind of laughed at them. I don't know why. We were not closely associated with them and we wouldn't have been there except that I was taking that census." When the mother of the impoverished farm household tried to join a country church, the pastor was so chilly that she gave up. Another woman, now gone from Boone County, recalled her early years of marriage to a tenant farmer: "The next-door neighbors . . . had nothing to do with poor trash like we were."

Even the Country Life Commission chaired by Liberty Hyde Bailey indirectly pointed to class differences in the countryside. Commissioners found that, although many farm homes had "all that can be desired," many others did not (Bailey et al. 1909, 46). Notwithstanding the robustness of the overall farm economy in the early years of the twentieth century, the main thrust of the commission's report was an enumeration of the problems of rural poverty and social disorganization. Hired laborers, according to the report, had special problems with intemperance, excessive mobility, poor housing, and lack of thrift. With its brief nod to the farms that were amply comfortable, followed by a longer treatment of the inferior living conditions on the majority of farms and a separate section on the special deprivation of hired laborers, the commission was implicitly acknowledging the presence of class inequalities in rural life.

Representations of poor people as dirty, intemperate, backward, or wasteful implied a moral judgment, a suggestion that poverty resulted from inadequacies of character. Such representations mask the economic dimensions of the perceptions people had about each other, about the possibilities open to them and others, and about the limitations they knew were there, even if they could not fully explain them. Class analysis connects these manifestations of unequal power to control of the production process. A schematic class outline divides the rural population into three major classes: (1) nonproducers who owned the means of production that others used to make a living both for themselves and for the owners; (2) workers who owned the means of production they themselves used; and (3) workers who did not own the means of production and were therefore subject to those who owned the land, raw materials, and equipment they used to make a living.[8]

Although these categories may apply to any kind of work, they may in this context be identified as capitalists, family farmers (simple commodity producers, or the traditional middle class), and hired laborers (working class). Much overlap and ambiguity is apparent when this division is applied to the people of Boone County, largely because an indefinite and changing number of farmers who technically owned their land were so indebted that this ownership was meaningless as a class indicator. But the significance of class as an ongoing factor involving the control of production does not depend on the unambiguous assignment of class agency to individuals, nor does the impossibility of assigning an unambiguous class position to each person preclude a class analysis.

Sociologist Patrick Mooney (1983, 1986) finds that the variables of hired labor, tenancy, indebtedness, and off-farm work have produced contradictory class alliances. One farmer might, for example, have been a tenant who employed workers on his rented farm. As a tenant wanting maximum land for minimum cost, his interests opposed those of the landlord. As an employer wanting maximum labor for minimum cost, his interests opposed those of his workers. These conflicting class affiliations—which shifted with economic swings that affected the variables differentially—account for the volatility in farm politics.

Some farmers persevered through the farm depression of the 1890s and realized a profit on their land sales when prices rose again after 1900. Others found themselves unable to hold on to their farms in competition with more aggressive dealers. The disappearance of the majority of farm households between 1900 and 1910 and the growth of a significant number of tenant farms point toward a sizable number of workers who did not control the means of production. The increase in the size of this class is indicated by the figures on farm tenancy alone: the incidence of tenancy among Boone County farmers rose from 39 percent in 1900 to 41 percent in 1920, 54 percent in 1930, and 70 percent in 1940 (Census 1902, 102; 1932a, 1204; 1943, 585). Not everyone who owned a farm necessarily controlled the production on that land; but most who did not own the farms they worked also did not have effective control of their own production processes. Their tenure on the land depended on their establishing production systems that would bring in the necessary cash or crops to meet the rising demands of farm tenancy. This promoted intensive exploitation of both family labor and the land, a situation that tenants might not have found to be fully in their interest if they themselves had controlled the production process. Midwestern writers Hamlin Garland (1969 [1891]) and Ruth Suckow (1926) powerfully depicted tenants' vulnerability.

Evidence that a small number of persons owned significantly more than the means of their own production may be found in an examination of farm structure, as seen in table 3-4. The largest farms, those consisting of more than 500 acres, were more than five times the size of smallest farms, those with less than 100 acres. Between 3 and 6 percent of the farms were larger than 500 acres, which, before 1940, would have been more land than could have been worked with family labor. The people who owned these farms would have controlled and profited from the labor of nonowners. Because many of Boone County's farms were rented rather than owned, the shape of the farm structure there minimizes class polarity.

A class profile of Boone County before 1940 may have revealed approximately 5 percent capitalists, something less than 50 percent middle-class owner-operators, and a substantial base of persons who owned no productive property. An examination of probate records from the 1930s supports this general outline. Only a minority of those who died in Boone County left productive property for probate. An estate would be probated if there were a will, if there were productive property, or if the deceased had left significant debts to be

[handwritten margin note: Tenants as a class]

Table 3-4. Boone County Farm Structure, 1900–1940, Percentage
by Size

	Less Than 100 Acres	100–259 Acres	260–499 Acres	More Than 500 Acres
1900	12	60	24	4
1910	12	60	23	4
1920	11	64	22	3
1930	11	65	21	3
1940	11	56	27	6

Source: Computed from U.S. agricultural census reports.

cleared. A few persons who left no more than their personal property
wrote wills, but usually the probate of an estate indicated that the
dead person had owned productive property sometime in the previous ten years before death. Only one-third of the persons who died
from 1933 through 1935 had their estates probated. Although many
people lost their property during the 1930s, those who had previously owned property generally would have maintained some ves-
tiges of it in the form of assets or debts. About 5 percent of the estates
were worth $20,000 or more, which signaled substantial capital in
the 1930s.[9]

The vast majority of Boone County women, those living in family
farm or working-class households, were workers. The household
economies could not operate without their labor. The women's income from their poultry, butter making, and other enterprises supported their households. Yet these women worked in different kinds
of family operations. Some families rented farms, some owned their
farms, and some farms were heavily mortgaged; some farm families
hired laborers, many families did their own farm work, while some
rural people worked as paid laborers. All these dimensions of class
division shaped the ways that the women lived and worked.

Food provision, a cornerstone of women's work, differed by class.
Some early Boone County women had adequate and nutritious food
to put on their families' tables; others did not. Meat, butter, sugar,
coffee, canned fruits, spices, and even flour and milk were luxuries

for some. Luna Kellie (1926, 31) wrote of how her family barely subsisted on peas, beets, beet greens, carrots, and other garden vegetables as they were getting their farm started. She had no flour to make bread. She craved bread, thought about it constantly, even dreamed about it. Although no one ever told me that my grandfather's family went hungry, I know that my great-grandmother cooked up meals of flour and water for her household, which was growing to include eight children. Insufficient or poor-quality food dampened people's spirits and energy, making them listless workers.

Along with the differences in food went a general difference in the farm women's homes and their furnishings. The better-off farmers built frame houses to replace their soddies, thereby changing the boundaries of women's work space from dirt to wood. The more fortunate women had better stoves and cooking equipment, more convenient water supplies, sewing machines, and warm clothes and shoes. Some women even had washing machines, organs, carpets, and factory-made furniture, while others walked on dirt floors and improvised their furniture. A few women had hired girls to help them, but this was rare.

Farm women expected to earn money from sales of butter, eggs, and whatever else they could manage to offer. The *Nebraska Farmer* ran frequent items by women asking questions and giving suggestions on how to develop or improve cash-earning enterprises (Hawks 1892b, 520; 1896a, 312; Vach 1930, 395). But for some women, just getting a good milking cow to launch a butter-making enterprise was impossible. Luna Kellie (1926, 43) wrote of her frustration at having inferior milk cows that did not give enough milk for her to make butter; her family had no money for good cows. Those with little money for buying chickens to start their flocks had to carefully tend the few birds they had and collect eggs for hatching. Without proper chicken feed, which an impoverished woman often lacked, she had to work harder to keep the chickens alive and wait longer for them to grow. If she did not have a good chicken house, she would lose many of them to coyotes, dogs, or even pigs. She had fewer eggs and fewer chickens to sell than she would have had if she had been able to invest in a good poultry enterprise.

Women in more marginal households were likely to be pressed

into service as field workers and assigned a greater share of livestock chores than were women living on farms that could afford to hire workers. Women picked corn, raked hay, milked cows, fed pigs, cleaned stalls, and herded cattle when they had to do it for their survival. One of my great-grandmothers, widowed at a young age, supported her family of three children by hiring herself out as a field laborer. Women's field work created a double burden. When household economies were more stable, women usually concentrated their efforts on children, poultry, dairying, gardening, sewing and mending, and food preparation—more than enough to keep them busy.

Check Extension Service documents,

Frequent moves were another disadvantage of being poor. People living on well-established farms tended to stay in one place longer than did tenant farmers or highly indebted farmers. Hired laborers also moved frequently. Beyond arranging a new house so that it was livable, the woman who moved had to find a school for her children, establish new links with neighbors (who might look down their noses at tenants or laborers), find a new place to sell her eggs and buy groceries, and locate a doctor who would be inexpensive and kind enough to treat the poor. She did not have the comfort of trusted social networks and established routines.

Blanche Pease, a tenant farm wife who wrote for the *Nebraska Farmer* in the 1930s, had this to say about moving:

Moving time is a heartbreaking time for farm wives. . . .

March first is so often a stormy, unpleasant day, and that makes moving time all the harder. . . .

Arriving at the new home, the farm wife goes into the cold and chilly interior and watches while they set up the stoves and bring in the piles of boxes, the beds and mattresses and the many odds and ends, setting them down in incongruous piles in the shabby, ill-smelling rooms. . . .

At times like this the farm woman feels like crying her heart out, but she seldom does. It does so little good. (Pease 1940, 10)

Although a few women lived on one farm or in one house nearly all of their adult lives, the high rate of mobility indicated that many—

especially many of the working class—repeatedly faced the emotional turmoil of moving.

The relative prosperity of a farm also affected the degree of isolation that women experienced. A woman with hired help probably found it easier to leave her home than did one without help. In addition, on a well-stocked farm she was more likely to have the use of a horse and buggy—later a car—to make short trips. The isolation and loneliness of poverty could be grinding and destructive.

The isolation experienced by women is a point of controversy that goes to the heart of the question of how farm women thrived. One view of plains women denies this isolation and emphasizes the ("neighboring") that women engaged in—helping, advising, consoling each other—and the political, religious, and social organizations they developed (Riley 1988, 173–93; Neth 1988). Several of these women's own writings confirm that they had happy and stimulating social lives (Kohl 1986 [1938]; Stewart 1914). Women valued their relationships with other women and sometimes walked miles to see and talk with one another. Luna Kellie said of Mrs. Stohl, whom she met her first summer in Nebraska, "Without that friendship that day begun I know I must have fainted and dropped by the way side eir many years had flown" (Kellie 1926, 13).

By the turn of the century, telephones were helping to put rural women in touch with each other. Frank Rice (1970, 60), in his reminiscences about growing up on a Nebraska farm in the early twentieth century, wrote that farm women were eager to get telephones and used them often. Men, on the other hand, disdained the use of the telephone and considered it to be a woman's instrument. By 1929 three out of four Boone County farms had telephones, often paid for with women's egg money (Census 1932a, 1280).

Still, evidence of women's isolation remains. If three out of four women had telephones, one out of four didn't. Storms often took down lines, and telephones could stay out for a long time before they were fixed. Luna Kellie, later known for her activism in the Farmers' Alliance and the Populist party, did not get to town once in the first eighteen months she lived in Nebraska. Although writers like Kellie often center their narratives around times when they had visitors or saw people from outside their households, weeks might pass between these visits. Men typically went to town or to visit neighbors without their wives. Men's farm work was seasonal, but childcare and domestic responsibilities tugged continuously on women, keeping them at home. Some women also dreaded being seen in shabby clothes and worn-out shoes.

Historian Elizabeth Hampsten (1982, 39), commenting on the writings of midwestern women from 1880 to 1910, said that "women were lonely, so lonely that some sickened and died or went mad." Women who had left their mothers, sisters, cousins, and friends behind when they moved to Nebraska could be intensely lonely; they felt isolated even when nearby people might have comforted them (Ritter 1982, 20–21). The hopscotch moving that took some farm families from place to place deepened women's alienation. Impoverished women were most vulnerable. As soon as they had begun friendships and collected a circle of kinsfolk in one location, it was moving time again. Some separate households of kin moved westward in tandem; others were totally alone.

Aside from their separations from kinsfolk, women's loneliness also grew from their physical isolation. Boone County was never as thickly settled as rural Iowa and was much more sparsely populated than the areas of Europe where the settlers had their deeper roots. Comparing the population of farming areas in Denmark, northwest Iowa, and Boone County, we can see a significantly lower population density in Boone County (see table 3-5). The sparse population in Nebraska meant that it took more miles of roads to connect people, making it more expensive to develop and maintain them. By 1939, only 17 percent of Boone County's farms were accessible by graveled or hard-surfaced roads (Census 1942, 644). Dirt roads became impassable for long periods in the winter and spring. When women could use the roads, their travel to visit other women or to town was more time consuming and expensive than it would have been had they had shorter distances and better roads to travel. Working-class women were forced to stay home more often than women living on economically stable farms.[10]

Although settlers initially believed that they would have closer neighbors as farming developed in the region, later Boone Countians were more rather than less geographically isolated. The poverty of the

Table 3-5. Population Densities of Møn, Denmark; O'Brien County, Iowa; and Boone County, Nebraska, 1900–1960

	Persons per Square Mile					
	1900	*1910*	*1920*	*1930*	*1940*	*1960*
Møn	42.4	42.4	46.6	47.9	46.4	43.0
O'Brien County	29.5	30.0	33.5	32.0	33.6	32.8
Boone County	16.9	19.0	20.4	21.3	17.5	13.2

Sources: Danish and U.S. censuses.

1930s intensified the isolation for most women. More than 60 percent of farm telephones were removed, and many farms were abandoned (Census 1942, 644). Although most farmers had cars, even when the roads were open the price of gasoline precluded all but the most essential driving for the majority of people.

In order to build their agricultural society in east-central Nebraska, European Americans removed the indigenous inhabitants and attempted to transplant a way of life from the eastern United States to the plains. Boone County was built on promises. The money for the buildings, roads, bridges, and farms that established the county and made it livable for whites came not from the bounty of the Nebraska land but from the East. Some people came from the East with enough money in their pockets to buy the iron, lumber, glass, and barbed wire that they needed. Others borrowed from eastern creditors. The biggest nonfarm area of employment was in construction—carpentry, well digging, railroad construction, road building— and these people got their money, directly or indirectly, from the farmers. Farmers might have repaid their debts given an economic system that worked to their advantage, but they had little more power than the native peoples to structure a system that would work for them.

The people who came west changed the face of the land; the land, in turn, changed the people. As agrarians, their presence in Nebraska depended on farming. Agrarian ideology was their charter, and eastern Nebraska represented one variation on the rural American theme. Although originally conceived as a haven for the small white farmer,

mennonits
true

rural Nebraska was immediately rent by class divisions. Ethnic homogeneity did not negate class cleavage.

Women did not live the same lives as men, and the myths and symbols of the land were different for them. Women centered their lives in the home; men outside. Women were less mobile than men, and class differences affected their lives broadly. The following two chapters discuss what these conditions meant for women as wives.

4 SETTLER WIVES

The order and economy of a house are as honorable to the mistress as those of the farm to the master.
—Thomas Jefferson to Nathaniel Burwell, 1818

If marriage were a proper contract, women would have to be brought into civil life on exactly the same footing as husbands.—Carol Pateman, The Sexual Contract, *1988*

The farmer was at the center of agrarian democracy, and such a person needed a good wife. Nowhere was this more obvious than on the farms of eastern Nebraska, where nature and politics conspired to keep so many on the brink. People worked and worked to settle the region and then they worked and worked again to keep it. Some prospered; most did not. Kinsfolk and family constituted the primary source of labor and the primary umbrella of social protection in hard times.

Although women were central to the family system, their legal inequality contradicted the folk belief in marriage as a freely entered contract (Pateman 1988). Marriage had legal, economic, and social ramifications for women that made their options different from men's. For a woman, adult entry into a kinship system was signaled most securely and definitively by marriage. Access to farming also came through marriage. On the farm the role of woman as wife was so central that the phrase "farm wife" became a generalized designation for farm woman.

This chapter explores the experience of being a settler wife in rural Nebraska, including the legal, social, and economic conditions that shaped women's choices and limited their opportunities outside of marriage. Court records and individual stories provide glimpses into the values and limits that structured married couples' daily interactions. Although newspaper stories, court cases, personal memoirs, and diaries characteristically emphasized unusual and memorable events rather than the tedious minutiae of daily life, this material nonetheless provides a valid representation of the principles, lessons, and boundaries that shaped women's lives.

Kinship among European Americans in the rural Midwest and plains country was part of an American system, and it took some of its rules and sanctions from this encompassing kinship pattern. On the rural plains, the attributes of kinship were related to the changing economy, demography, and the plains environment. In American society in general, sexual relations and beliefs about them formed a code organizing the kinship system. Sexual relations, legally constituted, defined the husband-wife bond and established children as blood relatives. As a symbolic system that interpreted and gave meaning to social life, kinship was highly charged emotionally. People held deep and intense feelings about it. The system codified family relations, which in turn constituted a base on which other institutions rested. Beliefs about marriage systematized a relation of difference between husband and wife (Schneider 1968).

What did this mean for women's daily lives? What kinds of marriages grew out of the conditions of farming and rural life in eastern Nebraska? What made these marriages beneficial or liberating for women? What made them oppressive? Did rural society, built around the farm, marriage, and family, support and protect women within the marriage?

A good wife was an asset to the farm. A woman like my great-grandmother Mary Lederer—strong, committed to the farm's success, and willing to sacrifice her own comforts—made things better for other family members in both good times and bad. Just as Seena Kohl (1976, 93) found in her study of modern women and family in rural Saskatchewan, the rural Nebraska wife was important to the success of the farm. The individualism that Jefferson believed would emerge from a small-scale, household-based farming structure could more appropriately be called nuclear familyism.

Historian Daniel Scott Smith (1974, 126) concluded that an in-

creasing emphasis on the conjugal family unit elevated the position
of women on the frontier. Women, together with their husbands,
could chart a new course as they separated from the established
social system. The farms needed women, and women developed their
roles as farm wives in response to this need. Unlike city women, who
were marginalized by the gendered division of industrial labor, farm
wives' labor placed them in the thick of the production economy.
Joann Vanek, who examined time-use studies of farm households in
the period 1920 to 1955, concluded that farming mitigated gender
inequalities:

> Since wives produced the basic necessities for subsistence,
> their husbands were dependent on them, just as they were
> dependent on their husbands. . . . The relationship of hus-
> bands and wives on the farm was not entirely equal, since
> according to custom and the law women were subordinate to
> men. But men's dominance was offset by the tangible value of
> women's contribution to the household economy. . . . [A]
> kind of symmetry had occurred earlier in the household mode
> of production of preindustrial economies and in an agrarian
> past. (Vanek 1980, 423)

According to Vanek, the gender division of labor on the farm
strengthened women's position by making them indispensable.

On the other hand, Sarah Elbert found the seeds of a farm woman's strength in her tendency to broach the boundary separating her
from her husband's work and business affairs. Rather than focusing
on the organic solidarity that grew out of mutual dependence, Elbert
discovered unity and similarity in men's and women's lives on the
farm.[1] This, she believed, was the reason for the power she found in
the traditional position of farm women. Separate spheres, as deline-
ated by the home economics movement, did not strengthen farm
wives' family position. It was the commonalities with their husbands,
rather than the differences, that gave farm women power: "To many
farm women, the phrase 'he's the boss' is of secondary importance to
the recognition that farm women play an important role in 'doing it'
[farming] and 'passing it on.' . . . For over one hundred years, they
have demonstrated a form of feminism that reaches beyond any sim-

ple definition of autonomy or individualism—farm women have claimed the right to integrate work and family life" (Elbert 1988, 263). By claiming their roles as producers and shaping their production enterprises to their acknowledged family roles, wives could relegate their second-class status to the fringes of their reality. Not only was shared labor a historical fact, Elbert pointed out, but egalitarian gender relations derived from that shared labor.

These egalitarian gender relations, according to Elbert, have offered the best hope of solidarity for farmers as a class. Husband and wife standing together have formed part of a "battle plan" for strengthening the family farm as farm people seek to extend their unique way of life into the future (Elbert 1987, 194–95). By learning the lessons of history, implies Elbert, farm women can solidify their roles as their husbands' equal partners and thereby stem the decline of the farm sector.

In a similar vein, historian MaryJo Wagner (1988) cites farm women's shared labor within the family farm—the blending of the public sphere of employment and the private sphere of domestic relations—as the reason why such women as Luna Kellie joined, and were accepted in, the Farmers' Alliance and Populist party campaigns. Wives shared farming tasks with their husbands and in this way earned power and respect, which they carried out of the home into the political arena. Their central roles as farm producers translated first to family power and then to political power. Like Elbert, Wagner connected gender equality in farm labor to political change for the benefit of farmers as a group.

Analyses that emphasize the degree of egalitarian relations possible in at least some farm marriages point to labor as the basis of this egalitarianism. The wives' sharing of work with their husbands overrode the political and economic factors that subordinated women. These wives found a distinct rural reality in which they could define equality on their own terms. This viewpoint, emphasizing the good things the farm did for women, relies on a vision of Jeffersonian agrarianism as promoting a gender-neutral domestic cooperation. The scholars who adhere to this theory tend not to view the necessity of marriage as a problematic requirement for women's entry into farming.

Looking beyond models of consensus and harmony within the family, other scholars have pointed out the existence of conflict as well as unity. What Elbert (1987, 185) described as an "all-for-one and one-for-all mentality" in farm families has tended to obscure inequalities. Although Vanek's (1980, 424) data indicate that house-wives and farmers spent approximately equal numbers of hours at work, her findings do not preclude the possibility that the greater income of men, among other factors, gave them more power in deter-mining who did what work and in allocating resources. The division of labor made significant differences in the experiences of rural wives and husbands. Women bore the continual responsibilities of caring for children and providing household food, whereas men's work was seasonal and left them free at certain periods of time. Unlike the time studies made in the twentieth century, studies of the nineteenth-century gender division of labor on farms have concluded that it was fundamentally unequal in that wives labored longer than their hus-bands. The labor of their wives freed men for leisure and political activities, a dynamic termed "the exploitation of women as wives" (Faragher 1981, 550). An analysis of the control of farm production and assignment of household resources indicates that the family farm historically has been a patriarchal institution in which the power of the husband was reinforced by his ownership of the farm property and his legal authority over family decisions (Faragher 1981; Sachs 1983).

Complementarity and interdependence existed in the rural household. The disagreement between a rosy assessment and a nega-tive assessment of this situation centers on the significance of the entailed differences between husband and wife. One perspective indicates that the particular circumstances of frontier farm life compensated—at least in part—for the jural inequality of wives, creating a separate system in which women's strengths and abilities earned their just rewards. Another perspective—the one I put for-ward here—places frontier wives in the context of the gender con-tradictions of U.S. society as a whole and denies the transforming power of the frontier and farming as gender equalizers.

A marriage was an economic transaction and more. Its legal, emotional, and sexual content came to bear continuously on a woman's daily life. The legal system defined the husband as head of the household and gave him rights to decide the place of residence, to invest or distribute family funds, to assign work to his wife and children, and to have sexual relations with his wife. Gender-specific sexual norms showed a certain uniformity across the country, but rural conditions produced distinct manifestations of these norms. Together, the separate strands of the marital relationship wove a tighter and less volitional institution than would be apparent in considering them in isolation. In rural Nebraska, almost every woman at some time decided that marriage was her best option and that divorce was not a respectable alternative.

The name on a homestead claim or land title was nearly always a man's name. The Nebraska legislature passed the Married Women's Property Act in 1871, giving married women a right to own property independently, and this applied to inheritance, gifts, or wages. But few rural Nebraska settler families had significant property to distribute to daughters, and almost no married woman had a job that provided her with individual wages. A wife retained her dower right, the right to one-third of her husband's property at his death. This right limited the husband's ability to sell or mortgage land without his wife's permission, as a buyer or mortgagee would usually require the wife to relinquish her dower right in a given property. Thus, a wife theoretically had the power to block a sale or mortgage. Records and reports of this actually happening are rare.[2]

A few Boone County women did file homestead entries, but these were taken out as proxies for brothers, sons, or others who had already filed homestead claims or were otherwise ineligible to file in their own names. Few if any Boone County women homesteaded alone and remained to farm on their own after receiving the land patent. Because a homesteader had to be a head of family, wives almost never filed homestead entries in their names.[3]

I have found no records or personal narratives mentioning single women who farmed on their own in Boone County or the surrounding area before 1940. During one of my interviews, two sisters, born in 1908 and 1913, spoke to the question of single women farming. Emma and Anna, both of whom remained single for life, were the only children in a family that owned two farms. They loved farming yet had never considered it a vocational choice. Their interview included the following exchange:

> *DF*: Did you ever think that you might like to farm?
> *Anna*: Yes. I know I might like to.
> *Emma*: The two jobs that I really loved were the farm and the school. You could make more at the school than you could at the farm.
> *Anna*: At the time Dad had to give it up women did *not* farm.
> *Emma*: That is, they helped, but they didn't take over the farm and do the whole operation.
> *Anna*: Frankly, the way we grew up we never thought of even trying it. It wasn't done and we didn't do it. We've thought, a lot of times since, we wished we'd stayed out on the farm.
> *Emma*: We worked on the farm during the summer and then taught during the school year.
> *DF*: But running a farm was something you never had thought about? There was no woman around here who'd ever . . . ?
> *Emma*: The first that I knew of a woman who took over a farm was probably in the fifties. Of course, we had been in the school then a long time.

A woman who wanted to farm was best advised to marry a farmer.[4]

From the earliest days of settlement, Boone County residents understood that a family farm, built around a farmer and his wife, was the way farming was done. This truth, already internalized by many European Americans, had been put into print in the yearly reports of the U.S. Department of Agriculture (USDA). The first reports of the new commissioner of agriculture assessed the potentials and problems of agriculture and indicated the general thrust of the department's plans. That women would enter farming as appendages or wives of farmer husbands was so taken for granted that no explicit discussion of the fact was necessary; what was necessary was to ensure that women's labor, like other factors of production, was fully utilized.

When women were discussed in USDA texts, their kinship status was usually included or implied. The section of the 1871 report dealing with the relation of women to rural industries contained the following paragraph:

> Of the six hundred millions of pounds of butter, worth $180,000,000, how much comes from the labor of *women* in milking and churning, and all the cares of dairy management? Of two hundred and forty millions of pounds of cheese, worth $36,000,000, how much is manufactured by the *wives and daughters of farmers*? The eggs and poultry, amounting to many millions more, are due to an industry in which the *farmer's wife* has by far the larger share of skill and labor. The sweets of the hive are largely collected under the directing care of *women*. Millions of dollars, many more than those appearing in the census of market-garden producers, are produced in kitchen gardens by *feminine labor*. No inconsiderable amount of small fruits, both for home use and for the village and city markets, is grown and picked by *feminine hands*; and the quantity and value of wild berries—strawberries, raspberries, whortleberries, blackberries, cranberries, and other kinds—would annually aggregate far more than the fortune of one millionaire. Then if the casual or regular labor of *women*, in *assistance volunteered or required* in planting, weeding, cultivating, haying, harvesting, and even the care of live stock, be computed at its true value, and its real percentage of our total farm production calculated, how would the figures swell the sum, and magnify the proportion of the wealth wrought from the mine of the farm by the hand of *woman*! (USDA 1872, 337; emphases mine)

These industries become factory → produced

"Farmer's wife," "feminine labor," "feminine hands," and "woman," were used interchangeably in this text. A farmer's wife (or a farmer's daughter—a future farmer's wife) was the only possible kind of farm woman. That her "assistance" was "volunteered or required" implies that another person appropriated the labor of the woman, this other person typically being her husband. She was an adjunct to the farmer rather than being a farmer herself. The USDA delivered this message in order to promote the full exploitation of women's labor potential on the farm. A farmer, it implied, should be fully aware of the benefits to be gained by having an industrious wife. ⚹

The exception to this rule of male farming, according to the 1871 report, was the widow who might manage property after her husband's death. A widow was usually elderly, a woman who had already put in her time as a wife. A maiden sister or unmarried daughter might, in rare instances, undertake to manage a farm by default, but her actual farm labor was usually limited to what were thought of as secondary enterprises: fruit, flower, butter, or honey production. Field crops and large livestock—the "real" business of the farm— would be tended by hired men. The report briefly mentioned a "muscular maiden" who stood six feet tall and did farm work with "masculine skill" but followed this oddity by stating, "Of course, her example is not to be commended" (USDA 1872, 341).

But the USDA believed women's frivolity to be a more serious problem than the occasional "muscular maiden." Officials feared that women's education too often emphasized arts and manners, a malignant European pattern that would ruin women for work. The United States, the department urged, should reject this type of education and train women in practical domesticity. Because they never disdained hard work, the people of the United States would acknowledge the benefits of women's labor on the farm as long as this labor did not violate the gender division: "Not that women should hold the plow, or dig ditches, or build fences; there are occupations pertaining to agriculture essentially feminine, and rural and household arts in which women are qualified by nature to excel, but for which only scientific and general culture and specific technical training can thoroughly fit them" (USDA 1872, 336). To force a wife to plow or dig was to misuse her; a wife misused would not serve the farm well.

In fact, an earlier USDA report on the hardships of farmers' wives had carefully cautioned farmers on this very subject. A farmer's wife probably worked hard, and her husband was reminded to speak to her kindly, provide household necessities for her, offer help to her, allow her to visit her friends, and humor her during her monthly periods of "lunacy" (USDA 1863, 462–70). This was similar to advice that a farmer might have been given about his livestock, or about his

Home Economics

slaves in earlier years. The USDA directed its farming advice to men, and it was not advice that could apply to women, who would not have wives. That a farm woman would have either a husband or some other substitute male was ensured by the ascribed inability of women to do the definitive work of men on the farm.

In the early years of settlement, almost all Nebraska women married. In 1900 only 2.4 percent of women over age forty-five had never been married (Census 1902, 284). In 1920 never-married women still represented only 3.7 percent of the total number of rural Nebraska women age forty-five and over (Census 1924, 594). John Mack Faragher (1979, 180) concluded that marriage was necessary in coming to terms with adulthood in the nineteenth-century Midwest; it was the norm.

A marriage was an economic relationship, and wives acknowledged their duty to accept the lives their husbands provided. The economic reciprocity entailed in a marriage varied according to class. The majority of wives of middle-range farmers did the kind of work described in the 1871 USDA report. The wives of the poor had more limited access to their own means of production and tended to join their husbands in doing stereotypically male farm labor.

The dual economy that I have elsewhere described for Iowa farms (Fink 1986) also prevailed on middle-range Boone County farms. Large livestock and crops, which brought in a sporadic but relatively large income, were men's responsibility. Daily provisioning of the household, typically with small egg-and-cream enterprises and home production for the family's consumption, was the farm wife's work. A woman who was married in 1915 described women's role in the dual economy: "The women had their own eggs and chickens and so forth. . . . I made better butter than we're eating today! . . . You took your butter and eggs to town and that's how you bought your groceries. Believe me! From the time we were married until I can't remember when we first got the separator and started to sell cream." This woman milked the cows and separated the cream, although not all farm women did that chore. Farm women, with the help of children, invariably made the butter. When mechanical cream separators became available, they also did the tedious but hygienically important job of cleaning the many blades of the separator.

Changing technology

↗ 1920's

Farm women expanded their poultry enterprises and maintained their dairy production during the early years of this century. Interview data for this period are sketchy, but statistics on poultry and butterfat production indicate that the sale of eggs in Boone County in the 1920s was approximately double what it had been at the turn of the century, while the sale of butter and butterfat together rose by 10 percent.[5] Boone County was situated more than a hundred miles from Omaha or Sioux City, the nearest primary marketing nodes, making marketing more expensive than it was along the more traveled roads and in the more densely populated areas to the east. Major Nebraska egg production was concentrated in the more populous southeastern quadrant of the state. Because of the less favorable marketing circumstances, Nebraska women never marketed the number of eggs that their Iowa neighbors did (Fink 1987a). Compared to Iowa farm women, Nebraska women reported a greater reliance on the labor-intensive processing of butter and cream for their weekly household monies. Individual Boone County women mentioned midwifery, making and selling soap, and dressmaking as further sources of income.

In addition to their dairy and poultry chores, many farm women—especially on the more marginal farms—did a considerable amount of what was usually thought of as men's work in the fields. Some accounts describe wives who were the major workers on farms that their husbands owned. Nebraska writer Willa Cather's (1918, 343) fictional Nebraska farm heroine, Ántonia Shimerda Cuzak, told an old friend that her husband knew little about farming and that she had been with him in the fields for the first ten years of their married life on the farm. Mari Sandoz, another writer who grew up in rural Nebraska, reported that her mother did most of the farm work on their western Nebraska farm as her father grew ever less inclined to turn his hand to practical farming matters (Sandoz 1935, 233). Other women pitched in when they were needed, for example in the long days of picking and husking corn by hand in the fall.

The wives of the elite were not supposed to work; in fact, one sign of gentility was a nonworking wife. John Turner, an early Boone County farmer, depicted his wife as a sheltered woman who was "so often unable to do anything" (Turner 1903, 200). In Turner's mind, his wife was morally superior to other people, but in coping with farm life she was timid, frail, and dependent on him. Cass Barns's description of his farming, medical practice, political work, and widely varying Boone County business ventures included little about his wife or children. Nothing in his book indicated that she figured positively in his business affairs. Yet one must wonder whether the wives would have described their lives in the same way if they, rather than their husbands, had written these books. It seems to have been fashionable for wives to be frail and helpless, and the books written by early male settlers (presumably among the educational, if not economic, elite) either omitted descriptions of wives' work or described such work in patronizing tones (Turner 1903, 165–66).

Although the wife of a large property owner might have spent a relatively greater share of her time in managing social relations than a poorer woman might, we need not accept at face value the dismissal by male writers of women's manual labor on the larger farms. The wife of a farmer with several hired hands would simply spend extra hours in the kitchen rather than going to the fields. Having more laborers to feed, a larger house to clean, and more clothes to wash and iron, she would be less visible as a worker than would a woman who worked outside or in a nonfarm business. Some women had hired workers in the home, but they themselves were not idle unless they were in some way disabled. Like the women on poorer farms and in the landless rural households, they worked hard for the improvement of the family economy (Papanek 1979).

Although men may implicitly have understood that they needed wives in rural Nebraska, women were not easily convinced that they needed to be there. Western settlement attracted more men than women. In 1890 the total population of Boone County was 54 percent male (Census 1895, 507). Rural Nebraska as a whole maintained a male majority from the time of the first white settlement through the 1980 census; within the rural population, farm residents have consistently shown the highest male-to-female ratios. Women were in short supply, and unmarried men were eager to court women they might marry and put to work on their farms. In 1900 in Oakland Precinct, a farming area in the northwestern corner of Boone County, there were twenty-seven single men age twenty-five or over and only six single women in the same age range. In Albion there were forty-five single men of this age and twenty-three single women.[6] Dances, one of the places where marriage partners might meet in rural areas, always had more men than women attending.

Unmarried farmers recognized the need for women on the farm: they corresponded with women; they tried to make their living quarters attractive to women; and they tried to convince women that they would have a good life in rural Nebraska (Sandoz 1935). Promoters, realizing women's necessary role on the farms, enticed unmarried women to go west to find husbands. One ditty used for this purpose went: "There is no goose so gray, but, soon or late / Will find some honest gander for a mate" (quoted in Fite 1966, 39). A 1903 advertisement in the *Nebraska Farmer* offered—for one dollar—to furnish the addresses of one hundred young women who wanted to get married. Still some men had difficulty attracting women to their Nebraska farms. Although most women wanted and expected to marry, few wanted to cut their vital links with women friends (Smith-Rosenberg 1982). This was one reason so many dreaded the move to Nebraska.

Marie Louise Ritter, a Swiss immigrant who traveled to Nebraska in 1893, was unable to replace her close Swiss ties with new relationships. Unlike her husband, who thrived in the new land, Louise mourned her losses for the rest of her life. In 1908 she wrote, "Had I known that you, dear ones, would not come here or we ever return, I believe I never would have come to America" (quoted in Ritter 1982, 24).

Similarly, Nebraskan Agnes Suiter Freeman—wife of Daniel Freeman, the famed first homesteader in the United States—maintained her closest friendships with those she left behind. She, like her husband, was a physician, and they eventually prospered as few others did. Yet her heart remained with her family in eastern Iowa. Unlike most rural women, Agnes was able to travel to see her family frequently as she grew older. Although her daughter felt that she would have wished to be buried in Iowa, her grave is beside her husband's in rural Nebraska (Hodgkin 1935a, 18).

Even those women who were willing to make new friends in rural

Table 4-1. Farm Household Composition in Oakland and Midland Precincts, Boone County, Nebraska, and Bruce and Homer Townships, Benton County, Iowa, 1900–1910

	Boone County n = 661	Benton County n = 499
Nuclear[a]	63.0%	43.7%
Expanded[b]	20.9	44.5
Smaller[c]	16.1	11.8

Source: U.S. manuscript censuses. See also Fink and Carriquiry (1990).

[a]Households consisting of a husband, wife, and child or just a husband and wife.

[b]Nuclear household plus other individuals.

[c]No married couple in the household.

Nebraska found it hard to do so. Not only were their homes more widely scattered than those east of the Missouri, but Nebraska women were also less likely to have sisters, mothers, or other female friends with them in their homes. A comparison of the composition of sample farm households in Boone County with that of a corresponding sample in Benton County, Iowa, at the time of the 1900 and 1910 censuses reveals that the majority of Boone County farm households were composed entirely of nuclear family members, whereas less than half of the Benton County farm households contained only a nuclear family. In fact, Benton farm households were twice as likely as their Boone County counterparts to include additional persons beyond the nuclear family (see table 4-1).

The nuclearity of the households meant that, in Nebraska, marriage insulated a woman to a greater extent than it would have even in neighboring Iowa. An extra person in the household, especially if she were a sister or mother, might have been a trusted emotional support for the farm wife. If (as was more likely) the extra person were a hired hand, the woman might well have enjoyed increased freedom to leave the house. In fact, any additional male or female adult in the house could have provided understanding, advice, support, humor, or orientation to a woman who was struggling to come to terms with her situation. Hired men may have created more work for a woman in cooking, laundry, mending, and cleaning, but this hired help might also have occasionally taken over some chores, leaving the woman or the whole family free to visit neighbors or kin or to attend meetings. A hired man might also have relieved the woman of milking or field work, giving her more time to devote to visiting friends or even to writing letters that would help her maintain ties with the extended family and friends she had left behind when she came to Nebraska.

Most of the time, though, Nebraska farm women worked without help. Manuscript censuses confirm that domestic help more frequently worked in Albion than on the farms. Hannah Patterson Johnson's diary describing her life on a Boone County farm in the 1880s revealed that she desperately wanted a "girl" to live in the house and help her with her work, but apparently it was difficult to find a woman who was willing to come to the farm and work for pay. Confined at home with a baby and a three-year-old daughter, Hannah noted in her diary, "Feel tired and useless" (Johnson 1883, 31). After a long search, the family located someone who might be willing to come and the hired man went to get her; he was unsuccessful, much to Hannah's chagrin. Two weeks later she wrote, "Pa was to get a girl but it was cold and she didn't come" (Johnson 1883, 34). After several more weeks she wrote again that "Pa" had heard about a "girl" and he would try to get her. He left before daybreak the next morning and this time succeeded in bringing the girl back before noon (Johnson 1883, 36). As this diary reveals, "Pa" was going to town, going to see neighbors, and doing his work with the help of two hired hands, while Hannah handled her work without the assistance or company of another woman.

Women typically stayed at home on the farms while their husbands went to town to do banking, buying, and selling. Women tended the house and took care of children. Not only was it hard for them to leave, but once they did make it to town they found that the social space—the pool hall, the saloon, the post office, the blacksmith shop—belonged to men. "A Day's Pleasure," a short story by Hamlin Garland published in 1899, portrayed a farm woman's visit to town. Although her husband saw no reason for her to go and found plenty of things for her to do at home, she was determined to make the trip, not having been to town for six months. But once there, she faced a long and tiring day alone with no place to be, very little money to spend, no crib for the fussy baby, and nothing to do while her husband saw his friends and transacted his business. In 1902 a woman writing to the *Nebraska Farmer* gave a similar account of going to town only two or three times yearly, although her husband went regularly. Paralleling Garland's story, she told about the difficulties in arranging to leave the farm household, the long drive, and the awkwardness of being in town. The farm woman who went to town could look in windows, see people, and shop; but her lunch would be only the crackers and cheese she brought with her. After the long day in town she would be faced with the chores that had accumulated in her absence (Durland 1902, 369).

Awareness of the difficulties facing farm women in town moved some town women to expressions of sympathy. One Norfolk woman, the wife of a prominent businessman, wrote an appeal for the establishment of town "rest rooms" for use by country women so that they could have places to rest, freshen up, eat their lunches, have their children cared for, and get some relief from their responsibilities. Farm women, as well as town women, needed a meeting place, and a rest room would give them all a chance to get to know each other. Other town women responded to this concern, writing of the common needs of town and farm women and of their understanding of the problems that farm women faced when they were alone with their babies away from home. A farm woman replied that she would indeed use a rest room, and that farm women might sell their fruits, vegetables, and eggs to town women if they would visit the rest rooms as well. These good intentions seem not to have produced many rest rooms, however. A notably successful civic project in Geneva, Nebraska, did provide a public rest room with an organ, rocking chair, cradle, sofa, and table, but this would have been woefully inadequate to meet the needs of even a moderate number of farm and town women gathering with their babies and children to rest, lunch, and converse. Such facilities never became common in Nebraska, and Boone County had no such room (Durland 1902; Edwards 1902; Potter 1902; Wyman 1909).

The isolation of the Boone County farms and women's special difficulties in getting away from them could only have heightened the stress on rural women and made them more dependent on their husbands. Many did try to reach other women to relieve the loneliness of the farm home. One woman I interviewed said that she would occasionally leave her work and walk a mile to have coffee with her neighbor. Another would climb the windmill and tie a dishtowel to the top as a signal that she was free to visit if the other woman could come. But some had no intimate contact with other adult women. When I asked two elderly women who their best friends were, they said there was no such thing as a best friend in those days.

If marriages were intensely encompassing for rural Nebraska women, was this good or bad? How did women themselves feel about their marriages? In general, they were not supposed to say anything that could be interpreted as being critical of their husbands. Nellie Hawks, who edited a regular household column for the *Nebraska Farmer* in the 1890s, invited women to write about their lives but then warned that she didn't want to read any complaints about husbands. She knew, she said, that many women were desperately unhappy and unloved, but this was no excuse for being critical (Hawks 1892a). What women did write and say about their husbands and their marriages filtered through their own and others' censorship and must be filtered back to be interpreted.

Even through the layer of censorship, though, we can read women's feelings in the things they did and did not say about their husbands. A few women wrote repeatedly of things they shared with their husbands—laughter, comfort, anxiety, sorrow, work—so that we feel the closeness between the two. In other accounts the husband is missing emotionally, and we sense that, although he was physically present, the wife had a separate personal life. A few women, or their children, broke the code of silence and revealed unresolved anger and disappointment that surfaced only seldom.

Luna Kellie convincingly described her lifelong affection for her husband, J. T. She referred to him as her "dearly loved husband" (Kellie 1926, 6) and maintained that however dissatisfied they were with their poverty, she was always happy to be with J. T. One summer night they were awakened by a downpour that leaked through their sod roof and soaked everything they had. J. T. called Luna to come and bring the baby, Willie, to a sheltered spot he had found. The three of them huddled together and laughed and laughed, finding it "ridiculously funny" to be there in rural Nebraska in the middle of a storm (Kellie 1926, 30). It was not hysteria—they laughed over that night for years to come. When Luna was overtired, J. T., although almost penniless, paid two women to help her with the work of feeding a threshing crew. He loved to hear her sing, she said, and wanted her well (Kellie 1926, 61). The solidarity, mutual respect, affection, and indulgence that linked Luna and J. T. are apparent throughout her writings.

Yet Luna's marriage was not as uncomplicated as it seems in places. Even as she wrote her memoirs for her children, wanting them to love and honor their late father, she subtly expressed persistent feelings of anger and resentment about her position as wife. After she got her laying flock established, her egg money was supporting their household, and she was making good money by selling chickens. Then one of J. T.'s sows developed a taste for chicken that could not be satiated. Even with a new pen Luna couldn't keep the sow from luring chickens to her corn and gobbling them up. (Pigs are intelligent animals.) J. T. refused to sell the sow to save Luna's chickens, and Luna called his refusal "heartbreaking." She had to sacrifice her lucrative enterprise to J. T.'s hogs because his farming was considered more important than hers (Kellie 1926, 86). Most hurtful to Luna, however, was when J. T., without consulting her, sold the homestead on which they had worked together for seven years. Although legally J. T. needed her signature to complete the transaction, he made the decision and closed the negotiation before discussing it with her (Kellie 1926, 89). Although the Kellie marriage may ✳ have been egalitarian insofar as both husband and wife worked and both knew they were needed for the survival of the farm, it was not egalitarian in terms of the power to make major decisions affecting their life together. Luna recognized this situation and grieved over it without attempting to change it.

The emotional warmth existing between Luna and J. T. seems to have been more the exception than the rule. Hannah Johnson's 1880s

Boone County diary reveals a relationship that was neither overtly hostile nor particularly warm. On May 1, 1881, she wrote, "Charles Crites home. Husband went up there A.N. [afternoon]. We were 2 years married today. Two years ago husband wouldn't have gone and left me alone. marriage changes men but poor women think too much about them and of them" (Johnson 1881, 19). She referred to her husband as "Husband" until two children were born, at which time he became "Pa" (Johnson 1881, 14, 19). By July 1883, now with two daughters, Hannah no longer remarked on his going places without her. In that month, he went to town thirteen times, taking her and the children with him twice (Johnson 1883, 27–28). Hannah wrote about her feelings for and reactions to her daughters, but her later remarks about "Pa" mostly noted his trips to town or what farm work he was doing: "[July] 30th. Rain, mud!! Men worked in orchard. Mowed, hoed, manured, etc. A.N. [afternoon] Pa went to town with Perkin's Mill. . . . Baby was so good. Lillie [older daughter] out awhile and got all muddy. She was glad to get out. Mr. Smith got a load of cobs. Baby understands lots I say to her. She knows 'there's Lillie,' and 'get up,' 'go to sleep,' 'come, Baby,' etc." (Johnson 1983, 29). Although we sense that her daughters gave her joy, this same emotion does not come through in the cryptic notes about her husband.

The *Nebraska Farmer*'s "Household" column—an upbeat, encouraging collection of household tips, recipes, and friendly advice on coping with farm life—published an anonymous letter from a woman calling herself "Penticost," who complained that she heard "the daily curses of a man who considers himself needlessly burdened with a woman and a houseful of brats." But then she defended her complaint by saying that she was entirely stoic in her suffering: "Never, not even to my mother, have I ever lisped that my life was other than a happy one" ("Penticost" 1896a, 328–29). Nellie Hawks, who objected on principle to remarks that reflected poorly on husbands, nonetheless opened herself up to this woman: "This is indeed another side to the matrimonial question, and we know there are husbands and fathers so steeped in selfishness and so unfeeling of the interests of wife and family that a woman's life is made to her a simple embittered endurance. *Yours is not an isolated case, dear woman*. . . .

Rest assured that in your own unhappiness you have the sympathy of womankind, myself among others" (Hawks 1896c, 329; emphasis mine). Other women wrote to sympathize with Penticost, saying that they understood her trials, because men so seldom showed their true natures before marriage. Readers tried to guess who Penticost was, some claiming that they knew her, but Penticost told them they were all wrong. No one would ever know her. But many knew women like her.

Some men physically assaulted their wives, a practice that seems to have been part of the high level of violence in rural Nebraska in the early years of settlement. Werner Einstadter (1978) has described a "subculture of violence" that pervaded the Great Plains in the period from 1863 to 1890. Contributing to a culture based on physical aggression were the violent removal of the native populations, armed conflict between farmers and ranchers, and the outlaw gangs generated out of the bloody guerrilla bands that fought over the slavery issue in Kansas and Missouri. In the absence of an effective legal system, the rules of the game were defined by the most powerful person in an area. Einstadter concludes that plains culture not only condoned but at times required violence. Commenting on crime in Boone County in the 1880s, Cass Barns wrote that murders were epidemic. In a county whose total population numbered about 5,000, a group of five men charged with murder at the same time once overcrowded the four-man county jail. Barns, a respected citizen, expressed his view that a murderer should not be prosecuted if he killed someone who was trespassing on private property (Barns 1970 [1930], 153–54). The theme of frontier violence is integral to the myth of the cowboy, which has been a central element of Great Plains culture (Lawrence 1982).

In her cross-cultural study of rape, Peggy Sanday (1981, 22–23) found that a high degree of interpersonal violence and an ideology of male toughness correlated with the presence of sexual violence toward women. The plains region, with its emphasis on both of these elements, would be among those societies that tended to condone rape.

In the character of her father, "Old Jules" Sandoz, Mari Sandoz (1935) drew a connection between the societal violence, male aggres-

sion, and domestic violence in rural Nebraska. As a newcomer, Jules
was both shocked and initiated to the region by an incident in which
a gunman murdered a young cowboy for mouthing off in a saloon.
Cattlemen killed farmers as they plowed their fields, and vigilante
gangs took revenge. Jules was caught up in the violence simply because he was there. This violence played out in different forms within
his family, which was far away from the people and the ways he had
known. An educated Swiss immigrant, Jules reveled in the study of
classical music, botany, fossils, archaeology, and other intellectual
pursuits. He was a lifelong friend to the Sioux. Wanting to found a
community in western Nebraska, he recruited and helped to establish
many new households. But his enlightened ideas did not extend to
his treatment of the women and children of his Nebraska family. For
them he had no respect. Married at least four times, Jules was crass
and brutal within his family and refused to do farm work. His first
three marriages ended in divorce; he succeeded in making his fourth
wife pregnant—and therefore tied to him—before she could make
the decision to leave. He beat and tyrannized his wives and children,
destroyed or appropriated their property, tried to keep his children
away from school, and consumed more than his share of scarce food.

Melody Graulich (1983, 1984), who has analyzed the violence
against women revealed in Sandoz's biography, cites the gruesome
and bloody scenes in which Jules subdued the spirits of his wives,
one of whom became insane and was eventually institutionalized.
Graulich believes that Jules was no more brutal than other men and
indeed was most typical of them when he was beating his wives.
Elizabeth Hampsten (1982, 120) cites some letters of midwestern
women describing marital violence, although she notes that these
scattered accounts do not establish a pattern of such violence.

Mari Sandoz's book, *Old Jules*, was widely read in Nebraska.
Boone County people identified with the realism of the book; men
admired Old Jules and sought to emulate him. Rose, born in 1906,
referred me to *Old Jules* as a good portrayal of the dynamics of
husband-wife relations. Asked if Jules was really typical of early
Nebraska men, she answered, "I don't think there were too many
men that were as embittered as Old Jules; I would say that there were
lots of families that the man was domineering." A local history of

Wheeler County, located just west of Boone, includes the story of a tyrannical husband who apparently at different times crippled his wife by breaking her arms, roasted her pet dog alive in the oven, and left her outside overnight with a broken leg until neighbors found and helped her (Day and Koinzan 1977, 173). He was not arrested or held accountable by the community for what he did to his own wife.

Such an incident as a woman lying outside all night with a broken leg could only happen in the isolation of a rural setting. The very isolation of farm women made them more vulnerable to their husbands' rages. A Boone County man born on a farm in 1903 estimated that his father had gotten drunk and abused his mother about six times, although he did not believe that they had a bad marriage. He explained that women couldn't leave the farms because they had no transportation of their own. Possibly, he said, a woman might "go home to Mama," but she had no option of living on her own. Even if she had transportation, a woman would not ask anyone for help, because the prevailing attitude held that she had made her bed and must lie in it. People didn't talk much about marital problems, because such things were private. Said one woman: "On those isolated farms, how would a lady get out to get a divorce? . . . Back in those days, I believe the man just managed things mostly on his own. I think he was the boss." For this woman, divorce was unthinkable from a practical standpoint, though not from an emotional one.

Drinking was commonly associated with domestic violence. The drinking question appeared repeatedly in the "Household" column in the *Nebraska Farmer* after an eighteen-year-old woman, using the pseudonym "Country Girl," indirectly broached the subject. Asking for advice about marriage, she described two suitors and wanted to know which of them she should accept. The first was good looking and well educated and had a nice home and farm. But he was known to take a drink occasionally; rumors were that he had been seen drunk. The second man was healthy, hard working, and frugal; he didn't smoke, drink, or chew. But he was not a church member and he was poor ("Country Girl" 1896, 216). The readers' responses poured in, warning her that she should never, never marry a man who drank. He would show his true personality after marriage. An occasional drinker today was a drunk tomorrow. The drinking vice far outweighed the other man's disadvantage in being poor and not being a member of a church. Only Penticost disagreed, saying an "occasional" did not inevitably become a drunkard. Many men, she said, remained occasional drinkers. She herself had turned down an "occasional," who was so distraught that he never drank again. Instead, she had married a poor but frugal suitor and had since regretted it ("Penticost" 1896b, 458). Penticost's argument in favor of the occasional drinker rested on her confidence that she could change him; most married women had no such illusions and considered drinking to be women's greatest bane.

Many women suffered from their husbands' drinking habits. The "Household" column had frequent advice on how to cure husbands of drinking, the most popular being the "Keeley cure," which involved injections of bichloride of gold. By 1891 "Dr. Keeley" reported that he had attempted to cure 5,000 cases of drinking, out of which only 5 percent suffered remission (Kirk 1891, 283). The frequency with which the Keeley cure was discussed in the "Household" column indicates that women were serious about confronting the drinking of the men in their families. Another cure, "Dr. Haines Golden Specific," was advertised as a remedy that would cure a man of drinking and return him to his family and friends a saved man. The Haines Specific had the advantage that, unlike the Keeley cure, a wife or daughter, as a "healing angel," could put it into the man's food or coffee undetected. The drinker need never know what transformed him (*Nebraska Farmer* 1892, 463). Liquor figured prominently in Cass Barns's description of business and government in Boone County, although he did not mention it in connection with domestic relations. Business deals were made over a bottle, political affairs got settled over a bottle, town characters drank too much, and a jury foreman needed a drink to see him through his deliberations. During Prohibition there were frequent convictions for liquor violations in Boone County (see, for example, BCDC 1931).

Farm women's enthusiasm for temperance is one sign of how much they suffered from alcohol and how pervasive drunkenness was. Although few women told me that they themselves had had problems with their husbands' drinking in early years, many mentioned the general problem of alcohol when asked about domestic violence. Men were most likely to be violent when they had been drinking. Drinking was also associated with quarrels over money and extramarital sexual relations.

Carol, born in 1927, connected her family's poverty and the violence she knew at home to her father's drinking: "I sometimes wonder if he and my mother were ever happily married. Really. Because he would holler and threaten her. We ended up hiding the knives and stuff because he was always threatening to kill her. That's the way I grew up. It was not a real happy marriage. . . . If he'd stay out of drinking, he was a fairly nice guy." Carol's mother was dead and unable to tell her own story by the time I was doing fieldwork. Although she died after her husband, I do not discount the possibility that her husband's drinking shortened her life. If women whose husbands drank excessively tended generally to have shorter lives than other women, they would have been disproportionately absent from my interview sample of women who remembered life in rural Nebraska in the early twentieth century.

Although beatings and drinking by a husband did serve as the grounds for divorce in a few instances (see, for example, Census 1908, 45), interviews indicate that it was more common for women to put up with the drinking. Sarah, born in 1914, said that the most typical marital problem in her youth was the combination of drunken husband and teetotaling wife. She continued: "It caused a lot of problems, but people didn't get divorced over it. People just stood it. . . . The wife couldn't have left. What would they have done if they had left? They didn't have welfare in those days. . . . Unless a woman had rich parents to support her she didn't have anywhere to go. The job market was bad. . . . Maybe some would have left if they could have raised their children."

By the Divorce Act of 1875, Nebraskans could be granted a divorce on grounds of adultery, physical incompetence, a jail sentence of more than three years, abandonment, alcoholism, or life imprisonment (Nebraska 1887). In 1903 husbands who did not support their wives were declared to be guilty of desertion (Nebraska 1907). Although legally permitted, however, divorce was not a common practice. In the early years of Boone County's settlement, wives more frequently than husbands were the petitioners, the most common grounds being cruelty, desertion, and neglecting their obligation of support (Census 1908, 45). Between 1887 and 1906, 114 divorces were recorded in Boone County, an average of 5.7 per year (Census 1908, 727). In a county that listed 1,755 families in 1890 (Census 1895, 923), this incidence of divorce was low, but it was increasing and continued to increase.[7]

The 1910 census schedule for Oakland Precinct in northwestern Boone County showed one divorced woman living on a farm. This was a thirty-five-year-old woman with two children, who kept house for her two unmarried brothers who operated the farm. In Albion there were three divorced women heading households and support- ing their children. One was a bookkeeper, another a photographer, and the third a domestic worker. In addition, a thirty-two-year-old divorced woman and her five-year-old daughter were living in her parents' household; this woman was not listed as having an occupa- tion. In a few other cases in both Oakland and Albion, married daughters and their children were shown to be living in their parents' households without their husbands, a situation that may have re- sulted from disrupted marriage relations.[8]

In general, however, divorced women must have left the county; otherwise, more than a hundred divorced women should be listed in the Boone County census record, assuming that these women gave the census taker the correct information. Although a woman who had received her divorce in Boone County probably could not have mis- represented her marital status while she was still living there, a wom- an who had been divorced before coming to Boone County might well have claimed to be single or widowed.

Divorce was a stigma. After Mari Sandoz divorced her farmer husband in 1919, she left the area and went to Lincoln. When she returned to teach in another part of rural Nebraska, she represented herself as single. Even though she kept her husband's name, she was known as Miss McCumber. She had never spoken to her parents or siblings about her trials in marriage. Mari's brother, Jule, remembered that her husband swore at her, but most men swore at their wives without having their wives divorce them. Mari's mother, who had lived for years with a violent husband, did not support her daughter's decision to leave the marriage. Jule reported: "Mama was terribly upset. She had never considered that way out of her own marital troubles and could not understand a daughter bringing such disgrace on the family. She always quoted Sophie Sears as saying, 'When you burn your hind side, you sit on it'" (Pifer and Sandoz 1987, 105). Jule also said that he would never have considered marrying a divorced woman (Pifer and Sandoz 1987, 117).

Even a bad marriage, people felt, should be preserved. In an 1896 article called "Absoluteness of the Marriage Tie," one woman talked about "demonic platonic love," which seems to have meant a husband's adultery. A woman was advised never to surrender her marriage. She must work ever harder to be worthy of her husband and must never allow herself to be jealous. She must always love him and be kind to him. As an afterthought, the author added that if the woman played her cards right, her children would eventually come to resent their father and devote themselves to her (Ball 1896). Nothing would justify a divorce. And although the existence of such advice does not indicate that women invariably took it, no countervailing popular texts existed to help women weigh the costs and benefits of maintaining sour marital relationships.

Those I interviewed told me that in the early years of the century people did not divorce. This was not true, but divorce was rare, and they might not personally have known those couples who divorced if they did not live in the same neighborhoods, or if the divorced people left the county at the time of their divorces. During interviews, women repeatedly answered my questions about divorce by explaining how hard it was for women to divorce rather than making the claim that women had no reason to want to be divorced. After Rose explained that a lot of men were domineering, I asked her how a woman would cope with a domineering or tyrannical husband. She answered, "That was the big trouble. . . . She had that family with those children. She didn't want to go off and leave them with this tyrant. It seemed that there wasn't anything for her to do but just stay there and try to deal with it. There wasn't any place to go. There wasn't anybody to call for help." As another farm woman said, you just never knew how violent or abusive men were on a farm, because each farmhouse was isolated from the others. Through hints and allusions, we learn that some husbands did beat their wives and that a woman's natal family was her best hope of protection. But many Boone County women had left their natal families to migrate west with their husbands and had no family help or protection nearby if they were beaten.

The social construction of sexuality reinforced women's marginality and lessened their power within marriage. Open discussion of sexuality was taboo for women, and girls learned to deny the reality of anything related to sex. Grace Snyder (1963, 39) wrote about a late-nineteenth-century social gathering of farm people at which a Swedish woman undressed a baby in mixed company: "Mama, who was so modest she probably never in her life saw all of her own body at once, had had a pink face all the rest of the afternoon." Grace's mother, who had babies every other year for twenty years, never discussed pregnancy with her daughters. Grace told about her and her sister's surprise when their mother brought forth another baby one day. Her older sister was eighteen and Grace was sixteen and they had not known enough about pregnancy to understand that their mother was expecting a baby (Snyder 1963, 194).

Writer Meridel Le Sueur, who was born in Iowa in 1900 and grew up on the plains, described her grandmother's attitude toward her body: "She wore a shift to bathe with; she never saw her body. Never saw it. I lived with her during my adolescence and she didn't know anything about menstruation, she just knew you did it and that you were in danger. . . . She didn't know how she got children or how she gave birth. She really didn't know. She said it was so disgusting" (quoted in Hoy 1987, 18). So modest was Grace Snyder's mother that once, when Grace and her sisters sneaked a dip in their pond while their parents were gone, their mother found out and beat them. They were not allowed to swim even with their clothing on. A wet dress clung to the body and revealed its contours. Women wore clothing that disguised the existence of legs, which were a source of shame. Although men and boys took the physical details of sexuality more in stride, a polite male referred to a "limb" of chicken rather than a "leg" of chicken in mixed company. He avoided using the word "stallion" and never, never said the word "bull" within hearing of a woman

(Johnson 1952, 36). The existence of her body was a woman's sinful secret.

By 1915, however, small signs of change were appearing, albeit as the result of urban outreach rather than rural innovation. The "Home Circle" column of the *Nebraska Farmer* recommended "purity books" for women wanting to instruct their children in morals and a booklet called "In Her Teens" for girls entering womanhood. These could be mail-ordered from New York City (*Nebraska Farmer* 1915). Although such material might not have answered all women's questions, ordering the booklets may have been a small step toward making the details of sexuality more accessible to women.

The suppression of women's sexuality limited their freedom and heightened men's sexual desires. Virginity was a prize that belonged to men. As Le Sueur claimed, "All those men, after they had made a success, married the leading virgin in town—you had to be a virgin—and then they just attacked you" (quoted in Hoy 1987, 18). The rituals of sexuality etched a pattern of male dominance onto women's consciousness. Men were the aggressors; they were the ones who were comfortable with their sexuality and ready to impose it on women who may or may not have been truly terrified. In describing his father's management of his cattle herd, Jule Sandoz tells how Old Jules insisted that the bulls have unlimited access to cows, even though the practice was weakening their herd, because he thought that males should never be sexually restrained (Pifer and Sandoz 1987, 77). An unmarried male gained prestige through his sexual conquests; an unmarried woman was ruined by the same actions.

As one woman explained, sex was private; for her, nothing resembling sex education existed. What girls knew, they were likely to have learned from siblings or peers rather than from more knowledgeable elders. Their other teachers were farm animals; a farm girl might manage to learn the rudiments of sexual intercourse in the barnyard. Alternatively, she might just as easily be forbidden to observe the sexuality of animals (Lawrence 1982, 122). Often she would receive hands-on instruction in her first sexual encounter with a man. However she learned about sex, it was not something a nice girl discussed or asked about. Sex, for women, was unspeakably bad.

This does not mean that sexual activity was confined exclusively to marriage and engaged in only for purposes of procreation. Some young girls were sexually molested by fathers, brothers, hired hands, or neighbors, and the trauma could be carried into their adult years. One woman, born in the early years of the century, told me that her father molested her repeatedly beginning at the time she reached puberty. Such a man probably would not have faced legal consequences had he been discovered, but he would have been subject to social censure, and this woman had never told another person of the sexual violation for fear of dishonoring her father. When Mari Sandoz was eight, her father brought a convicted child molester from the state penitentiary to work on their farm and live in their home. When this man tried to molest Mari, she locked herself in a room and defended herself with a gun. Only then did her mother's efforts to banish the man from the house prevail (Sandoz 1935, 271, 315). The few cases of rape and sexual abuse that reached the Boone County District Court were seldom fully prosecuted or resolved, and these undoubtedly represented only the tip of the iceberg in terms of the actual instances of sexual assault. In the 1980s, when one farm woman confronted her father-in-law about the sexual abuse of her daughter, he told her that sexual fondling of children on the farm was so common in times past that no one paid much attention to it.

Prostitution was also present in rural areas. Mari Sandoz (1935, 174) described prostitution in western Nebraska, and Frank Rice (1970, 115–16) wrote that there were houses of prostitution in Grand Island until the time of Prohibition. The loss of the liquor business apparently either drove them underground or forced them out of business. Nell, a woman born in 1941, said that her mother's mother had been forced into prostitution in the years 1915 to 1920. Nell's grandfather had deserted the family, and her grandmother was left with no other source of income for the support of a large number of children. Nell vividly remembered her mother's continuing anguish over this episode in her old age and approaching death. She was convinced that her mother had also been pressed into prostitution in her early teens, although Nell never found a way to discuss it with her mother. In contrast to the male response that some sexual activity was too common to arouse much concern, this particular activity, however common or uncommon, was something that haunted Nell's mother for the rest of her life.

Premarital pregnancy appears to have been common, though for the woman involved it was traumatic. Sequential census manuscripts reveal discrepancies in marriage and birth dates that would be consistent with attempts to hide a premarital pregnancy. Francis Long devoted a chapter of his book on early medical practice in rural Nebraska to a discussion of out-of-wedlock pregnancies. Upon discovering that an unmarried woman was pregnant, Long's standard practice was to go to her sexual partner to try to talk him into marriage. Only in cases in which a pregnant woman's sexual partner had left the county and could not be located did Long admit to performing an abortion (F. Long 1937, 106).

In the 1970s I knew a farm woman who had been faced with a pregnancy and forced marriage in 1914 at age fifteen. During her later years, she would call up mental lists of other women in the area who had faced the same humiliation. Many of these women avoided her rather than risk having their personal histories held up to them. Premarital pregnancy was a disgrace, and this woman did not want to suffer alone. While I was growing up in Boone County in the 1950s, I overheard various accounts of women who had been sexually active before marriage decades in the past, the point of each story being to discount the woman's moral credibility. No one was totally ostracized for premarital sexual activity or for having a baby too soon after marriage, but it was a black mark against a woman that the community noted and kept in its collective memory. Curiously, it was women themselves who kept these mental records, apparently in order to enforce the moral consensus that had hurt some so deeply and therefore must be shared. Only irregular sexuality such as intercourse with an animal or indiscreet public acts would stigmatize a man.

In the case of premarital pregnancy, it was the woman rather than the man who needed to get married for the sake of her reputation. The man characteristically was sheepish but could often joke about the matter over the years. This gender inequality in the symbolic structure of sexuality helped to erase the tactical advantage that women held by virtue of the demographics of the newly settled rural area. By the principle of supply and demand, the marriage market in the West should have been a woman's market, because there were always more eligible men than women. If a man could engineer sexual contact with a woman, he might turn her reluctance into desperation to marry (Sandoz 1935, 305). Moreover, the distinction between consensual and forced sexual contact seems to have had more to do with the relative ranking of the persons involved than with the nature of the contact itself. A married woman was out of bounds and could not be approached without giving deep offense to her husband. A propertyless male probably could not have sexually assaulted a banker's wife or daughter without answering for it, although this had more to do with the comparative status of the men involved than with respect for women. Within a man's own class he had more leeway with unmarried women. The way in which sexual subordination turned the tables on women can be seen in physician Francis Long's story about a young woman, whom he criticized as being boisterous and overindulged by her brothers. According to Long,

> A girl . . . came with a story of having missed several periods. Questioned she admitted that a lover had taken advantage of her, but stressed a story that she had been forced. I told her that was an unlikely story and that she could have protected herself but she pleaded that she fought until overcome, which I also told her was unlikely. I suggested that abortion was impossible to consider, that she must have the young man marry her, that she needed a husband and her prospective child a father. She blurted out that she did not want him, would not marry him. I again insisted that the child needed a father and she a husband, that she was in no position to choose—an attitude she had, apparently, assumed. I offered to talk to the young man if she wished me to do so. This she declined, but she promised me she would see him and report to me later. She returned with the report that the young man had said he would marry her if she would talk to her father and make him "come down handsomely." To this astounding

proposition she told him to "Go to h-ll," she would do nothing of the kind. (F. Long 1937, 104–5)

Unless the woman had submitted to the marriage plan she would have faced major dishonor. She might have thought it possible that she could stay on her family farm and retain the support of her indulgent brothers and parents, but in this respect she thought wrong. The man who had scored a sexual triumph was sure enough of his position that he could define the terms of the marriage, which he did to his advantage. The woman's father did present the couple with a farm, and they were married. She did not have an option. Whether we accept that the man had assaulted or seduced her depends on whether we believe her or Long's assessment of what happened. In any event, it was Long's response that determined that she would continue her pregnancy and thus inevitably marry.

Related to this social vulnerability arising from a double standard of sexual morality was the fact that single women rarely lived on their own or in any setting apart from a family-based household. The 1900 census schedules of Oakland Precinct and Albion town show a number of unmarried men living alone or in hotels. Only one unmarried woman, fifty-four years old, was living alone. In Albion there were two households composed of single sisters; one of the sets of sisters were milliners, the other had no occupation. Unmarried women typically lived with their parents or in the family households of siblings. Only in rare cases did working women board with nonrelatives, and usually these landlords monitored their schedules and visitors for them as if they were relatives. A woman might earn a living as a teacher, shop clerk, or even a domestic servant, but she could not translate her wages into the kind of independence and mobility that a single man enjoyed.

Both Mari Sandoz and her brother Jule eventually reached the point at which they no longer wanted to live in the same house and to be subject to the cruelty of Old Jules. Each had a final crisis of enmity with their father. Jule left home, worked as a hired hand, traveled on his own, and spent some time in Denver before returning as a grown man. Mari's escape was marriage, without courtship and apparently without any illusion of love, to a nearby farmer. Without money or some kind of support from her family, she did not venture away on her own. The added push of a disgraceful divorce, more maturity, and a little money took her away on her own a few years later. Unlike Jule, she did not return to live in the rural community.

Vera, born in 1909, told the story of her mother Edna, whose own mother died when she was young. Edna's father abandoned her when she was in her early teens, and she was left in rural Nebraska without a home: "My mother's [Edna's] sister was married and living in Lincoln, and Mother went to live with her. She [the sister] was married to my father's older brother. Then [the sister] said that, after all, she couldn't afford to keep her. . . . Dad happened to be down there and he said he'd take her. So he did and they were married. She was fifteen; he was nine years older. . . . She wanted a place to live. I guess she liked him." The implicit understanding is that Edna would have been faced with sexual vulnerability, possibly prostitution, and certainly loss of respectability if she had forged out on her own as a teenager. Edna's husband was a farmer, and they took up their lives on a farm. At age fifteen, this woman's life was already shaped by the structure of beliefs about sexuality. Because sex was taboo as a topic of overt discussion, much less political debate, no explicit formulation or negotiation on issues of sexuality could arise. Women stayed in their place.

Although all but a few women did marry at some time in their lives, a larger number were without husbands at any given time. Unmarried women up to their mid-twenties who stayed in the community would be identified as daughters, whether they lived with their parents or got jobs as domestic helpers. Widows formed an older category of unmarried women.

Husbands were, on average, five to six years older than their wives. Therefore, a greater number of women than men outlived their spouses. A farm widow with children at home might stay on the farm and operate it with the help of the older children or hired help. In Oakland Precinct in 1910 there were ten widows running farms, three of whom had also been present as widows or wives in 1900. All of these women had children who could do a substantial amount of the farm work; eventually one child, probably a son, would take over the farm. The widows ranged in age from thirty-six to sixty-one. Only six Oakland farmers, ages forty-two to fifty-nine, had survived their wives to run their farms and raise their children themselves. A larger number of widows were living in Albion, where eighteen, as opposed to nine widowers, were recorded as heads of households with unmarried children. Most of these women were said to be living on their "own income," which meant that they did not have formal occupations. Many of their children did have jobs of some kind. A total of fifty-two widows lived in Albion in various other household arrangements, including living with married children, working as servants, or living alone. In contrast, Oakland Precinct had no widows living alone and only four who were not heads of households. Rather than staying put, a farmer's widow was likely to move to town when no longer faced with daily responsibilities on the farm.[9]

A woman probably experienced her greatest freedom and power as a widow if she had enough money to maintain her independence. Anthropologist Judith Brown (1985), writing about middle-aged women, notes several factors that tend to produce an improved status for women in later life. These include reduced childcare and domestic responsibilities and enhanced authority in the family through control of the lives of the next generation. These advantages pertained primarily to women who had been married to men of some means. Although a Boone County widow would undoubtedly relish her reduced responsibilities as she got older, very seldom would she have had enough wealth to exert control over her children. More frequently, on becoming too old to subsist on her own labor, she would become dependent on her children. A widow was entitled to one-third of her husband's property, although normally she received only a life estate, which she did not have the power to sell or will. She might have been able to operate a farm until her son took it over, but she would have been dependent on his labor.

Nebraska's Married Women's Property Act of 1871 benefited the small minority of Boone County women who were in a position to own property, but not all of these women utilized their rights. Agnes, whose family had provided her husband with the initial capital for the large farming and ranching operation he put together, does not appear to have exercised property rights positively on her own behalf.

When her husband died in 1896, Agnes received a portion of his considerable property. In 1897 she signed this over to her oldest son, who took over the farm and ranch operation and continued to expand his holdings. Agnes kept only a house and a small income for herself. When she died in 1927 her estate was $720.17 in debt, and her oldest son paid this amount.

Although they did not have an egalitarian marriage, Luna and J. T. Kellie were among those couples who successfully reversed the forces that pushed them toward polarized marriage roles (Nelsen 1989). Katherine Harris, in her study of homesteading families in northeastern Colorado, concluded that in such families husbands and wives shared decision making and that women enjoyed a high status. If this pattern were to be found anywhere in Nebraska, we would look for it in the Kellie family. Luna was hard working and articulate. Active in the grassroots rural politics of the late nineteenth century, she was ready to challenge the status quo to fight for the rights of farmers. Depending on how status is defined, Luna may have enjoyed a high one; but she hardly shared decision making with J. T. in any substantive sense. Luna and J. T. were fond of each other, but the major decisions in their family were J. T.'s alone.

Many more couples lived some outward facsimile of contentment, only indirectly acknowledging the gap between their ideals and the mundane realities. More evidence remains of indifference or hostility than of closeness and warmth. Only occasionally, under stressful conditions, would underlying disappointment erupt into open expression.

Physician Francis Long described one such incident. Upon making a call to a farm home, he found a man dying of diphtheria. This man, who lived with his father, wife, and five sons, wanted to have the doctor write his will. An argument ensued. The man's father wanted his son to leave the land to him rather than to the wife. Apparently the wife's legal right to one-third of her husband's property was either not known or not acknowledged in this exchange. The father charged that the wife was young enough to remarry, and she would take the land out of the family.[10] At this the wife lost her temper and became, in Long's words, a "tigress." She erupted with what must have been a long-simmering frustration: "'I get married again? . . . Have I not had trouble enough with one man? I want no more the rest of my life! Take your property and do with it what you please! I can make my own living and support the children besides! I have slaved here all these years and if it had not been for my work Johannes would not have anything today'—and some other expletives, unprintable" (F. Long 1937, 63). Finally they agreed that the woman and the children would share the property equally.

This woman had power, but in exercising her power she became undesirable. The men could not trust her to carry out their plans. Although she had worked hard and borne five sons, she had not, in their eyes, earned a legitimate right to have a voice. In her frustration she complained of how hard her marriage had been for her over the years, when under other circumstances her husband's approaching death might have elicited softer sentiments. As if to justify the men's distrust, Long mentioned that she married the hired man nine months later. Although Long's sexist bias colored his account, as a doctor he was a respected, influential, and powerful person. His view was probably closer to that of the man in the street—and perhaps the woman in the street—than was that of the enraged farm woman.

Enduring the frustration of marriage was a woman's duty more than her pleasure. In 1896 a woman calling herself "Hired Girl" responded to the "Country Girl" debate in *Nebraska Farmer* by stating that, from all she could read of other women's responses, it didn't seem as if marriage were all that great for women. Why couldn't a woman remain single? ("Hired Girl" 1896). The answer, once again coming from women, was in essence that marriage was a categorical imperative. One woman responded, "Let me say I think if God had made a woman to live single all her life he would not have made her like other women, that is answer enough for that" (Taylor 1896b). And that was enough for that. The questions and complaints about marriage disappeared from the pages of the "Household" column, and it returned to household hints and bucolic images of how blessed women were to be wives in rural Nebraska. Although I have no proof, it seems as if the women had strayed too far from the fold for the tastes of the male editors, who insisted that their exchanges be more carefully weighed before they reached the journal's pages.

Diverse legal, political, and economic conditions worked against the "companionate marriage" that Suzanne Lebsock (1984, 28) found to be the emerging U.S. ideal as early as one hundred years before white settlement in rural Nebraska. The ideal promised more than it delivered. "Companionate marriage" may be an apt term for the conditions in rural Nebraska in that the nuclear family household there was probably more discrete, more set apart from the kinship and social nexus, than it had been in the more densely populated, longer-established areas from which the settlers came. Husband and wife did work together to negotiate their own power relations, their own division of labor, their own ways of answering the challenges of the plains environment. Fewer authorities were present to tell them how to do it. "Companionate marriage" is misleading, however, if it implies that husband and wife had equal power in these negotiations. They were not so far removed from civilization that they did not know how government, economics, and sexual norms worked in the United States. Just as Elizabeth Hampsten (1989, 196) concluded in her study of a North Dakota immigrant family, harsh conditions and poverty could alienate husbands and wives rather than bond them. Evidence that men brutalized women on isolated farms where by-standers and neighbors could not come to their rescue suggests that relative isolation from institutions of social order conferred even more power on the husband than he might have had in a European or eastern U.S. setting.

Marriage gave a woman a derivative status. In some instances she gained more power through marriage than she would have had as a single woman. But her position as a wife did not lend a woman power that she could detach and wield as an autonomous person in society. John Mack Faragher (1981, 550) found that the labor of women freed men from subsistence labor and allowed them to pursue their interests in the public world. This he found to be the central factor in the exploitation of women as wives. Marriage did not empower women in a parallel manner. Control of women's sexuality was a basic underpinning of their subordinate status.

Marriage was a relationship of difference and inequality, established and maintained by principles that were usually invisible, unspoken, and incompletely acknowledged. Both this invisibility and the underlying awareness of it may have removed the overt frustration and uncertainty of continually renegotiating the marital relation; it did not lessen the power of the principles.

5 RURAL WIVES, HARD TIMES

*[Rural Nebraska] women are doing much to ease the burdens
of the depression that their husbands are being called upon to
bear. It is their forbearance that is keeping up the stamina and
courage of the farmer and inspiring him with the hope of better
days that are sure to come. It is they who are insisting that, in
spite of heavy taxes, the standard of the excellent school
system it has taken years to establish must not be lowered. It is
they who are finding a way to make the home comfortable,
maintain a standard of living unequaled anywhere, and
provide nourishing food for the children and their hardworking
husbands.—Editorial in the* Nebraska Farmer, *1932*

The editor of the *Nebraska Farmer* celebrated farm women of the
1930s as wives who eased their husbands' burdens, maintained community services, and inspired others to carry on. That the women
themselves suffered hardship and discouragement went unaddressed.
Being beyond suffering themselves, they could minister to the needs
of those who did the real work; being wives, they had no needs of
their own. To some extent, women accepted the challenge of this
representation. Many did more work; they took pride in their ability
to withstand and survive; they were pillars of strength. They called
up physical and emotional reserves, and some identified with the
image of superhuman strength and resilience that would enable them
to face whatever came. Men needed wives more than ever; so women
became heroes in the depression.

Yet a counterimage, equally real, manifested itself through the
words and actions of rural women. Besides being stoic and unselfish,
women wanted changes. Although the depression strengthened family life in some contexts, it also prompted women to question the way
marriage worked for them. Evidence of this can be found in demographic changes, in new activities open to single women, in the

exploration of new ways of being wives, in different attitudes expressed toward rural life, and in a tentative redefinition of the agrarian message.

The years from 1900 to 1920 had been good ones for Nebraska farmers, in terms of both a favorable economy and a favorable climate with sufficient rainfall. The farm depression jolted rural Nebraskans in 1920, but it was the nationwide Great Depression beginning in 1929 and the drought beginning in 1934 that critically threatened the future of agrarian life in Nebraska. The population of Boone County, which had grown at every census since the original settlement, dropped by 17 percent between 1930 and 1940. The biggest loss was in the farm population, which declined by 25 percent in that time. Farming accounted for 65 percent of the county's population in 1930; by 1940 only 59 percent of the people lived on farms (Census 1932a, 89; 1943, 608). Because marriage was central to the family farm pattern, agrarian advocates formulated a pro-nuptial argument, which they directed primarily to women.

The women who might be expected to have experienced the most pronounced changes as a result of the depression were those who were young and facing decisions about work, education, and marriage in the 1930s. To ground my discussion in the concreteness of actual lives, I will begin by introducing three women who became adults and married in the 1930s. All three had been born on family farms and were trying to establish farm households with help from their extended families after marriage. They are all widows now, having lived through their marriages with no apparent ruptures or overt violence. They are not atypical. The variations in their experiences of work and geographic mobility show something of the differences that occurred even within similar economic frameworks.

With this grounding in the particulars of three women's lives, I can turn to the evidence of the strong economic and moral role of women in the rural family and the ways in which the depression reinforced this role but also challenged it. Many women left the rural area during this period; among those who stayed, a larger percentage remained single. Even those who married and stayed did not rely on their husbands as they would have in earlier years. In spite of efforts to keep Nebraska a farm state, women were being constantly pushed

and pulled away from farm life and its organic division of labor. Many
rural women, on farms and in small towns, looked to nonfarm occupations for better lives.

my grandparents

   Although the people whose farming operations were established
before 1920 might find a way to remain in farming, it was the new
generation of young couples who were critical for the future of
Nebraska agriculture. The couples who were newly married and were
attempting to farm or to run town businesses showed the direction of
change. Couples trying to establish themselves in Boone County
during the 1930s often coped with the difficult economic times by
sharing housing with relatives and moving frequently in search of
jobs. Many lost their farms and businesses. Even as the overall trend
moved away from farming and rural life, there was a great deal of
moving back and forth between town and country. Beth and George
moved in and out of farming; Nora and Sam left the farm and established a series of rural nonfarm businesses; Kathleen and Richard
remained on a farm that had been in Richard's family.

   Beth, one of six children, was born on her parents' Boone County
farm in 1908. Her father's parents had been among the first whites to
enter Boone County in the 1870s, and they had claimed some of the
rich bottomland in the south of the county. Beth grew up there, doing
chores and field work and being part of a local network of cousins
and assorted kin. She went to a country school and attended a rural
church. The relative prosperity of her parents' farm meant that she
was one of the fortunate youths who were able to attend high school
in town. She graduated in 1927, having taken a normal course that
prepared her to teach in country schools. The rural economy was
recovering from the crash of 1920 when Beth got her first job teaching school in 1927. She looked forward to a comfortable and secure
life in the country with her kin.

   In 1929, about the time of the stock market crash, when Beth was
in her third year of teaching school, George walked into a school
party and asked if she would play the piano for him while he sang.
George had lived in the neighborhood as they were growing up but
had left for Omaha some years earlier to study voice and try to
support himself as a singer. In 1929 he returned to Boone County to

work on his brother's farm. Beth and George married in February 1930.

George's family owned no land, and Beth's parents' land was going to her brother, so they were left largely to their own resources. Like many landless workers, Beth and George moved constantly during the thirties, trying to stay employed or to find jobs that paid a bit more than they were making. Although they hoped to farm eventually, they had only Beth's savings when they married. She had been making ninety dollars a month as a teacher, but a woman teacher lost her job at marriage. The best that George could do was to take a job as a farmhand for thirty-five dollars a month plus housing. They moved to the house of a bachelor farmer and George did farm work. But farm labor, like farming, was a family operation, and Beth was expected to keep house as her contribution toward George's keeping his job. The farmer supplied meat for their table, but Beth had to buy the rest of the groceries for the three of them out of George's pay. Even for 1930 it was not a good job. When a tornado struck the county, George was able to get a construction job repairing the damages, and so they left the farm and moved into an apartment in Albion. Their daughter Judy was born in this apartment in November 1930. George was looking for work again and in February 1931 he found another farm job. The three of them moved to the farm, where both George and Beth worked for a year and saved their money, hoping to be able to start farming on their own soon.

In 1932, thinking they might have enough money, they located an eighty-acre farm to rent. With six hens, a cow, two horses, and a garden they managed, barely, to survive as tenants during their first year. Beth remembers this as the hardest year of their marriage. Their only cash income was from the cream that they took to town each week, their highest weekly income being seventy-nine cents. Beth's parents gave them some potatoes, and they subsisted by eating lamb's-quarter and other wild greens, eggs, potatoes, skimmed milk, and garden produce. They were forced to sell their car, and George put together a makeshift buggy, to which he hitched his two workhorses so they could get to town. Their crops grew well, and they had a good corn harvest; unfortunately, the price of corn dropped to nine cents per bushel, and they ended up burning some of the corn as cheap fuel. After a long season of extreme poverty, hard work, high hopes, and devastating frustration, they tallied their first farming accounts with red ink.

In 1933, knowing they had to do something different, they decided to expand their farming. They managed to get a bank loan to buy six good milk cows and some hogs, and they moved to a 160-acre tenant farm. Franklin Roosevelt had been elected president, and farm editors declared that the depression was over and things were looking up. Beth and George bought another car and lived in comparative luxury with the cream income from six cows to support them through the summer. Unfortunately, 1933 was not a good year to be starting out in the hog business. When they sold their hogs in Omaha, the price had dropped so low that they did not even recover the shipping money. Beth's parents also went bankrupt. In 1934 they got another loan and bought thirty-five head of cattle. But in that year the drought hit with full force. What little feed they hoped to salvage for the cattle was annihilated by swarms of grasshoppers. They got through the winter and planted their crops in 1935 with the help of government feed and seed money. In addition George made a little money by cutting firewood from the grove of trees on their farm. But 1935 was a repeat of 1934. Although not exactly forced out of farming, they were discouraged and were ready to try something else. They sold their farm equipment, managing to pay off some of their debt and keep a little money.

Again they moved to Albion, where they put a downpayment on a service station. They fixed an apartment in the back room, where the three of them lived and ran the business. Beth set up a hamburger grill in the front room, and they tried to support themselves in a mom-and-pop business. It did not last long. Beth was pregnant again, and they had to find something else.

Their next move put them on the road. A relative working in Wyoming was able to help George get a job in a garage there. Beth, who had never been away from her family, was frightened and sad at the prospect of leaving, but she had no choice. A son, Ernest, was born in 1937 in Wyoming. But even though they had relatives in Wyoming, they wanted to go home. Later in 1937 they returned to Boone County, where George's brother was trying to start a service station. Having learned the mechanics trade in Wyoming, George was a skillful and careful worker. He worked for his brother for several months while he and Beth looked for employment that would support them.

George got a job as a ranch foreman, and it was time to move again. The ranch was forty-five miles from Beth's family home, and they had no close neighbors. Again, Beth was subtly included in George's job. Although George was the one officially hired as a foreman for fifty dollars a month, the understanding was that he was a married worker and that his wife's labor was part of the package. As Beth said, she was the "chief cook and bottle washer." In addition to doing the housework for their family of four, Beth had to take care of the bunkhouse, which held twelve seasonal haying workers each summer. Besides George, there was one additional full-year worker to help keep track of 2,000 head of cattle on 1,800 acres of land. Beth carried water, laundered clothes and linens in a gasoline-powered washing machine, and cooked for the family and work crew, a total of seventeen persons during the summer work season.

Beth had been terrified at the responsibility she was to assume, and she was afraid that her ineptitude would cost George his job. Finding food for the household was a major part of her worries. The ranch owner supplied them with a limited quantity of beef, but Beth was expected to provide the bulk of the food for her family and the other workers without any help from the employer. To do this, she raised a large garden, which provided fresh vegetables for the table in the summer. In addition, she canned large quantities of vegetables to be used for the rest of the year. She baked all of their bread, which usually meant firing up the oven every other day in the summer. To supplement the home-produced food, Beth shopped in Albion once a month, using their (actually, George's) wages to buy such items as cheese, apples, and flour in bulk. Despite Beth's fears that she could never measure up, the ranch owner found her efforts satisfactory enough to continue George's employment.

Although they did not mind ranch work, the intensity of the job, together with the loneliness, was a trial for both of them. Judy and Ernest were growing, and their care was a constant concern. Beth has never forgotten the panic she felt the time she looked up from her work to see Ernest, a toddler, inside a pen of bulls. She ran out and gently coaxed him to the fence, where she could grab him without disturbing the bulls. Her work for the ranch had taken her away from caring for Ernest and had put his life in danger. Working on the ranch had also separated her from Judy. The first year, Judy had gone to a local school, but it closed the second year and Judy had to go to live with Beth's relatives to attend school. Both Beth and George missed her.

Beth's family, although they had almost no money at this time, opened their doors to Beth and George. In 1940 they moved into Beth's parents' farm home, and George used their equipment to farm a 160-acre farm that he rented. Beth knew that the expense and confusion of their household weighed heavily on her parents, but it seemed to be the only realistic way of keeping the children with them. Indeed, they were luckier than those nuclear families that faced depression hardships without an extended kinship network.

The constant moving was the result of Beth and George's desperate attempt to support themselves and their children. A second couple, Sam and Nora, also moved around. For them, things worked out better. Nora's uncanny ability to do almost anything seemed to guide them through the decade.

Like Beth's family, Nora's had been early settlers in Boone County and owned some of the best flat bottomland in the area. She was born on their farm in 1910, when her father was still working the farm himself. In 1918 the family leased the farm and moved to Albion, where her father ran a retail business. Living close to her retired grandparents in town, Nora, like Beth, grew up amid the security of an encompassing community of kin and friends. After graduating from high school in 1928, she attended college for one year. She returned to Albion and Sam, her high school sweetheart, the following year. Living with her parents, she got an office job in an Albion business.

In 1931 she married Sam, who had abandoned his own college plans because of lack of money. He was living with his parents and farming when they were married, and Nora moved in with them. Her situation was exceptional in that she was able to keep her job and commute to town after her marriage. During their first year, Nora and Sam planned for their own farming operation and spent Nora's salary buying broken-down farm equipment at sales. Each night through the winter they worked together to clean, oil, and repair this old machinery.

By 1932 they were ready to farm on their own. Having no money, they negotiated a move to a farm owned by one of Sam's relatives. This farm was in the process of being foreclosed, and they understood that it would be available for only a short time. They were able to live on it and farm it for two years. In 1933 their first son was born. Nora quit her job in town and directed her energies toward farming and childcare. Knowing that they would probably have only a short time on this farm, they invested in a truck, and Sam did trucking on the side while Nora farmed. Borrowing Sam's father's tractor, she plowed, planted, and kept the farm going. As she did in most endeavors, Nora did well as a farmer, thanks to her special instinct for handling animals. She midwifed the difficult births of calves for her father-in-law, tamed an aggressive pig, and raised poultry.

But Nora's talents were insufficient to salvage their farming hopes. After two years the farm was foreclosed, and they moved into a country house close to a service station run by Sam's brother. There they could combine the trucking business with the service station operation. Nora took over the bookkeeping and managing. Sam did much of the trucking, but Nora would receive shipments and would occasionally pack up the baby and drive a truck to Omaha herself with the help of a hired man. Under Nora's management their business grew, in part through the trucking of hogs that the government was buying at this time to reduce the livestock population. When their daughter was born in 1936 and Nora was forced to spend ten days in the hospital in Albion, she had one of their employees report to her every morning so that she could continue to keep abreast of the business.

By 1937 Sam and Nora had enough money to take over an implement business in a nearby town. She worked through the birth of their second son in 1938. As Nora described the business and her role: "It was really rough times and we didn't have a whole lot, but we managed to make out. We would buy our parts and so forth on a time deal. . . . I always worked and ran the parts and ran the books and Sam sold the whole goods. We had help and so forth, too. I managed always. If I had to pull a string around my middle we managed. That [thrift] really helped of course."

In 1939 they were ready to take over a business in Albion. Nora recalled: "They had asked us to take over shortly after we had gone to [the first place]. We didn't think it was smart to change when we were just learning. Besides, we would have had to have taken over a lot of old stock. . . . So [later] we made the deal that we wanted to come and anything we wanted to buy we'd have first chance at it. We were not forced to take anything. Really, we came in with an advantage that way." They ran this business throughout the 1940s.

Nora's hard work, horse sense, and business savvy—along with a certain amount of luck—explain much of their success. If one couple in twenty was going to prosper during the depression, it would have to have been Nora and Sam—or maybe just Nora. The fact that she, unlike other women, did not lose her job when she married is an indication of her unique ability—she was not easily replaced. Although Sam and Nora received some family support in the form of housing and sharing of farm equipment in the first years of their marriage, its significance seems to have been that it enabled Nora to develop her broad-ranging expertise.

Nora, as the wife of a businessman, may well have been officially listed as economically inactive; but like farm women she was as much a worker as her husband. The key business role that Nora played can be judged in part by the fact that she ran the trucking business from her hospital bed when her second child was born. Not only did Nora make decisions in this nonfarm business, she had another employee report to her. Although she explained that Sam was having back trouble at the time, this is only half of an explanation if the starting assumption is that he was the businessman and she the wife/helper. In fact, Sam's health was never optimal, whereas Nora's health was excellent. Her family needed her intelligence and energy.

Couples like Beth and George or Nora and Sam would probably have stayed in farming if the conditions had been more propitious. Farming had been the first choice of both; but they, like many others,

shifted occupations repeatedly, and the general movement was away
from farming. Women's labor was critical both on the farm and in
leaving it. Even those who did remain in farming had different family
economies than those of their parents twenty years previously. They
were generating more of their income off the farm, and they depended on government programs that directly influenced the way
they lived on the farm. Kathleen and Richard were one such couple
who started farming and remained on their farm through the 1930s.
Working on his parent's farm, Richard was the only one of the six
young people described here who was able to claim family land at
this time.

Kathleen was born in 1914 on a farm in Madison County just east
of Boone County, and she graduated from high school in that county
in 1932. She taught in a country school for one year and then went to
work taking care of an elderly couple in their home until her marriage to Richard in 1936. At their marriage, Richard and Kathleen
went to live in a house on Richard's parents' farm. The first year, they
worked for his parents; after that they took charge of this farm,
paying rent whenever they could. In the fall of the year of their
marriage they counted two sows, three pigs, four calves, a hundred
chickens, and four cats, but they had enough corn fodder to feed only
two of the calves and so had to sell the other two. Kathleen took
charge of the chicken operation. With their egg money she was able
to buy weekly groceries in town. Dairy cows eventually supplied food
for the family table and additional weekly income. Having their own
butter, milk, eggs, meat, vegetables, and fruit on the farm, the couple's major staple purchases were flour and sugar, and they even got
some flour in a nonmarket transaction. In exchange for the work they
did for Richard's parents, his father gave them flour that he had
traded at a mill. Kathleen canned six hundred quarts of fruits and
vegetables each year, sewed and mended their clothing, made soap,
and baked bread. In addition, she wrote local news items for the
weekly newspaper, thereby making an additional small income.

Because of the drought, Richard was able to raise little grain or hay
on the farm, and it was left to Kathleen's enterprises to provide a bare
subsistence. Their farmhouse and wood for fuel were provided on the
farm, allowing them to live on a small cash income. In the dry years,

when ears of corn would not form, farmers would chop the corn plants for use as fodder for their animals. Richard had a silage cutter and was able to do a limited amount of custom work chopping silage for neighboring farmers. When WPA jobs were opened to farm men, he got temporary work on a road near their home. He also got seasonal work in the hayfields of Chambers, Nebraska, northwest of Boone County. Because the area around Chambers had a subterranean water supply that supported grass throughout the drought, it provided both jobs and livestock feed for a wider geographic area in Nebraska.

Horses were expensive to keep when farmers had to buy hay, and the drought hastened the conversion to tractors and fossil fuel. With a government loan in 1938, Richard and Kathleen bought their first tractor, along with a plow, cultivator, grain binder, and harrow, for a total of $765. With this equipment, plus a hay rake bought in 1939, they were ready to profit from the returning rains, and they continued to expand their farm during the 1940s.

Not only did Kathleen and Richard have the advantage of living on his parents' farm, but they also had the advantage of having to survive on the farm through only about half of the depression. A son was born in 1938, and Richard's relatives were close enough to offer help. When I asked if she worried about their economic survival, Kathleen said: "We never thought much about that. I think everybody was about in the same condition. We didn't think about how bad it was or anything. I just don't believe that we worried that much about it. . . . We were living on his dad's farm. I suppose we felt like we had a place to live. About fifty dollars cash rent a year and probably some of the crops. I suppose we didn't worry whether we was going to get put out or anything."

Kathleen washed her clothes in Richard's mother's washing machine during the first year of their marriage, and the households cooperated throughout the depression years. Although living on the farm was not easy for them, Kathleen and Richard did not face the constant worry or numerous moves that tenant and laborer couples like Beth and George had.

Rural Nebraska women had long done the daily work of provisioning their households, and the economic crisis of the 1930s intensified dependence on this subsistence economy. A study published in 1935 indicated that approximately two-fifths of the average Nebraska farm family's consumption was produced directly on the farm, and this production for consumption was inversely related to total farm income (Fedde and Lindquist 1935, 17). Although deflation necessarily entailed less available cash as well as a decrease in the assigned value of home production, in Nebraska the depression-induced decrease in cash expenditures was twice the decrease in the value of farm-produced consumption. A comparison with the situation in Illinois, which did not experience the ecological disaster of the plains region, showed that Nebraska farm families were consuming less than Illinois families but that a greater part of Nebraskans' consumption derived from home production rather than cash purchases (Fedde and Lindquist 1935, 39).

As in earlier years, sales of butter, eggs, and cream provided the household money in farm homes. Nora said of the time she and Sam farmed: "I sold produce. In fact, that's how we had enough money to live on the farm day by day. . . . I raised chickens and sold eggs. We milked the cows and so once a week we went to town with the cream and eggs. Then I bought my groceries. When I knew I was pregnant I saved up enough money out of the cream and eggs to buy a bolt of white flannel so that I could start making diapers and baby clothes."

Beth, on her farming years: "We sold the cream and that's what we lived off of—what little cream money we got. . . . Usually the cream check maybe brought fifty cents for the week."

Kathleen: "You could take the eggs into the store and trade them out for groceries. . . . The eggs and then after awhile we had a little cream. That was enough. The groceries didn't hardly cost anything then. . . . It was always about two dollars. . . . It helped take care of the groceries and a little extra for clothes."

A sample of other interview transcripts from the 1930s indicates the generality of this practice: "It seems like in the thirties the egg and cream check was what give you your weekly income." "The cream and eggs bought food, clothing, everything in the 1930s."

A woman who ran a grocery that exchanged food for cream and eggs said: "People used their egg and cream money to buy groceries. It was their only means of income. They never paid cash. . . . They

Women's Labor

always spent just enough for groceries so they had a little left to buy
gas so they could get home and back to town again."

Women almost always took care of the poultry and handled the
eggs. The 1935 study found that only 29 percent of farm women
milked the cows (Fedde and Lindquist 1935, 16). But women usually
handled the cream and washed the cream separator. A few farm
women were still churning butter to sell in the 1930s. Thus women
generated much of the family's weekly income in Nebraska, as they
did in Iowa and Illinois (Clark 1931; Fink 1986).

But in contrast to conditions in the farming states east of
Nebraska, the drought in the plains states threatened the subsistence
economy, even as families became more dependent on it. Women
gardened, canned, baked, sewed, gathered eggs, and milked cows
under the pressure of increasing economic desperation and decreas-
ing productive returns. Subsistence production became ever more
problematic in the light of the drought-induced reduction in livestock. With the longer distances involved and a less developed infrastructure, shipping produce from rural Nebraska was more costly
than it was in other places, a situation that compounded the depression price reductions. With these disincentives, the number of eggs
produced in Boone County declined by 30 percent from 1929 to
1939; butter production declined by 40 percent; and the amount of
cream sold decreased by 45 percent (Census 1932a, 1223, 1265;
1942, 602, 611). Farm women had to provide for their families; they
could not avoid that necessity. At the same time, their ability to
provide diminished. The drought and the depression combined to
make it increasingly difficult for women to manage on the farm.

In the early years of the 1930s, women's columns in the *Nebraska
Farmer* gave tips on raising poultry and eggs, along with success
stories about poultry operations that paid household bills (Biedermann 1930; *Nebraska Farmer* 1932c; McKenney 1935). When prices
continued low, the advice turned to alternative ways that women
could make money on the farm (*Nebraska Farmer* 1932b, 1935a). A
1938 article told the story of a woman who switched from chickens
to turkeys and was able to put two of her children through the state
university with the profits (Dobry 1938).

These projects for women were always described in the context of secondary operations that would make "extra" money to meet some of the "side" expenses, but never as business enterprises that would stand on their own. An article titled "Sheep Are Her Hobby" had a subheading that stated, "A Small Farm Flock Supplies Both Pleasure and Profit." It told of other women's "sidelines" that had rescued farm families during the depression; like the sheep raising featured in the story, these "sidelines" were presented as pleasurable hobbies. The woman with the sheep-raising sideline had netted $900 in cash "for miscellaneous things for the home" (Baier 1935, 6). Because the average farm income was negative at this time, her experience might well have been seen as a good way to make a farm operation pay its own bills and return an income. Had she been a man rather than a wife who was "helping out" with the bills, sheep raising would have had a different meaning. That it was considered pleasurable identified it as a woman's enterprise, a "sideline," a "help," and not a real business. As such, it was intended for family comforts rather than farm expenses.

Women's production also fed into a barter economy that existed outside of the money economy. With limited cash in circulation, an exchange of goods and services substituted for cash. After Helen's daughter was born in 1932, Helen dressed chickens each week and took them to the doctor until her bill was paid. The description of the household economies of Beth, Nora, and Kathleen provide some indication of the exchanges of goods and services within extended families. The Farm Security Administration's "Live-at-Home" project encouraged bartering as well as home production. The project report cited examples of a dressed goose being offered for a store payment, three chickens being traded for three brooms, and nine-and-a-half days of labor being exchanged for a veterinarian's services (FSA 1940).

The rural economy was moving away from its previous degree of agrarianism, and women were a major part of that movement. Beth grilled hamburgers; Nora kept books and managed a business; Kathleen wrote newspaper copy. All of these actions helped expand the agrarian base of the rural economy. But in each case the family economy was modelled on the family farm, where each person's work derived from that of the male household head. All three women were rural wives, but they were rural wives in a new way. The economic hardships of the 1930s removed the possibility of their being "only" farm wives.

Even as evolving twentieth-century changes in urban women's lives carried them into nonfamily roles, the role of wife was still emphasized for rural women. Notwithstanding the problems that rural women faced as farm wives in the 1930s, government agricultural officials and farm editors nonetheless looked to wives as the ones who could salvage rural life. Rather than the government's supplying relief employment for rural wives, as it eventually did for farmers, depression programs continued to locate rural wives in the home, doing work that did not pay. Private industry followed suit. Farm journal articles and advertisements addressed to women stressed their work in the home; advertisements for farm help specified married farm labor, which meant the employers were looking for men whose wives' labor would be included. While the number of urban Nebraska women statistically recorded as having jobs outside the home increased during the 1930s, the number of rural women working outside the family enterprise grew even smaller than it had been earlier (Census 1932b, 73; 1943, 602).

Just like their earlier predecessors, farm programs of the 1930s placed women in the home as wives. The Boone County Extension Service, organized in 1929, inaugurated a woman's section in 1931. Although single women as well as married women might work in the home, the extension's parallel programs were structured on the model of a marriage in which the husband worked outside the home and the wife worked inside the home. The program for the Women's Project Clubs Annual Achievement Day in 1938 included a recitation of the Homemakers' Creed:

> I believe that the home is the greatest institution in the world.
> I believe that the homemaker has the most important task in
>   the world.
> I believe that it is my responsibility as a homemaker:
>   To insure the purity and sanctity of my home,
>   To exert such a moral influence in my home that those

> lives I touch will be properly influenced thereby,
> To provide for the health of my family by cooking prop-
> erly and keeping my home clean and sanitary,
> To maintain a real home of cheer, comfort, and attractive-
> ness which my family will enjoy,
> To help lead my family in the paths of culture that it may
> seek and appreciate the better things in life.
> I believe that carrying out these duties will require an un-
> limited amount of determination, patience, perseverance
> and self-control, but I believe that for this expenditure I
> shall receive ample and satisfactory returns. (Mrs. Clyde
> Barkell, in Boone County Extension Service 1938)

That the homemaker would be a wife was too obvious to be stated.

Extension personnel believed that the material, cultural, and emotional support of a woman would carry a farm family through hard times (Fink 1988). If a rural wife worked hard and did things right, she could expect "ample and satisfactory returns." If a woman did not reap satisfactory returns, it must be because she lacked un-limited determination, patience, perseverance, and self-control. Even though the extension's home economics program elevated the status of rural wives by addressing them directly and by offering them a nationally recognized organization, it couched this honor in terms of intensified expectations of women as wives with unlimited resources to make things right for their families.

Other 1930s agricultural programs placed a parallel emphasis on the woman as wife. The Farm Security Administration (FSA), created out of the Resettlement Administration in 1937, took over that agen-cy's responsibility for rural resettlement projects, debt adjustment programs, rehabilitation loans, emergency loans and grants, and co-operative loans, in addition to administering the newly legislated Bankhead-Jones Tenant Purchase Program, which gave loans to ten-ant farmers to enable them to purchase farms of their own. The conditions for selecting applicants for the resettlement program had included the stipulation that the family be stable and free of dis-abilities, with preference being given to married applicants (FSA 1939). Before a farmer was selected to receive a Bankhead-Jones tenant purchase loan, every person in the family was required to undergo a physical and mental examination as part of the application procedure, which also included a home study in which a case worker assessed the personal relationships in the household. The primary personal relationship within a household was between husband and wife. A single person, although not expressly prohibited from applying for a Bankhead-Jones loan, was unlikely to receive one.

An FSA home supervisor narrative, written in 1938, began with the wife's history, noting the fact that she was one of eight children and had worked before her marriage. It commented that the wife seemed to be domineering—contrary to the usual preference that a husband control the household—but against this was weighed her strong commitment to her family, her satisfaction with farm life, and her enjoyment of poultry work (FSA 1938). A wife was supposed to be satisfied with country life, enjoy working, care for her family, and be subordinate to her husband; three out of these four assets were good enough if they were strongly pronounced. This case turned out to be a favorable one; the loan was repaid in full in 1945. The FSA, which presided over the future of many farms, thereby reinforced an orthodox marital relationship as part of an adaptive strategy for coping with federal personnel. A cooperative wife was obviously a plus for a farmer seeking a loan, and this was the image the family must try to project.

In another FSA loan case, the wife was a perpetual sore point. She had a job with the Agricultural Adjustment Administration and insisted that her wages be spent for the family. There were four children, and she wanted them all to go to high school, which in itself signaled a questionable elevation of individual ambition over the survival of the farm. In addition, she wanted to send each of the children to the university for one year, a plan that bordered on the frivolous. In 1939, when the FSA worker questioned her work for the AAA and the disposition of her salary, the wife angrily responded that she was working hard to support the family and pay the debts and that federal workers had no right to interfere in their family arrangements (FSA 1941). A 1943 notation indicated, "[T]his family has always been a problem case." The wife handled the correspondence, didn't complete records properly, refused to make a farm plan, and was delinquent on the loan. Although the husband might well have been more active in doing some of the paperwork, the home supervisor seems to have seen the main problem in the independence of the wife and her presumed lack of commitment to the family farm.

The Civil Works Administration (CWA), which was superseded by the Works Progress Administration (later the Works Projects Administration or WPA), represented another major relief effort in rural Nebraska. These federal employment programs served primarily non-farmers, although farmers were eligible for WPA work if they faced the imminent loss of their farms. Like the FSA, the CWA and WPA viewed the nuclear family as the basic unit of survival. They directed their relief efforts to individuals rather than households, but an individual qualified for government employment on the basis of being the head of a household. In Boone County, these agencies financed hundreds of public works projects. Although the majority of the jobs consisted of construction and maintenance work assigned to men, women also worked as seamstresses, housekeeping aides, librarians, nurses, and stenographers. Yet there was always a pressing demand for jobs, and a woman whose husband was employed could not get a WPA job. Although many women may have felt responsible to a wide group of parents, siblings, and other extended kin, the only responsibility that the WPA acknowledged was the nuclear family, and then only if the woman was, for some reason, the sole support. A woman could work for the WPA if her husband were unable to work or if she were separated from him, but if he was working she was supposed to be supported by him. Thus, federal jobs programs worked to channel and limit a woman's family responsibilities to her nuclear family and to reinforce the ideal of a wife supported by her husband (Scharf 1980, 153).

The farm press, closely allied with the extension service, used more and more ink to exalt the role of the farm wife, a relation that was taken for granted under the category of "farm woman." In the *Nebraska Farmer*, a series of letters from women readers on the question of "Why I Like Farm Life" addressed the topic from the perspective of a wife: "I can't help but rejoice because I am a farmer's wife. In no other business would I have the same opportunity to stand shoulder to shoulder with my husband as I do in farming" (Pease

1937, 16). Another letter likewise conflated living on the farm and marriage to a farmer: "I like the freeness, the health, the quiet of the country. . . . I like the friendliness of the country people. . . . So I am glad I am a farmer's wife" (*Nebraska Farmer* 1937a, 12). Wives should never forget that they were blessed in having husbands. Indeed, farm wives were uniquely blessed in standing "shoulder to shoulder" with men. Only by being a farmer's wife could a woman enjoy the unique quality of life in the country.

A woman must not let the chance to marry a farmer get by her. In 1935 the journal invited readers to respond to the question, "Should our young folks marry?" The answer was a resounding yes. Although the text indicated that some replies had come from "old batches," all of the printed letters were submitted by women and were addressed to imaginary women who were reluctant to marry. Noting that practical considerations dictated that a farm couple should be married only *if* they had money, a home, and help from parents, the editor titled the article "Young Love Laughs at If's." The winning entry came from a young married woman, who wrote: "Our home has been an ideally happy one and my advice to any young couple is this: Do not wait until your fortune is made and your young love has cooled, but grasp the happiness that is due you and enjoy life together" (*Nebraska Farmer* 1935c, 8). Abandoning caution and practicality, a young woman should claim the moment through marriage, even though love would cool with time.

Another woman, acknowledging the hard times and difficulties of marriage, nevertheless urged young people to surmount the obstacles: "I think that honorable marriages are the very foundations of civilization. . . . It is always a struggle to live with someone else, but do not life's struggles strengthen us?" (*Nebraska Farmer* 1935c, 9).

Not only did women hold the future of the family and the rural community in their hands, they also held the foundations of civilization. Being a good wife was an exalted calling. Little happily-ever-after sentiment can be found in these letters; but realism did not deflate their strong endorsement of marriage. None of the women denied that marriage was hard both economically and emotionally, but all believed it was necessary for civilization. A certainty that the foundation of Nebraska farming would crumble without marriage is implicit in these pleas for struggle and sacrifice from young people.

In 1937 the *Nebraska Farmer* printed a story about a rural University of Nebraska coed who won an interstate oratory competition with a plea for women not to become so engrossed in their educations that they neglected to get married:

> Every college girl has a right to question education on the grounds that it's interfering with her career. . . . Education ignores the marriage problem. . . .
>
> The college man doesn't forfeit his chance to marry, but at 30 he marries not the girl he loved in college, but a younger girl. . . . Marriage postponement definitely lessens the college girl's chances to marry. At 20, a girl has two chances to one to marry. At 25, the average age for college women to marry, the odds are only a little better than even. At 30 the odds are two to one against her. (Hannah Johnston, in *Nebraska Farmer* 1937b, 11)

"Against her" raised the specter of never being married. No mention was made of the possibility that an educated woman who could support herself might choose not to marry. Of course every woman wanted to marry. Those who chose education over early marriage might be making a mistake they could never correct. If farms needed married women, then women must understand the importance of marriage. They must not tarry in indecision but marry when they could.

The 1930s taught many married women their allegiance to the nuclear family. Just as in the settlement period, when women were uprooted from their kinship network to go west, many young families in the 1930s were uprooted and driven out on the road to try to find a livelihood. These wives, like the earlier women, were forced to weaken their ties to extended family members. Although many couples depended on parents and siblings for temporary shelter, exchanges of goods and services, and leads on jobs, geographic mobility generally reinforced the husband-wife unit. Whether George and

Beth were in Wyoming or Nebraska, running a store, working as farmhands, or farming with Beth's parents, they were a pair. They alone were responsible for Judy and Ernest. In 1940 Beth could look back on the previous ten years and recognize George as the only person who was a constant presence in her daily life. Crisis intensified their economic and emotional needs for each other.

Yet countering the factors that bonded wives and husbands in the 1930s were forces that pulled them apart. Rural society was shifting from its agrarian base, and women were seeking new roles. The mobility of couples like Beth and George might emphasize the unity of the nuclear family, but it was a unity forged in desperation and hardship. Those same factors might also complicate the bond between husband and wife in rural Nebraska.

The increasing rate of farm tenancy and the consequent mobility of the farming population loosened ties to the land. Many farm women lived for some time off the farm and found this way of life easier and more comfortable than what they had had on the farm. Vera, who married Adam and moved to his farm in 1930, found herself forced to move six times during the course of the 1930s. In 1934, when the bank had foreclosed on the livestock and equipment they were using to farm a tenant farm, Vera, Adam, and their son moved to Omaha and lived with her sister Dora, Dora's husband, and their two children. Adam worked at a packing house in Omaha and then, after he lost his job there, worked for the WPA and on various construction jobs. Dora's husband kept his creamery job, although his wages were cut to less than the family needed to live on its own.

In 1935 Vera and Adam had a second son, crowding the small house even more. Adam wanted to farm again, and in 1936 they had a chance to rent a farm and move back to the country. Vera seems to have wanted to stay in Omaha, although she said so only indirectly. In spite of being cramped and poor in Omaha, Vera had liked living with Dora, where the children could play together while she and her sister shared childcare. She recalled: "Adam wanted to go. I didn't care particularly. I liked it in town. There were so many things you could do in town that you couldn't do on the farm. . . . I hated to leave Omaha. . . . My sister was very nice; I liked her. I had four brothers and four sisters, but she was exceptionally nice." Adam,

Table 5-1. Population of Boone County Female Birth Cohorts,
1930 and 1940

Birthdate	1930	1940	% Net Decrease
1926–30	746	641	14
1921–25	821	601	27
1916–20	848	444	48
1911–15	740	401	46
1906–10	617	365	41
1901–5	480	337	30
1896–1900	461	335	27
1800–1895	2,366	1,630	31

Source: U.S. censuses.

Vera, and their two sons moved twice more to different tenant farms
in the 1930s, and Vera dreaded each move.

Settling down and getting married in Boone County was growing
more problematic. Indeed, many young women besides Vera were
leaving the county; most did not return. Not only was the county
population as a whole declining, but it was losing a disproportionate
number of young adults. During the 1930s there was a net out-
migration of nearly half of the women born between 1911 and 1920,
those who were ages ten to nineteen in 1930 (see table 5-1). Although it cannot be assumed that all the women leaving Boone County were rejecting life in rural Nebraska, it is a fact that the general
trend of rural women's migration from 1935 to 1940 was from farms
to towns and cities and from rural towns to cities. The greater a
woman's education, the more likely it was that she would leave (Census 1946, 159).

In contrast to the early years, when nearly all rural women married, Nebraska women's rate of marriage dipped below the national
average in the 1920s and still registered slightly lower than the average for U.S. women in 1930. This rate in Nebraska appears to have
remained at somewhat under the national rate, which itself declined
precipitously during the depression years.[1]

Single women in Boone County were finding new social space. A chapter of Business and Professional Women (BPW) was started in Albion in 1935 with fifty-five charter members. Not all of the women were single and not all were even employed, but single, career-oriented women formed the core leadership. The club president was single, and only six of twenty-five women listed in the newspaper as officers or active members in the first year used a "Mrs." title (*Albion News* 1936, 1937). These women, many of them teachers, included representatives of the middle-class farm and business families of the county. They had luncheons, went to conventions, and talked about women's place in the business world.

A more informal network united other single town women working as clerks, bookkeepers, waitresses, or at other occupations that did not require formal education or capital, forming a working-class counterpart to the BPW. A single woman who supported her widowed mother by doing office work described an active group of women who got together in the 1930s: "There were quite a few single women, . . . quite a few of us wandering around. . . . Some of them had boyfriends and we just always went together. We didn't seem to be unhappy at all. We would have picnics . . . There were fifteen of us. . . . I guess I was just born to be an old maid. It never bothered me. It never did."

Employers' depression-era practice of routinely dismissing female employees as soon as they married caused postponement—sometimes permanent postponement—of the decision to marry. Both public employers such as school boards and the WPA and private employers such as doctors and merchants dismissed women at marriage, a practice that undoubtedly saved payroll money even as it deterred marriage.

Young women from farms who were able to attend high school frequently took a normal training course, which allowed them to teach in country grade schools upon high school graduation. With eighty-five country school districts in the county, teaching was a common occupation for those young women who were able to go to high school but unable to go directly to college after graduation. A country schoolteacher earned approximately fifty dollars per month during the 1930s. Whether she lived with her parents or boarded in a home near her school, she paid approximately five dollars a week for living expenses. A woman who taught her home school from 1935 to 1910 while living with her parents remembered: "After I started teaching I bought the groceries every Saturday because it was hard times. And when we got a catalog I'd always send for things for my sisters. . . . I helped out. I suppose they would have made it okay, but this made it much easier." She was postponing marriage so that she could keep her teaching position; in 1940 she married a farmer whom she had dated throughout the years she taught school.

Another teacher kept her marriage secret so that she could keep her job until she and her husband were ready to give up her income. Beth, who was a teacher before her 1930 marriage to George, saw her monthly income drop by more than half when she got married. In the 1930s, women's teaching income afforded a security that few could equal as farm wives or in marriages to town dwellers. Although teachers' salaries declined in the 1930s, they continued to provide a significant source of income for single women, and this income kept some of them single.

Divorce was another negation of the rural wife role. Nebraska's divorce rate, which had been increasing since divorce was legislated in 1875, accelerated in the 1930s, with 75 to 80 percent of the cases involving the wife as plaintiff (USDHEW 1973, 36, 50; Stouffer and Spencer 1938–39, 553). In Boone County, divorces involved mostly nonfarm women. In a reading of twenty-seven Boone County District Court divorce cases filed in the 1930s, I found only one case in which a farm was mentioned as property in the petition. In this case the wife was charging her husband with an unusually violent pattern of drinking and battering that would have placed her in obvious and immediate danger. Notwithstanding this danger, the wife withdrew the petition within a week of filing it (BCDC 1930).

A common farm property seems to have forestalled divorce, as a woman in this situation would seldom find it to her economic advantage to leave a marriage. Although she might have been able to operate a farm with the help of her children if she were widowed, a divorced woman would rarely have had this opportunity. Only in an unusual case, such as one in which the husband was committed to a mental institution, would a separated wife take over the farm. When I asked Kathleen what a farm wife would have done if her husband drank too much, she answered: "I suppose in those days people didn't leave their husbands for reasons like that. They put up with it a lot. They probably didn't have any place to go. Now they can leave; they work or something and they can leave. It isn't so bad [now], but in those days women just kind of put up with some of this stuff. I think people thought they had to do that—put up with it."

A farm wife was more likely to put up with a bad situation than was a nonfarm wife, because she had invested herself in a joint economic operation that she could not hold on to if she dissolved the marriage. In 1933 one farm wife with five children asked that her husband, a "habitual drunkard and spendthrift," be given a guardian (Boone County 1933). In 1938 she charged him with abandonment, and the court ordered him to stop drinking and to support his family, orders that he repeatedly violated (BCDC 1938). Yet despite this ongoing problem, his ownership of the farm apparently deterred her from seeking a divorce. She seems to have run the farm while he moved between the county jail, the state penitentiary, and a state mental hospital.

Conversely, the decline in owner-operated farms in the 1930s may itself have made the option of legal divorce seem less catastrophic than it had for a number of wives in an earlier period, as nonfarm women usually had less to lose by divorce than did farm women. The absence of conjugal property may also have eased divorce by lessening the extended family's interest in the marriage (Goody 1976). One of the most common grounds for divorce was abandonment and failure to support. Not many farmers would abandon their own farm property, but the economic bases of many other marriages were less substantial. An indication of the economic marginality of many of the women seeking divorces is the fact that they usually received from ten to fifteen dollars monthly in child support and alimony, a meager sum for those not living on farms, even in the 1930s.

After 1935 a single mother could be supported at a subsistence level through the Aid to Dependent Children program provided by the Social Security Act. The increasing number of women who were divorcing and living without husbands appears to be related to the weakening of farm property rights among the population of Boone

County in the 1930s and to the possibility of even minimal support for a woman outside of marriage.

Even farm wives who seemed to do their work patiently and unselfishly often wished to move to town, to have an easier life, to be able to have a nonfarm job, and not to be forever in the grip of farm work. For these women, the possibility of eventually leaving the farm was the silver lining behind the cloud of hardship. Helen had one semester of college in 1929 before the bleak economy snuffed out her education plans. Married in December 1929, she moved in with her husband, his sisters, and his mother on their farm. During the 1930s she had two children, drove the tractor in the fields, and raised chickens—everything that a farm wife was supposed to do. Yet she never forgot that she had wanted to go to college; she had wanted to be a teacher. When her children were grown she was able to return to college and get a teaching certificate. About her years on the farm in the 1930s, she said:

> I kind of had teaching in the back of my mind. One thing I didn't really like to do was to raise chickens. I'd just get so disgusted with them. It was such a hard job. Because if you ever worked around a coop where you raised chickens, it's such a fine dust. It just bothered me to get in there to clean. You had to keep it nice and clean or else they won't do well. Especially when they're tiny, you know. I didn't especially like it. I did it, but I don't know that I was ever too successful. We sold a lot of eggs, and chickens, too.

That she survived on her husband's family farm, raised three children, and eventually remembered her years without bitterness did not erase the fact that she would not have chosen to live on a farm had she not married a farmer.

In an advice column, the *Nebraska Farmer* printed a letter from a farm woman who was heartbroken that her daughter, who had graduated from high school and was working in town, was determined to marry a farmer: "They will start farming with a load of debt. When I think of the struggle ahead for her, I actually ache. I didn't plan this kind of life for her, but what can I do about it. Has some mother had a similar experience?" (*Nebraska Farmer* 1938a, 8). Some of the readers who responded to her were sympathetic; others told her to mind her own business and let her daughter live her own life. But no one suggested that she misunderstood a woman's life on a Nebraska farm (*Nebraska Farmer* 1938b, 14).

How did the Great Depression change women's attitudes toward marriage? As in earlier times, the quality of the marital relation as experienced by women varied widely. Beth and George appear to have complemented each other well throughout their life together. George is now dead, but Beth's story contained numerous anecdotes that illustrated his unique personality, his strength and competence, his helpfulness to his parents and siblings, and his devotion to her. In other cases, the marital relation can be inferred from the woman's terseness when referring to her husband. One taped interview with a woman who was married in 1931 yielded thirty-nine pages of text on her family and work but only scattered and perfunctory statements about her husband. Among the snatches of information I elicited about him were these: he got dizzy when he tried to climb the windmill; he could not deal with their lawyer; he came home after she had finished the plowing; and he did not tend to their small son. Searching for positive statements about him, I found one and a half: he was good at finding bargains at sales; and he would be generous to a neighbor even when it meant depriving her. Without explicitly stating that her husband was irrelevant, she described a world that revolved around her work, her children, and her natal family—a world that largely excluded her husband emotionally.

As in the past, a strain of physical violence sometimes lay beneath the public face of a married couple. When I asked Nora about domestic violence in the 1930s, she said, "Oh, yes. That went on back in those years, but you hid that sort of thing." Helen said, "If anyone did get beaten up it would be the last thing she'd ever tell anybody." Although telling her friends might have elicited some sympathy for a woman, no evidence suggests that telling the authorities would have protected her. Divorce cases frequently mentioned battering as one of the grounds for divorce. But even when the husband did not contest the facts of the case, he was never arrested or held accountable for assaulting his wife. In general a husband could not be charged with the rape or assault of his wife, because these things were men's marital rights. Usually battering was only one of several stated grounds for a divorce, a sign that it may not have been considered a serious enough offense to have warranted a divorce by itself.

During the depression, a majority of Boone County wives—those who were becoming increasingly marginalized economically—found that they were more directly responsible for greater proportions of their families' livelihoods than they would have been in earlier years. The husbands of these women did not have the economic power that middle-class husbands formerly had and therefore could not control their households in the way they might have done, given greater economic power. Glen Elder (1974, 29), in his study of family relations during the depression, found that "wife dominance" was most common where the economic status of men was precarious, which was the case for most in Boone County. The relative power of poor women can be seen in their greater willingness to seek divorce. This is consistent with the theory that economic equality leads to a more general state of equality between men and women.

Yet this equality had limits. These women were equal to their husbands only because their husbands were poor and powerless. Sharing such an affliction would not confer significant power on a woman. In addition, the battering that was alleged in divorce petitions indicates either that men were physically claiming the power that they had previously held economically or that men's violence was a continuation of an existing pattern. Either way, it does not support an argument for egalitarian marriage. Nothing indicates that depression conditions produced less male violence than had existed previously. That the major economic position of a married couple seems to have come through the husband's employment is prima facie evidence of the husband's dominance. Beth worked beside George throughout the thirties, and her work was crucial for family survival. All of her work, however, derived from George's jobs. It was George who collected paychecks from his employers, even when both he and his wife were working. As much as she contributed to the household economy, Beth was economically subordinate, even though they

shared a meager income. She spoke of their occupational and geographical mobility as things that George wanted and she accepted:
"George and I did move around. He was a restless person. If things
looked too bad or got too rough he was willing enough, or daring
enough I guess you could say, to go look elsewhere for work. . . . I
went along with him. I guess it was hard to move away from the
relatives, mainly, but you just did. You'd get by." After her marriage it
became a question of what George wanted; George's attributes played
a primary role even in her description of her own life.

Women who lived in households in which the household members themselves controlled the means of their own production were
in a minority in Boone County, although the farms and small businesses of rural Nebraska afforded a greater access to self-employment
than cities did. Middle-class women provided the weekly grocery
money on the farms. Women like Nora who worked in small nonfarm
businesses were also essential to their families' economies. Even
though this position afforded a degree of economic security that the
majority of women did not experience, it did not translate into economic equality within the marriage or political equality outside of the
marriage.

Control of marital property among the middle class can be seen in
the pattern of estate probates in the 1930s, because by definition the
traditional middle class controlled productive property that devolved
onto heirs. An examination of estate probate records between 1932
and 1936 indicates that the husband usually held the property in his
name. It was his estate that would be probated, whereas the wife's
estate usually did not appear in the probate record. Of 135 probates
of the estates of persons who were married at some time, ninety-two
were of men's estates and forty-three were of women's estates. The
majority (65 percent) of women who had their estates probated were
widows at their deaths, while the majority (67 percent) of men were
married. In part this reflects the tendency of women to outlive their
husbands, but there were twice as many widowers as married women
whose estates were probated. This indicates that the husband would
have controlled the productive property within a family. When a
 woman obtained title to marital property, she was likely to be a
widow.[2]

The wife, who often survived her husband, had a statutory right to one-third of his estate. The majority of husbands died intestate, in which case the formula for dividing the estate awarded a third to the wife and two-thirds to be equally divided among the children. This would usually give a widow a small income from a farm being run by one of the children. Sometimes, though, a woman's statutory right to her husband's estate could be negated either by a prenuptial agreement or by a man who simply ignored the law and wrote a different will. In the latter case, a wife could contest the will, but in only one instance did this actually happen.

Of twenty-three married men who left wills at their deaths between 1932 and 1936, nine left their property to their wives in the form of life estates. With a life estate, the wife would have ownership of the property during her lifetime, but she would not have the right to sell it or to write her own will leaving the property to someone else. The husband specified who was to get his property at the wife's death. Frequently he would stipulate that she would lose the property if she remarried. For example, a man who died in 1933 leaving a widow and eight grown children left his seven acres, two cows, and his 1930 Chevrolet to his wife during her lifetime but stipulated that if she remarried the estate was to be divided equally among the children. Thus the husband's ownership of even a small piece of property could be used to control his wife after his death.

Only seven of the married men named their wives as executors of their estates; sixteen named sons or third parties as executors. Often a husband would will the bulk of his estate to his children, leaving the wife only a small pension.[3]

The control of property was even more explicit among those who had estates larger than family operations. Of the seventeen estates valued at over $20,000 that were probated in the 1932–36 period, fifteen were men's estates. Neither of the women who left substantial estates wrote a will; one of the men also died intestate. Nine of the fourteen testate men were married at the time of their deaths, while five were widowers. Five left their wives life estates or trusts that would not give them control of the property. Others divided their property, sometimes giving their wives a small inheritance, possibly a house and personal property, but willing most of the property to their sons and daughters. In only two cases did a husband will a substantial part of his property to his wife rather than to the children. Only four of these men named their wives as executors of their estates; one named his wife and son as coexecutors.

Herbert Lake, president of a bank and owner of a large ranch, was widowed in 1935; he remarried in 1939. In a prenuptial agreement, he and his second wife spelled out their expectations in detail. She was to inherit $1,000 for every year that he lived after two years of marriage, thereby giving her incentive to care for him well. This money was to be forthcoming only if she continued to live with him during his lifetime; if she left him, she would receive only the sum that would have been due to her if he had died the year they separated. The prenuptial agreement superseded her right to a statutory share, and the bulk of the estate was to go to Lake's son by his first marriage. This agreement came close to explicitly defining the wife as a paid nurse and concubine, a relationship that balanced his personal neediness against her economic neediness.

Propertied males left little to chance where their wives were concerned; they left little room for their wives to wield economic power at their deaths. That the wives were comfortably provided for does not mitigate the lack of control they derived from being wives.

Sons fared better than wives. Not only did they inherit property that they could use for productive purposes, but they were also beginning to be accepted as their fathers' business partners. A 1941 article in the *Nebraska Farmer* described a wife's involvement in her husband's cattle-raising venture. Like many farm wives, she provided strong support and expertise for making important farm decisions. After noting her participation, the author stated, "Some day the firm may be H. H. Forney and Son, because young Donald, just out of high school, is wrapped up in the purebred Hereford business, too" (Weaver 1941, 13). "H. H. Forney and Wife" or "H. H. and Mary Forney" were beyond imagination at that time, and the writer, herself a woman, was apparently unaware of excluding the wife.

Being a wife could be comfortable and emotionally rewarding. A married woman might gain economic security, respectability, and prestige. What she did not gain was economic or political power through marriage.

Gender norms discouraged a woman from asserting her independence, and sexual independence was probably the most undesirable characteristic a wife or potential wife could have. If the 1930s brought any relaxation of sexual restrictions on women, it applied only to nonpropertied women. Unlike respectable men, respectable women limited their sexual expression to marriage. Strong sanctions enforced the control of middle-class women's sexuality. Teachers, the most numerous and public of unmarried middle-class women, were subject to stringent controls. Town teachers were not allowed to go dancing locally, to smoke, or to drink. If a town teacher were dating a man, she had to be very careful of her reputation. The rule requiring a woman to quit her teaching job when she married existed because it was thought that her husband should support her and that no couple should claim two jobs when others had none. But another effect of the rule was to ensure that female teachers would be asexual. As one former teacher explained: "They wouldn't hire married women. They were afraid of pregnancy. That should not have been in school." Pupils should never guess that their teachers could be sexual. Although unmarried women did engage in sexual activity, it was always in secret. A young unmarried woman was always under the cloud of suspicion. She removed herself from the suspicion of illicit sexuality by marrying.

John Burma, writing in 1941 about the 1930s out-migration from Clay County in central Nebraska, stated that out-migration, for all the trouble it had caused, cleared out some of the "ne'er-do-wells," including "three girls strongly suspected of immorality" (Burma 1941, 164). Immorality, in the case of young women, never meant stealing or lying; it clearly meant that they were sexually active—presumably with numerous males rather than one boyfriend, although these males do not seem to have incurred any social stigma. By including the young women in the category of "ne'er-do-wells," Burma implied that the town was well rid of them. Their sexuality, unlike that of males, was a social rather than a personal characteristic. By being sexual they had rendered themselves ineffective, even harmful, as rural women, and they were not considered a loss to the town even when out-migration posed a serious threat to the future of rural Nebraska.

The double sexual standard symbolized the intense pressure on a woman to marry in order to remove herself from public scrutiny. As in earlier years, the double standard functioned as a disadvantage to a wife within marriage. A woman's sexuality was tainted and unclean; in marrying she was lucky to be able to turn it over to a man, who would manage it for her. Her husband, who was not under a corresponding cloud of sexual pollution, might need a wife for many practical reasons, but one of them was not to save his sexual reputation.

Throughout the 1930s, women were attempting to build economic bases that did not depend on marriage. Agrarian ideology, with its emphasis on women as farm wives, remained a fundamental and unchallenged principle in rural Nebraska culture, but some women reworked this ideology so that it said what they wanted it to say. The Business and Professional Women of Albion found a new way to praise their rural roots. At a 1939 meeting two women spoke—one on pioneer women and one on modern women. The first speaker cataloged the ways in which rural women of the past had been limited by the traditions and prejudices of their day; the second speaker talked about modern women and named some who had made impressive strides in science, business, and other professions. A summary of the meeting stated:

> The members of the club were indeed grateful to these ladies for the beautiful picture each painted; the pioneer woman in her coarse, homespun gown and heavy shoes with a child under one arm and a staff in the other, on the pioneer trail with her steps leading ever westward, marking that trail so painfully in order that the woman today might lead a richer and fuller life; the other a picture of the successful business and professional woman who has been accepted by man because of her worth and ability. (*Albion News* 1939)

The revised view held that women of the rural past were models of strength who persevered through all difficulties. These women had borne children, sacrificed, and claimed the land that would someday support the office buildings, schools, and laboratories where women could continue their achievements in more favorable surroundings. The daughters of pioneer women would reap the fruits of their mothers' sacrifice in the form of lives that were not tied to farms. In modern life they would relate to men not as wives but as colleagues and competitors. This rendition of agrarian ideology put farming at the chronological base of social development. It did not encourage women to stay on the farm if they were ready to leave.

The BPW program included campaigns for economic security, for repeal of all legislation that discriminated against women, for the election of women to public office, and for the reemployment of women in private business (*Albion Argus* 1935). These women saw their lives not as a break with tradition, but rather as fulfilling the dreams of their pioneer mothers. Farming, to them, was a step toward a better world for women, not an end in itself. Rather than defining a successful woman in terms of her husband, these women looked to other women for support and inspiration.

Agrarianism was alive and well in the 1930s, in spite of the unfavorable environmental and economic conditions in rural Nebraska. Women were central actors in the farm economy; everyone realized that things would not work without women. Insistent voices praised the beauty and moral stability of family life on the farm. Much was expected of rural wives. The family was compressed and forced to depend on internal resources for those things that the nonfamily economy could not provide; as a result, wives' responsibilities intensified. Yet agrarian life was crumbling, and the patterns established in the early years of the century would not cohere in the 1930s; rural people had ever fewer resources to tap. As hard as women worked, they could not maintain their production, ease the burdens of the depression, and make everyone comfortable, as they were supposed to do.

The strains caused a shift in the foundations of Boone County society. Women said "no" to the agrarian pattern in a number of ways: they left the farms in large numbers; more women who stayed remained single; more married women divorced their husbands; and women who stayed married were less tied to the farm economy than they had been previously. Married, single, or divorced, these women who expressed the coming changes found their voices not as dutiful wives, but as women who quietly and subversively insisted on the validity of their own experiences and aspirations.

Family of Charles and Mary Lederer, circa 1896. Many Nebraska farm
women had large families, and the care of these children dominated their
lives. Mary Lederer's childbearing stretched over twenty years. Standing:
Cleo (author's grandfather), Louis, Noah, John, Charles. Seated: Walter,
Mary, Ruth, Charles, George.

Sod house farmstead of Levi W. Huffman, near Callaway, Nebraska, 1892.
(Nebraska State Historical Society Photograph B983-1636)

Frame farmhouse. A few Nebraska farm families had comfortable frame houses like this one. (Nebraska State Historical Society Photograph B355-4-19)

Fourth Street, Albion, Nebraska, 1911. Boone County's political, commercial, and cultural center drew farmers and supported a population of construction workers, government officials, doctors, lawyers, merchants, and clergy. (Courtesy of Geo Stewart)

Main Street, Albion, Nebraska, 1917. (Nebraska State Historical Society Photograph A337-8)

Populist convention at Callaway, Nebraska, 1892. Although scholars have argued for the prominent position of women in the Farmers' Alliance and Populist party movements, this picture of a local gathering does not support that judgment. (Nebraska State Historical Society Photograph B903-2185)

Jules and Mary Sandoz, 1926. The parents of Nebraska writer Mari Sandoz were the subject of her book Old Jules. *(Nebraska State Historical Society Photograph S218-8a)*

School in Buffalo County, Nebraska, 1907. Young unmarried women often taught in one-room, eight-grade country schools. The press of farm work kept some children, especially boys, out of school for much of the year. (Nebraska State Historical Society Photograph B983-2777)

Dust piled against a snow fence. When the grasslands were plowed, they became subject to severe wind erosion during times of drought. Dust storms of the 1930s left drifts of dust covering fences, buildings, and equipment. (Nebraska State Historical Society Photograph D974-19)

Wife of a homestead farmer in Kearney, Nebraska. The New Deal Resettlement Administration supplied some landless families with farms, homes, and equipment. Through the program, this woman found comfortable housing, adequate food, and improved household conditions for herself and her family. (Nebraska State Historical Society Photograph R433-50)

6 MOTHERS, CHILDREN, NEW FARMS

> *What will theologians say to a hell where the childless woman feels unsatisfied the pangs of heart-hunger, an endless yearning for the mother love that on earth they ever scorned and shunned? Could anything be more terrible?—G.S.H., "The Mother's Joy," 1906*

Most of the women who moved onto the Nebraska plains had large numbers of children. The relation between a woman and her children gave meaning to her life in the new territory. Her children, in turn, formed the backbone of the rural workforce. The agrarianism that propelled the westward expansion into the farming frontier had particular implications for mothers and children. The popular belief, as expressed in the well-loved "Little House" books of Laura Ingalls Wilder, was that rural children grew up ruddy-cheeked, healthy, industrious, happy, unselfish, good humored, and honest. Rural mothers were self-sacrificing, uncomplaining, and mystically able to make things right for everyone. Such images of rural mothers were widely disseminated in popular magazines, newspapers, and promotional literature on the West (Juster 1979; Rasmussen et al. 1976). As an ideal place for raising children, the family farm was unsurpassed.

Yet the substance of motherhood was beset with contradictions from the earliest years of settlement in Boone County. The very intensity with which women approached mothering produced conflicts that were especially painful for the majority of Boone County mothers, who lived an economically precarious existence. Trying to be a perfect mother within the framework of late-nineteenth-century European American culture—an impossible attainment anywhere—

was hopeless on a marginal farm. Often the children were over-worked, poorly educated, and isolated. The prescribed organization of motherhood, by which each mother was separately responsible for tending her own children within the nuclear family farm household, conflicted with the raising of healthy and well-integrated children. And although ideology detached mothering from economics, the re-ality was that both women's and children's labor was crucial to the success of family farms. Because of this need, women's childbearing had an instrumental dimension. Women as mothers were at the cen-ter of a contradiction, and mediating this contradiction was a funda-mental part of their work in establishing a new society on the plains. Some women embraced the possibilities and promise of raising chil-dren in the new environment, but others resisted.

A mother was closely attuned to her children, sensing their needs and tending to them so that they would survive and lead the best possible lives. More than anyone else, a mother knew the pain of her children and made it her own. The mother's story blends with those of her children.

The childbearing of white women was a major factor in winning the West for commercial farm production, because women's fertility swelled the labor force so vital to the success of plains farming. In this respect, the women's own emotional and economic needs con-verged with the interests of agriculture. Children supplied emotional gratification for women isolated on the newly established farms and in nuclear family households. Children's dependence and trust gave women, at least temporarily, the power and authority that were other-wise reserved for men. Children also represented a mother's hope of being cared for in her old age. Given a situation in which women could not express their gender identity in terms of the conventions used by middle-class women in areas of longer settlement, mother-hood told them they were women. With all its attendant problems, having children was an integral part of the emotional and economic security women worked to establish. Wife and mother were separate, and at times competing, roles.

A woman's responsibility for bearing and nurturing children shaped her work both within the household and within the community. The women of Boone County, like women of every society, had children, but the configuration of motherhood there developed in terms of historical, geographical, social, and economic specificity. The division of labor, access to birth control, household income, beliefs about children, the rural economy, and the interaction among households all affected the way women viewed motherhood and carried out mothering tasks.

Women's work as mothers meshed with the intensive farming pattern being established in Boone County. Studies of fertility in the United States have shown higher birthrates in rural areas than in cities, a fact linked to the greater economic value of children as workers in rural settings (Okun 1958; Hammel et al. 1983; Folbre 1983). In turn, caring for a large number of children limited the kind of work women could do. The need to stay close to small children usually kept women in the vicinity of the house, where they tended to the poultry, milking, and other chores. But some women managed to combine their childcare with a considerable amount of productive labor away from the house, particularly if they had daughters old enough to press into service as substitute mothers. Children were enculturated with a sense that constant work was a fact of life; they assumed farm labor roles at an early age. In this way, family members supplied the farm with an efficiently produced, low-cost, highly intensive labor force. In no other sector of U.S. industry could the labor of women and children be so fully utilized.

This total-exploitation-of-resources analysis of household farming operations, although probably valid, leaves open the question of why things worked the way they did. Why did rural Nebraskans emphasize labor over leisure, education, health, or other values? Why did they not integrate diverse values into their routine? Why did they believe it was their destiny to claim and populate the land?

The earlier presence of Native American peoples with different family structures underscores the varied possibilities for plains culture. Anthropologists have documented widely differing ways for women to be mothers (see, for example, Mead 1935; Tanner 1974; Goody 1976; and Yanagisako 1985). Even in European American history, nannies, slaves, and grandmothers frequently shouldered much of the burden of caring for small children (Drummond 1978).

In some societies the care of children has been seen as a widely shared duty and pleasure (Lee 1979; Weltfish 1965). These anthropological studies de-emphasize hormones and biological imperatives and point to the wide variety of cultural interpretations of biological processes.

Although Jeffersonian agrarianism is part of the liberal tradition that separates public and private spheres and places motherhood in the private sphere, the state has always had a policy in relation to reproduction. Regulation of birth control measures is just one way in which the public arena has spilled over into the supposedly separate world of motherhood and private life. The division between the spheres has always been permeable and subject to political intrigue and manipulation (Petchesky 1984).

European American mothers, for their part, generally acquiesced in furthering U.S. political goals. Linda Kerber (1980) concluded that the "republican mother" solidified political consensus in the early years of the nation by inculcating in her children the piety, obedience, self-discipline, and sacrifice needed for service to the state. The uplifting image of the pioneer woman marching westward with a child under her arm softened the brutal reality of the genocide that occurred as whites took over the plains from the native peoples. Motherhood took the hard edges off a sordid undertaking. Women's willingness to lend their spiritual capital to this campaign inevitably ensnared them in a web of violence.[1]

The fiction of the separation between public and private spheres has tainted women's efforts to be good mothers. One part of the problem with recent European American motherhood is that it has taken so much of women's time and energy that they have been unable to attend to their own sanity, their own economic needs, and their own varied social contributions. Too often they have looked to their children to fill impossible chasms in their lives. The common practice among mothers of manipulating their children to satisfy their own latent ambitions has been but one example of emotional violence. Mothers have nurtured their children, but at the same time they have used their power over them in socially and personally destructive ways (Rich 1976; Gordon 1986, 1988; Dinnerstein 1976; Chodorow 1978).

Although the validity of public and private spheres as a prevailing model cannot be denied, analyses of the interpenetration of motherhood and public politics blur this distinction. A consideration of mothering in Boone County will show the continuing interconnections between the home, the community, and the state. Even though motherhood was culturally defined in the context of a home and family separate from the rest of society, the many inconsistencies in this model reveal an underlying unity of public and private life. Mothers responded to economic, ideological, and social pressures; in turn, mothering affected the community and the world beyond it.

Mothers did good and bad things for their children, themselves, and their society. Recognizing the historical and political contingency of the motherhood configuration allows us to acknowledge its complexity without concluding that it has been inevitable or beyond questioning.

Nineteenth-century North America witnessed a major transformation in the popular ideology of domesticity and motherhood. The cult of domesticity was a pattern of social attitudes concerning women, home, and family that blossomed in the northeastern states during the late eighteenth and early nineteenth century. It exalted motherhood as the special calling of women. Before this time, the rearing of children had been closely controlled by the father, and hands-on childcare had been accomplished by a diffuse group of kin and servants; but according to the emerging wisdom on motherhood, raising children was something that only a mother could do properly. Premised on the Lockean concept of the child as a blank slate, the new view of motherhood assigned to mothers the responsibility for shaping the characters of totally malleable children. The cult of domesticity downplayed the role of father except as a distant authority figure. Mothers' work became the salvation of children and, through them, the salvation of the world. Motherhood required continuous commitment and sacrifice; in turn, it would provide fulfillment for women. The rise of the moral mother upgraded woman's status by assigning her authority in the new domestic sphere. Most nineteenth-century women, including feminists, accepted motherhood as a woman's primary definition of worth (Bloch 1978; Cott 1977; Ryan 1981, 1983; Stetson 1896).

The acceptance of this new understanding of motherhood was accompanied by a birthrate decline that focused public attention and controversy on childbirth and birth control. The declining birthrate seems to have resulted more from an acceptance of the expanded demands of good mothering than a rejection of the existing mother role. Although separate strands of the rationale for limiting births divided advocates into different political groupings, a pronatalist backlash lumped them together and found the new and frightening label of "feminist" to be an effective means of coalescing opposition to women's control of birth decisions. The pronatalists won a legal victory with the Comstock Law of 1873, which banned the distribution of birth control devices or information. Abortion also became illegal. Although these measures curbed birth control research and practice within the medical establishment, knowledge of birth control could be only incompletely suppressed, because women themselves controlled and retained rudimentary contraceptive practices. The specter of even this much control kept pronatalist ideologues active (Gordon 1976, 1982; Mohr 1982).

Although most specific birth limitation measures were not universally known or accepted, in general they had long been employed in varying degrees regardless of the legal or social stigma attached to them. The development of birth control technology was not a primary agent in the declining birthrate of the nineteenth century; the critical factor was the social consensus about birth limitation that governed the distribution of existing knowledge. A demographic study of a rural Massachusetts community suggested that the population there was deliberately limiting births in the early nineteenth century, and a fertility study of the Mormon population indicated that fertility regulation was used even among populations in which the rate of childbirth would suggest the absence of birth control (Bean et al. 1990; Osterud and Fulton 1976, 1988). But whatever birth control methods were being used in these places, their application was contingent on the particular circumstances of a time and place and would not automatically be diffused to other areas or to succeeding generations. Political and economic expansion in the late nineteenth century depended on a rapidly growing population of loyal citizens and workers, and therefore a partial suppression of birth limitation practices within the dominant social group was seen as a necessity.

Pronatalist polemics flourished among the Yankee agricultural entrepreneurs who spearheaded the late-nineteenth-century frontier expansion. Although the nineteenth-century birthrate decline crossed racial, ethnic, and class lines, as early as the 1860s middle-class whites were being encouraged to see themselves as a beleaguered minority doing battle with dark forces to maintain control of their country. Keeping control of the rapidly breeding hordes of immigrants, blacks, and other poor meant that native-born, bourgeois women could not shirk their duty to reproduce their own kind (Gordon 1976, 138). White mothers were needed to rescue the uncivilized West and bring it into the ideological and economic fold. An essay that won the special prize offered by the American Medical Association in 1864–65, comprising an extended argument against abortion, concluded its case with a reflection on the necessity of populating the farming frontier with proper U.S. citizens:

> All the fruitfulness of the present generation, tasked to its utmost, can hardly fill the gaps in our population that have of late been made by disease and the sword, while the great territories of the far West, just opening to civilization and the fertile South, now disinthralled and first made habitable by freemen, offer homes for countless millions yet unborn. Shall they be filled by our own children or by those of aliens? This is a question that *our own women* must answer; *upon their loins depends the future destiny of the nation.* (Storer 1974 [1868], 85; emphasis mine)

Native-born white children were to form the backbone of the future midwestern population, and settler women's work was to mother these children. Peopling the West with white family farms would secure this vast territory and its wealth for the politically dominant group. Significantly, the essay writer believed that "our own women" must answer the question of the future birthrate, indicating some ambiguity about where the control lay. If the emphasis was on "our own," it implied that men must control their women. If the emphasis was on "women," it implied that European American women controlled a key factor in the success of frontier expansion.

In the early twentieth century, President Theodore Roosevelt lent his political weight to the white pronatalist movement by popularizing the term "race suicide" as part of a campaign that nurtured the fear that white women who limited childbirths endangered themselves and their families. Such pronatalist sentiments also found expression in rural Nebraska. Cass Barns, the doctor-farmer-businessman who migrated to Boone County in 1878, emphasized the significance of rural-born children in shaping Nebraska's early history: "Maternity came often to those sod houses. . . . Large families were common. . . . Nothing else did so much for the upbuilding of the state. Without those troops of boys and girls the prairies of Nebraska would have been barren wastes and the sod house homes but dreams" (Barns 1970 [1930], 248–49). In using the phrase "troops of boys and girls," Barns implicitly associated children with soldiers conquering the land. Children raised by attentive, prolific mothers, the theory went, would both build and inherit the state.

European American mothers and children secured the state in a social and moral as well as an economic sense. Charles Wesley Wells, who came to Nebraska as a railroad worker in 1867, complained that most women around the railroad camp were of a "baser sort" (that is, living independently of families). Lumping together a diverse collection of undesirables, he wrote, "With the Indians, the murderers, horse thieves, prostitutes, and drunkards, this country was a hell to live in" (Wells 1902, 171). Wells married and moved to Albion as a clergyman in 1877. In recalling the development of the area, he underscored the importance of white mothers and children in making Nebraska a suitable place to live: "The Red Man's pony has yielded to the plow-horse and the roadster that is driven by thousands of cultured wives and daughters of white men. . . . In place of the dirty, half-naked children of the desert, playing and growing up in ignorance, our own children are making the schoolgrounds ring with their merry laughter, while both mind and body are being trained for usefulness" (Wells 1902, 312). Usefulness meant that, in contrast to Native American children, "our own" children, those born to "cultured wives," would be working on family farms and in other rural businesses.

Despite all of the emphasis placed on children as building blocks of the future, few details about actual pregnancies and childbirths have come down to us from the women themselves. Nearly all of the women who were having children during this period are now dead; few left any form of written record, and those written records that do exist rarely mention pregnancy and childbirth. The diary of Hannah Patterson Johnson, written in Boone County in the 1880s, tells of differences between Hannah and her husband, conflicts with hired workers, and various personal health problems, but it does not mention her pregnancies. Although she frequently noted that she was tired and ill starting at the beginning of her diary in March 1880, it was not until September 28, when she mentioned that she had a baby in the night, that she revealed to the reader that she had been pregnant (Johnson 1880). Although we can surmise that the awareness of her pregnancy and her forthcoming relation to descendants might have prompted her to begin her diary as a link to the future, Hannah herself avoided discussing the intense feelings she must have had on facing motherhood.

Avoidance of discussions of pregnancy might also have stemmed from its close association with sexuality, a topic even more rigorously avoided than pregnancy. Carol Fairbanks and Sara Sundberg (1983, 55) link the absence of sexuality in frontier women's diaries and letters to the fact that their writings were often intended for parents, children, or grandchildren rather than agemates.[2] Even if women were able to share information and feelings about childbirth with their close personal friends, their disinclination to pass information to succeeding generations indicates that childbirth, despite its central role in society, was still viewed as a problematic and tainted experience. The impropriety of mentioning any body functions associated with reproduction meant that some women entered marriage and faced childbirth with only a vague knowledge of what they would be experiencing. Grace Snyder's (1963, 108) ignorance about her mother's pregnancies, even in her later teens, shows how women learned not to acknowledge the biological reality of childbirth even as it unfolded.

Notwithstanding this silencing of women's voices on the sexual reality of having babies, the dominant ideology of motherhood became the axis around which nineteenth-century rural Nebraska women plotted their lives. Luna Kellie, who in 1876 traveled with her husband J. T. and infant son Willie to central Nebraska to homestead, believed that the West was a good, healthy place to raise children. Luna and J. T. wanted a large family—twelve children at least, and preferably fifteen. Large families were a blessing (Kellie 1926, 22). Kellie accepted that motherhood would be central to her life in rural Nebraska. In fact, a search for the space and economic means to have a large number of children was the major factor in Luna and J. T.'s decision to migrate to Nebraska (Nelsen 1989). Luna eventually had thirteen children, eleven of whom survived infancy.

Although such large families as that of the Kellies were not uncommon, individual families varied greatly, and some women appear to have deliberately limited their births. One example of contrasting practices of birth limitation can be seen in the 1900 Boone County census schedules. Two married farm women lived near each other in the eastern part of the county. The first woman, forty-two years old, reported nine births and eight surviving children, these having been born in 1884, 1886, 1888, 1890, 1892, 1894, 1896, and 1900. The other woman, her forty-three-year-old neighbor, reported having four children, these having been born in 1877, 1878, January 1881, and December 1881. Because the second woman appeared to possess unimpaired fecundity, it can be inferred that she deliberately chose to limit the number of births, but only after she had had four children, all of whom survived. This practice would still be consistent with a strong commitment to mothering, as the second woman may have chosen to channel her resources toward her four children rather than to distribute them among more children. Like Luna Kellie, both of these women were U.S.-born migrants to Nebraska.

For mothers, having children was a way to partly fill the emotional void created by leaving kin and familiar surroundings in eastern North America or Europe. According to Mary Hargreaves (1976, 183), large numbers of children helped to relieve the loneliness that women felt when they settled on the large, isolated plains homesteads. Once she became a mother, a woman's time, physical energy, social relationships, fear, anger, and hopes all centered on her children. Many women's accounts, although they record misbehaviors and illnesses, also record the humorous things children did, the warm affection freely given by small children, and their own pride in their children. A toddler's smile could lighten a trying time (Kellie 1926, 41). One Boone County settler called his daughter a "sunbeam" and declared that she was "a good thing to have about the house, especially a sod house, away and alone on the prairie" (Turner 1903, 353). "The childless woman only half lives," declared another woman in a letter to the *Nebraska Farmer* (Alcott 1906, 412). In a lonely environment with little entertainment or leisure, children provided diversion and company. As they grew older, they might furnish important personal support for their mothers. Mothers cherished their children.

Mothers assumed almost total responsibility for childcare. When John Turner described his work as a Boone County census taker (apparently in 1890 or 1900), he noted that men often did not know basic household demographic information: "I found that the women knew more about such matters than did the men, anyway, especially with regard to ages of the children. When I applied to the men for the information needed, they would almost invariably refer me to the wife and mother, saying, 'O, you'll have to ask the woman about that; she knows more about them things than I do'" (Turner 1903, 181).

Affection for their children may have lightened the drudgery of caring for them, but the work itself was monumental. After the demanding round of nursing and cleaning a baby—carrying water from the well, heating it, washing linens, carrying water out—a mother had to scurry constantly to watch over a small child just to keep her out of the most immediate dangers. When a mother had both a baby (or two) and several small children at the same time, it complicated her situation exponentially. Mothers were subject to continual demands on their time and attention, even as they tried to sleep at night. After the birth of her first daughter in 1880, every entry in Hannah Johnson's diary talked about what her children were doing— whether they slept or stayed awake, where they played, whether they were well or sick, and what mischief they got into. Hannah noted with regret the time her baby cried herself to sleep alone because Hannah was too busy to tend to her.

Primitive housing conditions only complicated childcare. Living in one- or two-room sod houses, small children had ready access to kitchen knives, food supplies, and fires, among other inviting potential disasters. Luna Kellie (1926, 30–35) told of struggling to keep her baby dry in their leaky sod house. After her second baby was born, she and J. T. made a canopy to protect her and the new baby when it rained. Another woman told of placing her baby in a box under the kitchen table to keep her dry (M. Long 1937, 166). Besides being leaky, many houses were cold and drafty, making it necessary for women to provide heavy bedding and clothing for their children in cold weather. Lacking screens or tight-fitting doors and windows, sod houses attracted fleas, bedbugs, mosquitoes, flies, rodents, and snakes, all of which posed threats to the care of children.

A mother, more than anyone else, sheltered her children in their middle childhood years and prepared them for adult life by giving them the knowledge they needed and by standing up for their interests. If she died or abdicated this responsibility, her children might be forced to fend for themselves at an early age. They might be adopted and cared for by someone else, but this was not assured.

Rural society of the nineteenth and early twentieth centuries offered few social services and little economic support to those in need. The key role that mothers played can be seen in the story of a motherless home. Vera, born in 1909, told me about her mother, Edna, whose stepmother deserted her family. Then Edna's father left also, leaving Edna, age fifteen, and two small half-brothers with no home and no source of support. The two boys were put up for adoption in Omaha, one of them eventually being adopted by a couple who also housed, but did not adopt, the other. We can only imagine the continuing anguish of the boy who lived alongside his favored brother without himself being accepted as a family member, but this concern was not a social reality on the plains in the nineteenth century. The mother was responsible for providing the personal love and care that prepared children to cope with the uncertainties of life; in her absence, society appointed no one else to do it. Widowed fathers frequently sent their offspring to be raised by relatives or others, an action that tended to be attributed to deep grief for the deceased wife.[3] Seldom did fathers themselves take over the mothers' responsibility of loving and caring for their small children.

For all the trouble and expense they entailed, children, in turn, contributed to the development of family enterprises. From an early age both boys and girls put in long days on Nebraska farms. Nebraska author Mari Sandoz, born on a homestead in 1896, gave the following description of children's work:

> All of us knew children who put in twelve-, fourteen-hour days from March to November. We knew seven-, eight-year-old boys who drove four-horse teams to the harrow, who shocked grain behind the binder all day in heat and dust and rattlesnakes, who cultivated, hoed and weeded corn, and finally husked it out before they could go to school in November. And even then there were the chores morning and evening, the stock to feed, the cows to milk by lantern light. . . .
>
> Often there was no difference in the work done by the boys and the girls, except that the eldest daughter of a sizable family was often a serious little mother by the time she was six, perhaps baking up a 49-pound sack of flour every week by the time she was ten. (Sandoz 1970, 21)

Sandoz herself was blinded in one eye as a result of riding over bright snow all day rounding up cattle for her father after a storm.

Beth, born on a Boone County farm in 1908, recalled being in the fields, where she and her younger sisters worked as soon as they were big enough to handle the horses and machinery. Beth was constantly fearful of the possibility of a runaway team or of an accident:

> The hay rake was the most dangerous thing I rode on because you had to trot the horses to get it to dump right. . . . If you'd have fallen off you'd have fallen right down into that rake thing. . . . It was kind of scary. Of course, I was younger then, but I realized the seriousness of it later. I think that was the job I hated the worst, except driving a stacker team. That was what we always started with, because it wasn't supposed to be

a very difficult job. But with the men up on the stack stacking the hay you had to get that load of hay up there just right. If you didn't throw it far enough it came down between the stacker and the stack. Or if you got it a little too far—threw it a little too far or fast—you would throw it over the stack and cover the man up. It was kind of hard. . . . You just had to do it because Dad couldn't afford to hire help. I was the oldest and of course the younger girls did it too after I got a little older.

Life was not easy for children pressed into service as farmhands at an early age.

An astute farmer/businessman might depend on his children to run almost the entire farm while he pursued other trades. A *Nebraska Farmer* story on a successful immigrant farmer described his resourcefulness in setting his sons to farm while he made money as a shoemaker (Hodgkin 1935b). My great-grandfather worked as a carpenter and a teacher while his sons worked the farm. A woman I interviewed said of her father, "He was not a good farmer. I think if it hadn't been that he raised three sons, [he wouldn't have stayed in farming]. From the time they were little they took charge of most of the farming."

Daughters and younger boys frequently contributed to the farm operation by helping their mothers with their work. In 1883 Hannah Johnson's diary mentions that her daughter, barely three years old, dampened clothes for ironing, picked feathers when Hannah butchered chickens, dried dishes, and laid fires (Johnson 1883, 31–32). A woman with an older daughter would assign even more of the women's work to her.

Children's labor—and hence women's fertility—was a crucial factor in the success of Boone County farms. Consistent with the historical pattern of rural U.S. women as a whole, rural women of central Nebraska had more children than did urban women. (Okun 1958, 67, 78, 85). Newly settled areas seem to have shown especially high fertility levels (Easterlin 1976, 605). The 1900 federal census schedules show that farm women living in Oakland Precinct, which was just being settled between 1880 and 1910, had higher fertility levels

Table 6-1. Number of Children under Age 5 per Thousand Women
Ages 15 to 44, Albion Town and Oakland Precinct, 1900 and 1910

	1900	1910
Albion	486	435
Oakland	857	702

Source: U.S. census schedules.

than the women of Albion. In Oakland Precinct the married farm
women between ages thirty-five and forty-four had an average of 6.1
children, whereas those living in Albion had an average of 3.8 children. None of the farm women in the 1900 Oakland census had
reached the end of her childbearing years with fewer than two children, and only two women stopped at that number. As seen in table
6-1, the fertility ratios in Albion were about 60 percent of those in
Oakland Precinct.[4]

Census schedules offer evidence that the labor of these children
functioned as an economical alternative to hired workers and extended family members. Table 6-2, which gives the correlation between a household's composition and the number of children in
Oakland Precinct and Albion, indicates that women ages thirty-five to
forty-four who lived in nuclear family households had more children
than did married women of the same age range who lived in households that included extended family or nonfamily members. Although the majority of households in both Albion and Oakland Precinct were nuclear in composition, the farming precinct, which
shows a higher rate of fertility, also had a larger share of nuclear
family households. Fertility in extended family households was 55
percent that of nuclear family households in the farming precinct, in
the town of Albion it was 62 percent of nuclear household fertility.[5]

Several explanations, not necessarily mutually exclusive, may account for the higher level of fertility in women of nuclear, as opposed
to extended, family households. Considering first the difference in
women's choices, it is possible that women living in isolated nuclear
family households were particularly anxious to fill the social and
labor voids in the sparsely settled area and were, accordingly, more
inclined to want children as both companions and helpers.

Table 6-2. Number of Births and Surviving Children per Ever-Married Women Ages 35 to 44, in Nuclear and Extended Households, Oakland Precinct and Albion Town, 1910

	Births	Surviving Children	N
Oakland			
Nuclear	6.4	5.4	32
Extended*	3.5	2.8	10
Albion			
Nuclear	4.2	3.5	57
Extended*	2.6	2.2	27

Source: U.S. census schedules.

*Extended households are defined as households including extended family members, multiple family households, or households containing a nuclear family and nonrelated persons such as servants or boarders.

Another explanation focuses on the extent to which a woman would have seen herself as rightfully having her own voice and having access to birth control technology. Historian Glenda Riley (1988, 82), having researched women on the Great Plains, stated that women avidly discussed the issue of birth control, exchanged advice, and purchased various devices that were marketed illegally. In 1896 the "Household" column of the *Nebraska Farmer* published an exchange of opinions on woman's right and obligation to have children. All the women who wrote to the journal said that women should have children, but many felt that they were justified in limiting the number if they could not take care of them properly. A woman wrote that she had read about President Roosevelt and race suicide, but that having babies was not as hard on Roosevelt as it was on her. It was one thing for the rich to bring babies into the world and watch them thrive; it was another for women like her to bring babies into the world and watch them suffer. She wrote, "A little baby is the sweetest thing possible, but like candy, too much cloys the appetite" (Sparks 1903).

Although the Comstock Law prevented any explicit discussion of birth control methods from appearing in the *Nebraska Farmer*, women could still debate the morality of birth limitation. "Household" columnist Nellie Hawks (1896b) came down squarely in favor of women's controlling their own reproduction: "We say let every woman become so educated in all the mysteries that envelope maternity that she may be a law unto herself." Abortion, she said, was not the only remedy. But then she avoided giving the specific information that so many women must have wanted. They would have to find this elsewhere. A number of women responded to the discussion and debated the use of "regulators" to prevent pregnancy (Miller 1896a; Lambrigger 1896). Advertisements for regulators stated that they would produce regular menstruation: "LADIES. Our harmless remedy relieves without fail delayed or abnormally suppressed menstruation" (Nebraska Farmer 1903b). By being advertised as a remedy for menstrual irregularity rather than as an abortifacient, this product circumvented the Comstock Law, although most women would have understood that the primary purpose of regulators was to block pregnancy.

It is impossible to know how widely birth control technology was distributed, but a woman would probably get her most useful and explicit information from other local women. Close friendships and intimate sharing with other women could have provided crucial information about and moral support for birth limitation, and it was precisely this intimate sharing that many Nebraska farm women living in nuclear family households missed. One of the women I interviewed said that her grandmother had taught her mother how to induce an abortion with a buttonhook. But not every woman had a mother or even a friend on hand to pass along information. A woman's isolation from other women would have impeded this kind of access to birth control, and the greater the isolation, the less likely a woman might have been to limit her births. Such a woman would have been less able to talk over her feelings about childbearing and, therefore, would have been less likely to have these feelings mirrored and reinforced by other women.

An economic explanation for higher nuclear household fertility would suggest that, because children's labor on the farm seems to have been used as an alternative to the labor provided by hired hands and extended family members, supporting children as workers may simply have been cheaper than supporting other relatives or hiring labor. It may have been easier to create a dependable farm workforce composed of children than to recruit labor from outside the nuclear family.

Correlations between the number of children and the viability of the farm are consistent with the hypothesis that children's labor was a critical variable in the farm economy. A demographic study of a Kansas farm community in the period from 1885 to 1905 indicated that the presence of children on a farm was positively correlated with the success of that farm (Flora and Stitz 1988). Comparing the Oakland Precinct farm households that persisted from 1900 to 1910 with those that disappeared from the census in the intervening years supports this finding. The persistence rate of farms over the ten-year period was less than 50 percent. Those families that survived on the farms consistently had more children than did those farm households that disappeared between the 1900 and 1910 census. Considering the households containing married farm women between the ages of thirty-five and forty-four in 1900, as indicated in table 6-3, the ones who were also present in the 1910 census had an average of 6.3 surviving children in 1900, as compared with 4.7 surviving children for women whose families would not last the ten years as Oakland farmers.[6] Approximately 20 percent of the farms listed nonfamily hired laborers, but their presence was not correlated with the persistence or disappearance of a farm.

Child labor may have made high fertility an efficient farming strategy in Boone County, although the mere presence of a correlation demonstrates neither causality nor the presence of a conscious strategy.[7] Whether or at what level of consciousness pronatalism constituted a farming strategy, statistical evidence of high birthrates, together with ethnographic evidence of substantial child labor, argue in favor of a high birthrate as a contributing factor to farming success. Women thus contributed significantly to the farms with their frequent childbearing and with their feeding, washing, chasing, nursing, clothing, and disciplining of the people who were, or would soon become, the farm workforce. They bore the costs of childrearing in their lengthened and intensified workday and in the physical jeopardy they incurred through frequent pregnancies and hard labor.

Table 6-3. Comparison of 1900 Fertility of Oakland Precinct
Married Farm Women, Ages 35 to 44, by Households That Did and
Did Not Persist to the 1910 Census

	Births	Surviving Children	N
Persisting	7.1	6.3	15
Disappearing	5.5	4.7	19

Source: U.S. census schedules.

Child labor on the farm benefited the farm. But what did the farm, in turn, offer to children? Agrarian ideology promised health, wealth, and wisdom for children growing up on the farm. Farm work, however, limited children's school attendance. Building schoolhouses was usually one of the first farm community efforts, and one-room elementary schools soon spread across Boone County. Theoretically they offered a formal, if limited, educational opportunity for all children. But not every family could spare its children from farm work even for local elementary schooling. When Grace Snyder was nine years old, she was herding cattle for her father in the mornings and afternoons, so she could attend the country school only between the morning and afternoon recesses (Snyder 1963, 101). Even more frequently, boys stayed home to help with farming, so that by the time they were eighteen many had had only a few months of schooling. If a household needed money, a boy as young as ten years could be sent to another farm to work as a live-in hired hand.

Keeping boys on the farm put them behind in their schoolwork, which often produced negative feelings toward school and disruptive behavior when they did attend. This in turn made it easier for parents to justify keeping them out of school. Hattie Byfield, a regular "Household" correspondent, argued against giving in to one's children's reluctance to attend school by pointing out that no one gave in to children's reluctance to do farm work. Mothers owed it to their children to provide the discipline that would benefit the children themselves, not just the discipline that would benefit the farm (Byfield 1906),

But just attending a country school did not in itself imply that a young person was gaining even rudimentary literacy. Country schoolteachers did not always have high school diplomas, and women as young as fifteen sometimes had charge of teaching whole schools, in which some of the male students were older than the teachers. Alvin Johnson, founder of the New School for Social Research and an editor of the *New Republic*, was born on a Nebraska farm in 1874 and recalled his country school days without nostalgia: "We expected to learn nothing in school, and we were not disappointed" (Johnson 1952, 40). In Johnson's school, the eighteen-year-old boys would deliberately foment mischief in order to be kept after school by their sixteen-year-old teacher. Although attending school may have rescued some children from some long days of farm work, the only students who were able to proceed to higher education were those who received basic instruction from their parents. In contrast, children growing up in rural towns went to elementary school and continued on to high school if their families could support them. Few farm youths could go to high school, which usually entailed commuting several miles to town. As seventy-nine-year-old Sigrid recalled her schooldays in a 1987 interview, "Going to high school was quite a thing in those days. Very few farm girls got to go on to high school. Very, very, very few boys [did], because when they became high school age they didn't have the chance to go to school. They had to stay home to help farm. That was customary."

Farm children did not always accept the hard work and lack of education passively. Some fathers and mothers used buggy whips on their children's bare backs to enforce demands for heavy farm work. Not all parents did this, but whipping was considered to be a parent's right. It did not bring social censure. Many of the women I interviewed told stories about uncles and brothers who ran away from home because of the hard work and beatings they were subjected to.

Vera, born in 1909 as the second youngest of nine children, was allowed to graduate from high school, but most of her older siblings were not. She talked about her brothers and sisters and the conflicting claims of school and farm:

Most of them didn't stay in school very long. Ellen went some to high school. So did Nancy. And then Bill, the youngest, I think he had a year of high school. But the boys Mick and Kit didn't get to go to high school at all. I think they probably finished grade school and that's about it. . . . They didn't mind working, but they would have liked to have had more school, too. 'Course, Kit didn't like the farm at all. He kept running away. He ran away when he was eleven, thirteen, and so on. Finally at fifteen Dad let him go. It wasn't worthwhile trying to bring him back, because he'd run away again. I have no idea what happened to him. . . . Tom didn't like the farm, either. He ran away from home rather than have to work in the field. Tom left when he was about fourteen. Eighth grade. He went to Omaha and [then] he and another boy went to Kansas City.

In 1896 Hattie Byfield wrote to the *Nebraska Farmer*, declaring that farm children were being sacrificed to the needs of farming. On the farm, she wrote, a boy of ten might be forced to work ten-hour days, seven days a week. Farm children had old and resigned looks on their young faces; they had bent shoulders; they missed school. "Our children have just as good a right to a little of childhood's pleasures as have the town laborer's and just as good a right to education" (Byfield 1896). Another woman wrote to agree but said that girls worked even harder than boys. Their work in the house and in taking care of young children was as destructive to them as was boy's work (Taylor 1896a).

Some fictional descriptions written by people who grew up on Nebraska farms confirm the impression of the mother as a buffer between her husband's desire for child labor and her children's needs (Sykes 1935; Winther 1976, 1979). On the other hand, Willa Cather portrayed a shrewish mother, Mrs. Shimerda in *My Ántonia*, who bullied her gentle husband, overworked her children, and kept them from school. Without blaming either fathers or mothers, we can nevertheless point out the apparent incompatibility of farm life and formal education for the majority of children. Running away seems to have been the most effective means of resistance available to children. Because of the sexual vulnerability and social censure facing young women outside the family, however, running away was a more viable option for adolescent males than for adolescent females, although both were known to have left their families.

The subject of health represented another conflict between the reality of farm life and the welfare of children. The medical establishment had accepted the germ theory in the 1880s, and doctors were beginning to connect the unsanitary conditions on frontier farms with the epidemics of diphtheria, typhoid, cholera, and diarrhea that plagued the settlers. Many farms lacked even outdoor toilets, and excrement attracted insects and contaminated open wells. Homes were poorly heated, and in many cases the family's diet was meager and poorly balanced. A doctor who tended a family in which ten children all had typhoid fever insisted that the family drain its well. They found corncobs, corn husks, dead rats and mice, and a dead rabbit in the well (F. Long 1937, 64). Another pioneer doctor wrote: "[T]he wonder is not so much that disease and infection took a heavy toll, as the wonder that so many survived to spend their later lives in modern homes where the laws of ventilation, sanitation, heating, internal toilets and bath rooms replaced the half barbarous homes of the young settlers" (Barns 1970 [1930], 247).

The 1909 Country Life Commission report noted the particular health problems of tenant farm households:

> Theoretically the farm should be the most healthful place in which to live, and there are numberless farm-houses, especially of the farm-owner class, that possess most excellent modern sanitary conveniences. Still it is a fact that there are also numberless other farmhouses, especially of the tenant class, and even numerous rural schoolhouses, that do not have the rudiments of sanitary arrangement. Health conditions in many parts of the open country, therefore, are in urgent need of betterment. . . . In general, the rural population is less safeguarded by boards of health than is the urban population. The physicians are farther apart and are called in later in case

of sickness, and in some districts medical attendance is relatively more expensive. (Bailey et al 1909, 45)

Widespread rural poverty, with the accompanying poor housing and
poor sanitary conditions, overwork, and inaccessibility of medical
care, shortened the lifespans of some Boone County children.

Census information on births and surviving children indicates
that in the early years of settlement approximately one in five Boone
County children died in early childhood. A 1920 report by the Department of Agriculture stated that infant mortality during the first
month of life was forty-six per thousand in rural areas of the United
States, compared to forty-three per thousand in cities (Ward 1920,
56; Jensen 1981, 151).

Besides the persistent threat of infectious disease, numerous sad
stories were written or told of children who were killed or severely
injured in accidents while their mothers were away doing farm work
(Kellie 1926, 76; Fairbanks and Sundberg 1983, 49, 54). Living far
from medical help, mothers were often the ones who provided first
aid when their children were injured, cared for their illnesses themselves, and worried about the real possibility that their isolation from
help could cost their children's lives. Having a neighbor nearby could
be critical.

Luna Kellie, who wanted as many children as she could have, was
picking broom corn when she went into labor with her second child,
Jimmie. Luna rejoined her husband in the field three days later. She
returned to the house only when her father dropped by and insisted
that they get a hired man to replace her. While J. T. was working in
the fields, she took care of watering and moving the cows. The hard
work of handling cows in the summer heat exhausted her and diminished her breast milk, leading to the death of her beloved Jimmie
(Kellie 1926, 44).

Although nearly every nuclear family with a large number of
children could expect to lose some of them, this did not make the
grieving any easier or more routine. My great-grandparents suffered
the loss of their first daughter in 1885. Almost sixty years later, their
son Louis—eleven years old at his sister's death—remembered that

loss as the time when he and his brothers began to understand the depths of the hardships their parents faced as pioneers (Lederer 1944). After Jimmie's death, Luna and J. T. Kellie also lost their next child, Susie. Again Luna grieved deeply, blamed the death on her lack of faith, and resolved to care less about her children (Kellie 1926, 72). Although infant and child mortality was not limited to rural areas, it was worse there than in cities. The poverty and hard work of rural life conflicted with the agrarian vision of healthful, vigorous rural citizens. Mothers worked hard to keep their children healthy, and their anguish and worry may be counted as another facet of the costs that children and farm labor exacted from rural women.

Yet as difficult and risky as it was to have children in Boone County in the early years, not having children also created difficulties and risks, especially for the poor. Mothers hoped that their children would repay their years of care by providing emotional and material security for them in their old age. The nature of the mutual dependence and the way that children provided for their parents varied according to class. Only those who owned significant productive property at the end of their working lives could wield economic power over their children in their old age. A parent with a farm might decide which child would take over the farm, how the farm and household would be operated, and what services the children would render to their parents. Children contributed to the continuity of a farm when one or more of them took over the operation and kept it within the family. In a few households, an aging parent actually lived with grown children.[8] More frequently, a retired parent lived in a separate house within a short distance of a grown child. As the prospective heir took over the farm, parents initially would help with farm work, sewing, and childcare. Gradually they would move toward greater dependence on the labor and income of the next generation. Sometimes sons or daughters would buy the farm from their parents and make yearly payments for it; otherwise they could rent the property until they inherited it. Regardless of the residency arrangements or terms of land transfer, parents who were transferring land to their offspring were deeply invested in their children's economic survival.

Frequently a wife, who was usually several years younger than her husband, would outlive him. When a man owned a farm or other property, he typically willed it to a son or divided it among his children; sometimes the widow got a life estate, but seldom did she actually control family property. Even on a family farm, a woman relied more heavily on her children's gratitude and devotion than on her legal rights for the care she needed in her old age. Whereas a father could, and sometimes did, negotiate with his children over their inheritance, no one I interviewed or talked to told me that her or his mother had been instrumental in determining matters of inheritance. Some mothers may have exerted indirect and subtle pressure for specific property arrangements, but real property does not seem to have been a major link between mothers and their children. I heard several stories about fathers who used their property to manipulate their children, but these stories had no counterparts featuring mothers. Such behavior would have been unmotherly and would have tended to cancel the emotional capital that was a mother's major leverage for controlling her children's lives.

Most Boone Countians left little, if any, property for inheritance. Often a heavily mortgaged farm was the closest thing to an estate that farmers left. The lack of material property meant that growing old was an underlying worry for many Boone County people, and local society made little provision for support of the aged. For the majority of mothers, who would not accumulate any capital in their lifetimes, children who stayed in Boone County and were earning a living there were almost the only hope. Over time, then, the mother-child dependency relation was a reciprocal one, and this probably affected the way that mothers related to their children throughout their lives.

The distress of children on the farms spurred women's much-feared and much-studied dissatisfaction with rural life. Being a good mother in rural Nebraska was just too hard for many women, and life on the farm was not what they wanted. Gilbert Fite (1959, 174), in his essay on flight from the farm, stated, "It seemed to be almost a passion with many farm women that their children should pursue some occupation other than that followed by their parents." In his autobiography, Alvin Johnson made clear that it was his mother who pushed him away from rural Nebraska: "On almost all matters my mother and I had the same point of view. There were rare exceptions. Whenever I expressed enthusiasm for farm life and its possibilities, my mother would douse my ardor with cold water. She did not want me to stay on the farm. I'd wear myself out prematurely with hard work. . . . In the end my chief business would be bringing up a household of children inevitably inferior" (Johnson 1952, 23).

Herbert Quick, who in 1913 articulated the problems caused by farm women's chronic dissatisfaction, wrote: "*I have found the men on farms much more contented and happy than the women.* My mother wanted my father to leave the farm, and move to a college town where the children would have 'a better chance'" (Quick 1913, 427; emphasis in original). Similarly, when John Ise (1936) described his widowed mother's departure from the Kansas farm she and her husband had homesteaded, he noted that it was the children's need to live in a city in order to get an education and move up in the world that finally convinced her to sell the farm and leave. Although women's dissatisfaction with farm life—the "woman problem on the farm"—was broader than their concerns for children, the children nevertheless loomed large in their complaints during the early twentieth century. Many mothers living in farm households simply could not meet the cultural standards for mothering.

Motherhood in Boone County was not an activity that fit neatly into a private sphere. It was public policy, because children were the building blocks of the rural economy and the expanding state. Farm production for the market and women's reproduction in the home fused in the agrarian model of the family farm. Although the benefits of children's labor accrued to the public economy, the costs of childrearing were extracted privately from women within the family. The sentimental celebration of the pioneer mother obscured the economic connection by representing motherhood as a sacred calling that existed apart from the economic calculus of the market.

Agrarian ideology failed mothers except as a sentimental sop. A number of disjunctures between the needs of the farm economy and the needs of mothers and children caused difficulties from the beginning of the settlement of Nebraska. Because they cared deeply for their children, women often wanted them to have opportunities not open to them on the farms. The model of the family labor farm thus contained a contradiction that women faced squarely and unavoidably as mothers who loved their children.

But women were more than selfless victims. They pursued their own interests within the limits they experienced. They looked to their children to meet their needs both in youth and in adulthood. Many women did not passively sacrifice their children to the agrarian dream. Some resisted the life that rural Nebraska offered for their children. Although encouraging children to leave might have negated the accepted strategy for preserving family ownership of a farm, a child who succeeded in business or in a profession could provide just as reliable a system of old age security as a child who stayed. Mothers had their children's futures on their minds, even as they tended to their own interests as mothers.

old—
age

7 MOTHERS AND THE DEPRESSION

The world broke in two in 1922 or thereabouts.
—Willa Cather, Not Under Forty, 1936

The depression that began in rural areas in the 1920s changed the course of rural life for the rest of the century. For the majority of Boone County women, raising children became more difficult. The Boone County farm economy became unable to sustain the reproduction of the population. Although mothers in middle-class homes could continue to feed and clothe their children, the children of single mothers, marginal farmers, farm laborers, and the poor were destitute. People went cold and hungry; many left the area; the birthrate fell. The government entered the picture to assume limited but continuing responsibility for maintaining the mother-child relation among the rural poor. Motherhood remained the central axis of women's identities. Mothers and children counted on each other for shelter and comfort, and they pooled whatever income or resources they had so that one would not be cast adrift while the others had anything.

New contradictions arose out of these economic changes. Although the family farm continued to absorb the labor of many children until the environmental breakdown of 1934, only a small fraction of these children would grow up to become adult farmers in Boone County. Most would leave to join the urban industrial labor force. Motherhood was still ostensibly patterned within the nuclear

family, but the tasks of providing food, shelter, education, companions, and opportunities for their children necessitated a larger social
network than that nuclear grouping. Despite the isolation of the
majority of Boone County family farms, the needs of children challenged mothers to construct a wider social circle. A tension existed
between politicians' tendency to regard children as social resources to
be generated within private households and mothers' tendency to see
children as a personal value to be supported, if necessary, with public
resources.

The Progressive period of the early twentieth century, which produced a broad range of social reforms, addressed child welfare as a
central issue. Reformers pushed for better schools, compulsory
school attendance, child labor laws, higher standards for child nutrition and health, and mothers' pensions. Concern for the health and
welfare of children heightened when World War I military recruits
were found to have a variety of health problems that could be traced
to poor nutrition and poor medical care in childhood.[1] Rural recruits
were particularly disadvantaged, with disproportionately many showing physical deformities, mental slowness, and lack of agility (Fuller
1923, 40–42). The federal government began to distribute pamphlets
on childcare. *Parents* magazine (directed primarily toward mothers)
was started in 1926 to publish articles and advertisements related to
children's health. Instructions on feeding children, sterilizing baby
bottles, and elaborate sickroom techniques appeared with advertisements for new children's food and health products, including such
things as sunlamps, Vicks Vaporub, children's laxatives, and Listerine
antiseptic (Cowan 1983, 192). Articles on child psychology stressed
scientific theory and urged less reliance on instinct and custom.

The movement reached rural as well as urban mothers. The
Country Life movement and the USDA Extension Service that
emerged from it were the major rural manifestations of Progressive-
era politics. Extension literature on nutrition and childcare taught
rural women about vitamins and emphasized the importance of milk
in children's diets. By the 1930s, the *Nebraska Farmer* had a regular
column featuring information on child psychology and nutrition.

Childrearing became more complicated and time consuming as

new activities for rural children appeared. Four-H clubs, organized by the county Extension Service, offered agricultural and home economics lessons to rural children and gave them chances to show their projects at county and state fairs, win prizes, take trips, and attend summer camps. In school children were encouraged to participate in sports and to take drama and music. Girl Scout and Boy Scout clubs were established in some towns.

Mothers were increasingly pressed into such efforts as trying to secure books for school libraries, financing and overseeing piano lessons, leading 4-H and scout clubs, coordinating arrangements for children's high school attendance, and enabling children to participate in sports, drama, and school clubs. The changes were both economic and organizational. Money was required for children's transportation, equipment, clothing, and fees, and the new activities took children away from their income-generating farm work. Women could not begin to provide these new opportunities from within the nuclear family. Although the nuclear family had never organized all childcare and socialization, the welfare of children was becoming increasingly tied to institutions beyond the family. Mothers who accepted the modern childcare standards found themselves challenged to participate in school politics, extension work, church committees, and various clubs. Many farm mothers took on extra work both in the home and beyond to make it possible for their children to participate in the new activities.

Wilma, who married a farmer in 1915, had daughters born in 1917, 1919, 1922, and 1926. Recalling their activities, she said:

> I had to use the old push-pull washing machine. Our four girls were in a music club and the teacher had them doing athletic things—stunts and things. They had white outfits. The music club had a white skirt and blouse. . . . They would appear somewhere and I had to wash all four suits. They had to be ready for next time. . . . The same way for outfits they wore for tap dancing and these athletic things. Those had to be washed and ironed about every whipstitch, too. . . . I did all that. We used to take the girls to Girl Scouts and ball

games. . . . We used to just about run the wheels off the car driving.

Wilma had encountered new mothering tasks, different from what mothers had done in the past but every bit as intense and demanding.

In 1930 the *Nebraska Farmer* "Home Circle" section requested responses to the discussion topic, "My Biggest Job." The "Home Circle" editor wrote: "Judging from the letters received, . . . children are the greatest problem homemakers have. Canning, sewing, and gardening are difficult, but when these tasks are completed we know when we have succeeded. That brings satisfaction. Child training is never completed. . . . The modern mother is never satisfied with her accomplishments. She is constantly seeking something better" (*Nebraska Farmer* 1930).

Beyond feeding them and taking care of their physical needs, modern mothers accepted responsibility in ever-increasing measure for their children's social, intellectual, and emotional health. As one mother wrote: "My biggest job is feeding my child properly. Not only should he have the right food for his physical needs, but for his spiritual and mental needs as well. . . . Child raising does not end with food and clothes. I wish we mothers could study more child psychology. Many mothers think it is foolishness. One woman said to me, 'I was able to raise my children without reading books.' But she didn't raise them they just 'grew up'" (*Nebraska Farmer* 1930). This mother, who apparently had only one child, was setting a standard. The newer childrearing tasks, like the old ones, were mothers' responsibility. With scant social support, mothers themselves would have to realize the new expectations for their children.

The higher standards of childcare were on a short collision course with the realities of the depressed rural economy. Wilma, although even she said that finding money for everything was "nip and tuck" during the depression, had more money and more security than most women in Boone County. For her, the new standards of childcare were a challenge. They were impossible for most rural women. While magazines and lessons showed happy children with all the new advantages, economically disadvantaged mothers were painfully aware that their own children worked on farms without access to the pro-grams and products that they were learning they should have.

Sharon's story about her farm life was in stark contrast to Wilma's. Born on a farm in 1916, Sharon knew nothing about tap dancing or Girl Scouts. Although her family owned their farm, they were impoverished owners. Sharon milked cows every morning be-fore going to the country school and in her teen years was doing much of the outside farm work. Sharon's mother died long ago and was unable to tell her story of being a mother, but Sharon told about her own work and life as a teen:

> I didn't go to high school. We didn't have money enough to go to high school in the thirties. We only went to town once a week to get the groceries that we needed. That's all. Then we stayed home. . . . Dad wanted me out in the field. We went out there and I cultivated a half a row of corn out and he got mad at me. I said, "To hell with it, I'm going back to the house." I could of, he just didn't take enough patience with me. . . . So I didn't go out and help him that way, but I pitched hay and milked cows and got the cows home. If the calf pen needed cleaning I came out and piled it all on a pile in front—a manure pile. . . . I cleaned up the sheep. . . . We had chickens. Chicken house to clean out. We were busy out on that farm.

Much of Sharon's work on the farm was done with her mother and her sister. They did livestock chores and housework:

> On the farm where I was you got down and put your bucket between your legs and milked. Take it up to the milkhouse and run it through the separator. Then you had to wash the darned separator. Then you had dishes to do. You didn't have time to get your work done. If I didn't get the separator washed it was so stinkin' sour. No, heck, I'd run the separator and take the milk out to the calves. Mom would start washing the separator right there. If you were like a team it works, but if you ain't—. . . One time with the sheep, the gate was open, Mom said, "Now they can go through the gate and we've got

to go out and fix the gate." Mom could do that. I got boards
for her and stuff and nails. She hammered and I hammered
and we got it fixed. . . . We'd get a threshing machine and
we'd have to get all the neighbors to help. They'd do a run.
They'd start maybe at your place and they'd just go down the
road. They would come to us and we'd feed then. Gosh, oh
man, I thought they'd eat until they died. . . . Everybody
come in for eats. It takes all day long and all the day before.
We cooked and cooked and cooked and cooked and
cooked. . . . Then they come. Quarter to eleven. Mom says,
"Oh, my god, now what?" Well, we had the potatoes all peeled
and had the water on. We knew we was going to have them
that night for supper, see, and in the afternoon . . . I don't
know how we done it but we got it done. Mom would say,
"Run this, run that, get me some more water." . . . No water in
the house, no toilet, no nothing. We were so darn tired we
couldn't hardly go no more. Mom was so tired I don't know
how she stood that. . . . I was just a kid.

When Mary Meek Atkeson (1929, 189) wrote about women's problems on American farms, she said that the prosperity of American
agriculture rested on the backs of women and children who worked
without pay. Sharon worked without pay and without realizing the
presumed prosperity of American agriculture. Sharon's family was
more representative of the majority in Boone County than was
Wilma's.

Wilma's daughters all graduated from high school, whereas the
three children in Sharon's family were all forced to quit school to do
farm work. A compulsory school attendance law had been part of the
Progressive period child reform measures in Nebraska, although it
was weak enough to satisfy the farm interests of the state. The Compulsory Attendance Law of 1905 required children to attend school
from age seven through age fifteen, the exception being that children
age fourteen and over were excused if they were regularly employed
in economically necessary labor. In addition, children living more
than two miles from a school were not required to attend unless the
school provided free transportation. These exceptions meant, in prac-

Table 7-1. Percentage of Boone County Children Ages 14 to 17
Attending School, 1920–1940

	Ages 14–15	Ages 16–17
1920	79.5	41.8
1930	84.7	54.1
1940	88.8	69.5

Source: U.S. census reports.

tice, that farm parents were able to keep their children out of school
if they wished.[2] Federal census data on the number of Boone County
teens attending school indicate a steady increase in the years between
1920 and 1940 (see table 7-1). According to these figures, the majority of fourteen- and fifteen-year-olds were staying in school by 1920,
and the sixteen- and seventeen-year-olds' attendance increased until
by 1930 the majority of them were also attending school.

I believe these statistics show a higher rate of school attendance
than actually occurred. It would have been tempting for a respondent
to misrepresent this information to an educated census taker, particularly if the child's absence from school was of questionable legality.
Even when children were technically enrolled in school they might
be kept out for long periods of time. Kathleen said of her husband
Richard's school attendance in the 1920s: "He had to stay out of
school three months out of every year and help his folks when he was
quite small already. . . . He never did get to go to high school. He
went to eighth grade two years. . . . He missed so much. I don't think
they'd allow that nowadays at all. They did then."

Harriet gave a similar account of her brothers' staying home to do
farm work in the 1920s:

It was just customary in the schools in those days that the
boys stayed out and worked on the farm. They just went to
school in the winter months, you know. Some of them boys
would be sixteen, seventeen, eighteen years old and go to
these country schools where you already were swamped with
children. I think they'd cause problems in the school. My
father, he used to keep my two brothers out with the corn-

picking and things like that. They'd get so far behind they'd never want to go back to school. . . . It kind of goes back to the pioneer days when everyone stayed out and helped with the work.

Going to a one-room country school, these nearly grown boys would be in a classroom with one teacher and classmates as young as six years old. Even when these students were formally enrolled in school, their farm work responsibilities took first priority, and their education was minimal.

Further indication that the census figures for school attendance may afford a misleadingly rosy view of rural children's education may be seen in the figures showing total number of years of school completed. The 1940 federal census, which was the first to solicit information on completed years of education in addition to formal enrollment in school, showed that, for persons in Boone County over age twenty-five, 70 percent of the farm population and 53 percent of the nonfarm population had completed eight years or less of school (Census 1943, 649, 655).

When I asked Harriet who made the decisions about children's school attendance and farm work, she said, "Back in those times, I believe the man just managed things mostly on his own. I think he was the boss. The women, I guess, more or less went along with it. . . . My father was that way." The depressed farm economy narrowed the choices open to the father, but he still made decisions about the allocation of family labor. Mothers who would make decisions on behalf of their children were confronted by their own isolation and powerlessness in setting priorities. Those least able to make free and informed decisions on their own behalves were the children. The agrarian model held that farm children were learning the most economically, spiritually, and intellectually significant things in the wide open, healthy air of the farm; the reality was not so nice.

The reformers' attempts to change the working conditions of farm children represented a threat to the farming interests of Nebraska, and farmers resisted. The question of who owned and controlled children was addressed in the debate over the federal Child Labor Amendment, which was proposed in 1924. Under terms of the

Amendment, Congress would have the power to limit, regulate, or prohibit the labor of persons under eighteen years of age. Between 1919 and 1924 the National Child Labor Committee completed numerous studies of children who worked on farms and found that most of them suffered ill health from overwork, stoop labor, exposure to bad weather, and accidents (Trattner 1970, 153). Yet opponents of the Child Labor Amendment defended farm labor by mounting agrarian ideological appeals for the benefits of fresh air, healthful work, and usefulness. Agricultural economist Charles Galpin of the University of Wisconsin wrote:

> The labor of the child on the farm in America, with some few localized exceptions, has about it a minimum of child-labor features dangerous to the child and to society. Work in the fresh open air, attended with great variety of movement both from place to place and from task to task, has none of the hazards of mines and factories to the growing body and soul. Farm life is lavish with space in which the child may grow. The open country is a large mold, and the child's nature fits the mold. The vigorous use of the muscles induces the maximum growth and power of the great organs of the body. (Galpin 1923, 120–21)

Debate on the Child Labor Amendment called on empirical studies, but no opposing ideology could be found to counter the agrarian myth of the broad benefits of farm life.

The amendment came before the Nebraska legislature in 1935, at which time the *Nebraska Farmer*, which vigorously opposed its ratification, put forth a number of arguments focusing primarily on the question of parents' rights and secondarily on the benefits of farm work to children. An editorial entitled "Shall Congress Control Our Children?" labeled the amendment an affront to "state rights and individual liberty." Continuing, the editor claimed, "The experience of most successful farm families will verify the assertion that a large part of their success and material wealth came from the combined work of the father and family. Without denying that some farm parents overwork their children, it is still reasonable to contend that the cases of such injury are far less numerous than those of heartaches and wrecked ambitions from instances of wayward youth with too much idleness" (Leadley 1935, 1).

The call for responses from readers brought a flurry of letters from farmers. A typical one read: "My 82 years of observation on earth shows me that more children are harmed by not working enough than are harmed by overwork. Nebraska being an agricultural state, the help of children on the farm is absolutely necessary, therefore we hope that the proposed 22nd amendment to the federal constitution will be defeated" (Sturdevant 1935).

Farmers generally asserted that the work needs of the farm coincided with the best interests of children. One farmer summed up his children's well-being as follows: "I have raised five children, three boys and two girls, and they helped me on the farm from the time they could walk. The three boys husked more corn on Saturday than I did, and after school they helped again. I don't think it hurt them a damn bit, because they all weigh around 200 pounds each now" (Quinowski 1935). Although this letter implied an absent mother, such would not necessarily have been the case. She may have been a silenced mother and wife. The father in this case took credit for raising the children, claimed their labor, and was himself the arbiter of their welfare. All the letters published in opposition to the Child Labor Amendment were followed either by men's names or by "Mr. and Mrs." The one woman who wrote on her own also supplied the only dissenting voice, saying that children belonged in school and that serious problems would arise from their being worked too hard.

The editors, however, responded with the last word: "Any time the farmers of America leave it to Congress to regulate the hours and conditions of labor of their children the most cherished right of parents on the farm has been swept away. This is a vital issue and the determination of it should not be left to thoughtless sentimentalists" (*Nebraska Farmer* 1935b). The "cherished right of parents" was a euphemism for the authority of fathers over their children. In practice, though, it was the mother who was most often closely attuned to the everyday life of her children. She worried, argued, sacrificed, and anguished over what would happen to them. Yet mothers did not have an independent collective voice. In their extension clubs, farm women expressed commitment to the farm programs laid out by male extension leaders. They did not support the Child Labor Amendment, but neither did they appear among its vocal opponents.

The Nebraska legislature finally rejected the amendment in 1937, and it died for want of ratification by enough states. When Congress subsequently passed the Fair Labor Standards Act of 1938, child labor was effectively banned on goods shipped in interstate commerce, but agriculture was exempt from the child labor limitations except for the hours in which a child was legally required to attend school. In Nebraska this affected only those children from ages seven to thirteen.[3]

The collapse of the farm production system, extensive out-migration, and the destitution of most Boone Countians interrupted the internal flow of goods and services that had undergirded social relationships. Farm prices had fallen drastically in 1920, annihilating the profits that farms had reaped during World War I. In 1934 the drought threatened the gardens, milk, potatoes, and the meat supply that had heretofore fed farm families when they were not making money. Many mothers could no longer feed and clothe their young children; many adult sons and daughters could no longer meet the needs of their aging parents. Government intervention during the 1930s prevented the complete economic and social dislocation of Boone County. Of the various forms of federal intervention, it was the Social Security Act of 1935 that most directly affected mothers and children, particularly the sections having to do with Old Age Assistance (OAA) and Aid to Dependent Children (ADC). OAA released children from the support of aged parents, most of them mothers; ADC reinforced the mother's role as the caretaker and primary parent of minor children.

Farmers and farm laborers were not originally included in the retirement insurance provisions of the Social Security Act. Even those few rural nonfarmers who did enroll in the social security retirement program would not immediately realize the benefits. OAA, however, was available to all indigent elderly persons. More Boone County people received OAA than any other form of federal relief except for Farm Security Administration (FSA) grants. In January 1939, 342 OAA recipients received an average of $32.19 each month from the government. OAA was means-tested, a recipient being required to have assets below a set level, which was subject to verification through checks of bank records. An OAA recipient could own a house that brought her total assets over the limit if she gave the county a lien on it. Applicants' children who were living in Nebraska were required to sign a short statement attesting to their inability to support their parents, but their finances were not subject to investigation, and adult children were rarely pressed for support.[4]

In her book on the Social Security Act, Mimi Abramovitz (1988) has emphasized that it was working-age people who advocated Social Security for the elderly as a means of releasing them from the responsibility of supporting parents, rather than as security for themselves in the remote future. In earlier years, adult offspring had represented almost the only source of support for the working-class elderly. Because of the massive wage cuts and unemployment of the 1930s, this line of support was becoming thin and tenuous. In addition, people were living longer in the 1930s, in spite of the hard times. Caring for the elderly was becoming a greater personal and financial burden to their children. Abramovitz quotes from a 1935 report of the Committee on Economic Security (CES), which drafted the Social Security Bill: "Old age pensions are in a real sense measures in behalf of children. They shift the retroactive burdens to shoulders which can bear them with less human cost, and young parents thus released can put at the disposal of the new member of society those family resources he [sic] must be permitted to enjoy if he is to become a strong person, unburdensome to the State" (Abramovitz 1988, 242; [sic] in original).

The majority of elderly were women, and OAA kept some Boone County women from starvation in the 1930s. It injected needed cash into the local economy, and it released grown children from bearing the responsibility for indigent mothers. If an aging mother had a home, she could survive on OAA with little help from or interaction with her children. As the CES report indicated, the tie to the ascending generation was loosened in order to allow "young parents" to spend more money on the succeeding generation.

Impoverished parents of young children needed all the help they could get. Some of the most dire instances of rural poverty occurred among widowed, divorced, or deserted mothers with children to support. Farm creditors and such federal agencies as the FSA assessed family labor resources in processing loan applications. They were reluctant to extend loans to farms that had no adult male workers. The majority of self-supporting farm mothers lost their farms and were forced to move into town to live on the small incomes they earned as laundresses, waitresses, or housekeepers, or to apply for ADC. Frequently their young children earned supplementary money doing odd jobs or domestic labor; teenagers would drop out of school to take jobs.

Boone County court records show an increasing rate of desertion by husbands in the 1930s; I did not find any verified reports of women deserting their children. Although some deserted mothers went to court and were awarded nominal child support, never did a mother receive more than twenty dollars per month in the 1930s, and collection of this amount was unreliable. A typical case involved a couple married in 1923. In 1930, when the two children were ages three and five, the husband abandoned the family. The mother supported her children and herself by working in domestic service. In 1935 she was awarded a divorce and four dollars per month child support, a sum far below the costs of raising her children. The court record does not state whether or not she actually received her money (Boone County District Court 1935). The mother was the one usually faced with supporting her children after the dissolution of a marriage.

The state affirmed this link in the ADC section of the Social Security Act. ADC was an extension of the Progressive period mothers' aid pensions. The Nebraska mothers' aid legislation, passed in 1913, had provided a small income to mothers who were widowed, deserted, or divorced or whose husbands were physically or mentally incapacitated or imprisoned. By the 1930s, mothers' aid recipients were receiving approximately fifteen dollars per month to support their children. ADC, which became available after 1935, increased the amount of money that mothers could obtain. In January 1939 fifty-three Boone County ADC mothers received an average of $48.16 each in monthly benefits to support a household of 3.4 persons. It was impossible to provide a well-balanced diet, a warm home, and warm clothing on this amount. An ADC mother might have supplemented her pension with assistance from her family, income from her children's labor, intensified subsistence activities, and the occasional illegal wage income, but she could not provide a comfortable living and secure future for her children.

Recipients of ADC were subject to more oversight than OAA clients. Like OAA applicants, ADC applicants were subjected to a means test. ADC mothers, being younger, would have been less likely than the elderly poor to own houses that they could keep, and so they would not have had this property exemption as a buffer to provide them minimal protection and security. Both OAA and ADC applicants were assessed on the basis of personal qualities such as gratitude and thrift, but ADC mothers—other than widows—were accorded no initial assumption of merit. They often appeared to case workers as slovenly, irresponsible, and unintelligent. These women had to prove to their case workers that they were deserving mothers. No welfare rights existed. In practice, an indigent mother's access to ADC depended on her relationship with her case worker. If the mother qualified economically and personally, the case worker would forward the case to the county welfare director, who would submit the application to state offices and to the county commissioners. As Abramovitz (1988, 319) notes, the pattern was to always keep ADC benefits low, to aid only "deserving" mothers, and to make selective suitable home rules. ADC was not intended to be an attractive alternative to marriage.

In theory ADC money, unlike mothers' pensions, could be awarded to single fathers, grandparents, aunts, or uncles as well as mothers, but in practice nearly all of the recipients were mothers. The dispensing of relief checks to mothers emphasized the prevalent view that feeding and clothing children was the mother's responsibility. If she was unable to earn her own living, her access to subsistence income was as a dutiful mother. Conversely, her children's survival rested with her. Saving the family meant keeping the woman at home, and ADC payments helped to do this.

There was always some tension between the goal of keeping mothers in the home and the disinclination to support those not recognized as being truly worthy. Most unattached mothers fell into the latter category. Widows consistently had readier access to ADC than did single or divorced mothers (Abramovitz 1988, 317–19). But even though the majority of impoverished mothers could never measure up to the standard of nobility that mothers were supposed to meet, no other social provision existed for the support of their children. Stretching her tiny income to provide a living for herself and her children, a welfare mother was faced with a long workday spent in sewing, baking, laundering, cleaning, shopping, disciplining, and worrying. Shabby and inadequate household equipment and stringent limits on consumption made her work harder. She often had no sympathetic supporter to assure her that her maternal decisions were right or to share the responsibility for hard decisions. Although marriage was the most likely way for a woman to escape being on welfare, keeping company with men was not a way to be a respectable mother. As a result of this double bind, welfare mothers were often demoralized and vulnerable.

Deserted mothers and their children were obvious victims of the hard times, but even having a husband was no guarantee of an adequate income. The depressed economic conditions meant that even those women whose husbands stayed with them were often unable to provide adequately for their children. Some married farm women, particularly those in tenant families, were desperate. With no way to pay rent and no money for food or clothing, they had nowhere to turn but to the government (Cape 1931). But initially the federal government did nothing for them, and it provided only limited help after New Deal and Social Security legislation took effect. In 1938 a Nebraska farm mother with thirteen surviving children committed suicide by walking into the side of a train (*Albion Argus* 1938). This was one mother's way of saying she had had enough. Increasing numbers of rural people were losing access to the piece of land and the personal property that placed them in the traditional middle class; many lost hope in the future.

child
Labor

The economic return that childbearing paid to the family farm operation was diminishing. Although Boone County farms remained labor intensive until the 1940s, children provided less of the economic balance after 1920. Progressive period programs and literature pushed the basic standard for child nurture upward. The increasing pressure for children to attend school limited the amount of work that could be expected from them. Even in poverty, more women tried to emulate Wilma's model of childrearing than that of Sharon's family; but no one with more than five children could do the things that Wilma did.

Not only did households benefit relatively less from children's presence, but the long-term prospects of establishing them on farms or in town businesses also weakened after 1920. The majority of Boone County farm families could offer, at most, a highly mortgaged farm to one child, or possibly only a little livestock and machinery. One heir had some chance to make the farm business work, to remain in Boone County and look after aging parents, and to continue the family farm. Multiple heirs had almost no chance of doing so. With no new farmland to be claimed, rural youths found their way to the cities.

The number of births in Boone County decreased during the 1920s and the 1930s (see table 7-2). From 392 births in 1920, the numbers reached a low of 204 in 1938. Yet there continued to be a natural increase every year, and this helped to maintain the population base as out-migration accelerated. Women's childbearing in those years was still adding some child labor to farm production, but it was adding more future adult labor to the urban industrial labor force.

The migration of farm-reared youth to the cities was a twentieth-century way for farming communities to contribute to urban development. Midwestern farms supplied native-born, white labor to the cities. This new laboring class was well disciplined and not culturally predisposed toward collective action. As expressed by agrarian politician Henry A. Wallace, farms should be given credit for solving the labor problems of the cities:

> The farms of the Middle West and the South are literally the breeding grounds of the Nation. The farms of the United States produce every year from a third to a half million more children than is necessary to maintain the farm population. . . . These extra hundred thousands are sent to the cities. . . . The future of the cities of the United States seems

Table 7-2. Births, Deaths, and Natural Increase in Boone County, 1920–1929 and 1930–1939

Year	Births	Deaths	Natural Increase	Year	Births	Deaths	Natural Increase
1920	392	95	297	1930	300	114	186
1921	379	87	292	1931	334	108	226
1922	391	92	299	1932	296	94	202
1923	377	99	278	1933	293	109	184
1924	354	104	250	1934	282	98	184
1925	296	97	199	1935	255	83	172
1926	330	97	233	1936	254	103	151
1927	346	77	269	1937	220	85	135
1928	324	105	219	1938	204	105	99
1929	308	100	208	1939	214	58	156
Total	3,497	953	2,544	Total	2,652	957	1,695

Source: U.S. Bureau of the Census, Vital Statistics, various years.

eventually to lie in the quality of the blood sent them from the farms. The native-born in the cities are not producing enough children to maintain themselves. (Henry A. Wallace, quoted in Wallace 1925, 25)

Ignored here is that it was farm women, not farms, who were producing children.

Charles Galpin, applying pre-Mendelian genetic reasoning, argued that rural children would enrich the genetic vigor of the urban labor force by infusing it with the strength and health acquired from their hard work in the open air of the American farm: "The farm-bred child, therefore, is the contribution of rural life to the human stock of society. . . . Society will be exceedingly wary of any plan for the rural child which may jeopardize the future of carrying the stamina of the race from generation to generation" (Galpin 1923, 121). In other words, reformers should stay away from farm families, because farm children would be the salvation of the degenerate urban population. A steady stream of labor from the farms allowed society to neglect some of the problems of the cities. Just as farm products provided

Table 7-3. Comparison of General Fertility Rates of Boone County and U.S. White Women, 1920–1940[a]

	Boone County	U.S. White	% Difference
1920	126.5	115.4	8.8
1930	93.1	87.1	6.9
1940	90.6	77.1	17.5

Source: U.S. Bureau of the Census, Vital Statistics and Census Reports, various years.

[a]General fertility rate is 1,000 times the number of births divided by the number of women ages 15 to 44.

underpinnings of food, raw materials, and a favorable currency balance for urban industry, so did rural children provide the population base for the growth of cities. The immigrant populations who had come to the United States up until World War I were not seen as being as vigorous and good as the native-born farm population.

The decrease in the number of births indicates that women were more concerned with the living standards of their offspring than they were with responding to the needs of urban industry. Yet much of the decline in the number of births resulted from the out-migration of women of childbearing age. Table 7-3, which shows general fertility rates, indicates that the biggest drop in fertility in Boone County came during the 1920s, when the depression first affected agriculture and rural areas experienced poverty in the midst of a generally prosperous economy. Rural women would have been most painfully aware of the contrast between what they, in their poverty, could offer their children and what the Progressive reformers told them that children should have. The Boone County fertility decline in the 1930s was less than that of other U.S. white women, so that by 1940 the difference between the fertility of Boone County women and that of other white women widened. Although Boone County women were having fewer babies, motherhood remained as an emphasized and central part of their lives. They lowered the birthrate in response to social and economic changes, but they did not reduce the rate as drastically as white urban women did.

While a few women continued to have babies regularly, other women were seeking ways to limit childbirth, and some of the information about women's birth limitation strategies can be pieced together. Hannah, a farm woman who had three children by 1920, remembered taking great care not to get pregnant during the depressed economic period. Constantly fearful that she would conceive, she practiced a form of rhythm control and became pregnant only once again. A neighbor woman performed abortions for other farm women, but Hannah chose to continue her pregnancy and gave birth to her last child, who was considerably younger than her first three children. Sigrid, married in 1927, said that she always felt sorry for women who got pregnant, and she thought herself lucky to have avoided pregnancy during the depression. Nevertheless, several of the women I interviewed who were married in the 1930s reported that they conceived within days of their marriages and gave birth within the first year because no birth control measures existed at that time. Yet none of these women had the large numbers of children that Boone County women of thirty years earlier had. Most of these women's second children were born five or more years after their first, suggesting that the women might have investigated birth control after their first experiences with sexual intercourse and caring for a baby under depression conditions.

FSA home economists worked in Boone County, offering education on health matters among other household concerns. Some FSA home economists taught birth control, but I have not been able to determine whether this was part of the Boone County program. Historian Linda Gordon (1976, 321–23) described a grassroots demand for birth control during the 1930s and said that support for government birth control programs was surprisingly strong in rural communities. The Comstock Law banning birth control was overturned by a federal judge in 1938, removing the vestige of illegality from federal birth control efforts. One Boone County woman, born in 1923, said that her mother used a contraceptive sponge moistened with liquid from a bottle, but she did not know where her mother got these things. Condoms had come into more common use after World War I, and traveling salesmen sold them from farm to farm by the 1920s. Most women considered condoms too expensive. The most common form of birth control seems to have been some combination of abstinence, rhythm, and withdrawal.

Alice, born on a Boone County farm in 1919, was the oldest of nine children born over a twenty-one-year period. Alice's mother had died over twenty years earlier and was unable to tell her story for this study, but Alice talked about her mother's childrearing:

> Ellen was born in 1932 and then she didn't have any babies for awhile. That was really good. She said, "I can do something." She was president of the Ladies Aid, for instance. She had time to do that. Then when she found out she was pregnant with Sandra she wasn't very excited about having another baby.
>
> Dad said, "We haven't had a baby for awhile."
>
> She said, "He was just trying to cheer me up, but it didn't work."
>
> I'm sure she had started the change already. She had Sandra and then Andrea afterward. She was forty-one when Andrea was born.

Her mother made and remodeled all of their coats and shoes, fixed pancakes for their meals, and did extra washings so that her children would always wear clean clothes to school. Alice remembered that for a time her mother refused to go to town with the family because it made her sad that she couldn't buy things that her children needed.

Alice also discussed birth control and abortion: "I don't suppose they knew that much about birth control. I remember Mom saying, 'Well, if you love your husband. . . .' She would never, never do anything like abortion! My son once asked me what abortion was and I told him it's murder. No, she just didn't do that. She would have liked birth control." Still, Alice's mother had only three children in the 1930s, compared with five in the 1920s. Her desire to limit childbirth makes it likely that she was practicing some rudimentary birth control in spite of her "if-you-love-your-husband" statement.

Although abortion was not openly available to all Boone County women in this period, it was an option for some. One woman said that if a woman were afraid she had become pregnant she could go to a doctor and he would give her something so that she would not be pregnant. Although she did not define this as abortion, that must have been what was done. Hannah's mention of the possibility of a home abortion left unclear the extent to which women used this service. A Boone County chiropractor was found guilty of abortion in 1937 when one of his patients brought charges against him (BCDC 1937). Other possibilities for abortion undoubtedly existed. A woman with money and determination probably did not have to bear a child she desperately did not want; but finding the money, the will, and the courage to probe into the dusty corners of rural society was not something that many rural women could manage.

Not every Boone County woman believed birth control to be a healthy, ethical, and socially acceptable option. Unwanted pregnancies occurred. Like Alice's mother and Hannah, most women probably carried them to term. Not every woman would have thought to ask her doctor to keep her from being pregnant. Probably not every doctor would have complied. Home abortion may not have been safe. Given this situation, women's reproductive control depended on a number of variables, including her relations with her husband, her ability to pay for medical service, moral support that would encourage her to follow her own inclinations, and access to information shared within the women's community about birth limitation options. However, the cumulative pressures to have fewer children seem to have spurred women toward more diligent and conscious cultivation of the birth control technology within reach of the women's community.

What were the benefits of having children in the depression? Children's wage labor sometimes provided income for their families. Although the prospect of children's wages might suggest that more children would bring more money, one or two good incomes would probably offer parents more support than would more children doing agricultural or domestic labor. Parents were not always able to claim their children's pay, but in the 1930s a daughter was more likely to channel her earned income back to her parents than was a working son (Scharf 1980, 147; Helmbold 1987, 646).

The most prestigious and remunerative job open to a working farm daughter was teaching in a country school. The country school was the social center of the farm community, with its spelling bees, school programs, and parties bringing everyone in the surrounding area together. The teacher was a community leader and a source of pride to her mother and father. To become a teacher, a young woman attended high school and took a normal training course. Out of the Albion High School class of 1932, approximately thirty-five of the seventy-one graduates had taken a normal training course. Each normal training graduate would then take the state teachers' examination. Upon passing this, she could get a temporary teaching certificate that would allow her to teach if she attended summer classes at college or evening classes at the study center that opened in Albion in 1933. With a certificate, a young woman who was well respected by people in the community and who was willing to work hard might, with luck, land a teaching job in a country school. Teaching in a one-room school with eight grades, carrying water and fuel, and managing the discipline and community relations centered around the school was hard work, both physically and mentally. Some teachers would be so exhausted that they spent their weekends in bed trying to recover from the previous week and fortify themselves for the next.

But they made money. Teachers' salaries approached $100 per month in the 1920s, but dropped to $50 or less in the 1930s. One woman said she was paid as little as $27.50 per month for teaching in the years from 1936 to 1939. If a young woman was lucky enough to teach in her "home school," she could live with her parents and thus keep her rent money within her family.

A teacher contributed to her parents' household economy by paying generous rent money or by paying for other household items. Yvonne, who taught from 1935 to 1940 while living in her parents' farm home, told of buying groceries for the household and clothing for her sisters. Barbara, who taught from 1932 to 1939, said that she loaned her father money to buy a tractor so he could continue farming. Rose, another teacher, borrowed money from the bank on the basis of her salary so that she could buy five hundred sheep to replace the cattle that her father lost in the drought. The sheep—which he called those "damn snottin' sheep"—pulled him through the depression. Rose was exceptional in that she was a married teacher whose husband was a school administrator in town; in most instances a

married woman was not allowed to teach. That the general rule banning married women from teaching could supersede the married
couples' interests in having the wives earn income during the 1930s
underscores the importance of daughters' incomes to the middle-
class family farmers who represented the political power in farm
neighborhoods.

As a high school graduate, a teacher was a privileged woman
within the rural community. Usually she had grown up in a relatively
prosperous farm household and was likely to have had the music
lessons, 4-H, and athletic activities that required dedication and sacrifice from the mother. All of Wilma's daughters taught school after
their high school graduation. Sharon, by contrast, did not even begin
high school. With the number of positions limited to one per farm
neighborhood, teaching was not a job that many mothers could or
would prepare their daughters to fill, but by concentrating attention
and care on a smaller number of daughters, a middle-class farm
mother might experience the pride and satisfaction of seeing them all
do well and contribute income to the household.

A more common source of income for daughters was domestic
work in farm, town, or city homes. There was always more demand
for domestic help than there were domestic workers, and such wom-
en tended to drift away from their farm communities. During the
1930s, more and more young women found their way to Omaha,
Chicago, or Kansas City, where they could always find jobs that paid
more than they could make in Boone County. Alice, who got a domestic job in Chicago through family friends, sent some of her ten-
dollar weekly paycheck to her parents' farm home during the 1930s:
"I could send money home. I didn't send much, but I would buy
clothes for my sisters—sweaters and skirts and things like that. . . .
[My brother] was in high school. I sent him money. I know he bought
his suit for graduation and he was real pleased because of that."

Alice maintained a close and supportive relationship with both of
her parents. She returned home between jobs, looked to her parents
for advice in making decisions about jobs, and stayed closely attuned
to the financial problems of her family and to the lives of her siblings.
She emphasized that her parents never forced her to give them
money: "I never *had* to send money home—nothing like that. Some

of our neighbors, the girls would go to work during the winter and they had to send the money home. When spring came they had to go home and help on the farm."

Parents' control over their daughters' lives was primarily exercised through moral authority and custom. Although the loss of an inheritance might theoretically have represented economic control, this threat would logically have affected sons more than daughters, and sons typically did not share their income with their parents unless the parents were destitute. Daughters were raised to be more attuned to family needs and willing to sacrifice for other family members, and they carried these traits into their roles as mothers.

In spite of farmers' last-ditch efforts to control the labor of their children, by the 1930s childrearing was beginning to be disconnected from the farm economy. Farm children were going to school more, doing less farm work, and looking toward nonfarm jobs. Even impoverished rural people had radios in the 1930s, and radio programs brought news, music, and ideas from beyond the rural neighborhood into the home. Women still shouldered the major costs of raising children, but children's labor could no longer be as efficiently processed by the family farm. Young children worked on the farm until they came of age, and then they expected adult autonomy. In economic terms, children who were raised to look for horizons extending beyond the family farm cost more than they returned. Women were having children for no economically rational reason. Given the devastating depression, the question is not why women were having fewer children, but why the birthrate declined no more than it did. The rewards of children's wage labor or children's assumption of family support in the future could hardly be overriding the more immediate economic disincentives of having children.

As Nancy Folbre (1983, 279) wrote, the "intrinsic" rewards of parenthood must have been a factor in the persistence of childbearing. The difficulty of securing reliable birth control may explain some of the higher rural fertility, but not all of it. Women had babies, in part, because they wanted them. In an era when a woman had little hope of happiness or accomplishments in her own life, she could center her hope for achievement and her vicarious experience of joy in a child. A woman could prove to herself and to the world that she was not a loser if she could produce a child who was a winner. Eventually some children returned their mothers' devotion by helping them, defending their interests, and loving them. Few others did.

Although many women appear to have limited their childbirths after 1920, they did not totally reject motherhood. Sigrid, married in 1927, got through the depression without becoming pregnant. But when she discovered she was sterile, she was devastated: "It was hard times. We felt sorry for the mothers, our friends, when a mother became PG. We thought we were fortunate not having a family. By the time we were financially able to have a family we were too old to adopt. It really hit us. We had no family." She remembered a woman's club meeting at which members were supposed to answer roll call by naming a gift of God. Almost all of the women answered by recounting an achievement of one of their children. Then Sigrid's name was called: "I answered, 'I'm just at a loss at what to say. I have no gift. I have no family to brag about.' That's what this roll call was—bragging about their children. I said, 'I just have to answer present.'" Having children was hard, but not having children was harder. Few if any married women remained childless by choice. Boone County women of the 1930s chose to focus rather than to abandon their commitment of resources to their children.

Children represented a mother's hope and dream. Bess Streeter Aldrich, a resident of Elmwood, Nebraska, wrote popular novels about Nebraska women in the rural depression period. Her novels celebrated the simple joys of fresh-smelling laundry, clean houses, and, most of all, motherhood. My grandmother, who graduated from high school and was married to a businessman, had both the education and the leisure to read novels. She had grown up in Elmwood, and Aldrich was her favorite author. Living in the town of Tilden in Madison County, she read all of Aldrich's novels as soon as they appeared in the public library. Her favorite was *A Lantern in Her Hand*, published in 1928 when my father, her fourth and last child, was eight years old.

A Lantern in Her Hand is the life story of Abbie Deal, a rural Nebraska mother. Abbie, born in Scotland, is half aristocrat and half peasant. Her father, a handsome Scottish nobleman, had gotten lost while hunting, fell in love with a peasant girl who gave him a drink, and took her to live in his mansion. When he loses his fortune through a fluke he takes his poor-but-genteel family to the United States, where he soon dies, leaving Abbie's mother to rear their children alone. Abbie, the daughter who has inherited his long, white, tapering, aristocratic fingers, is a beautiful and talented singer and painter. A rich doctor woos her and offers to take her to New York City, where she will have the finest teachers available, but Abbie chooses to marry strong, silent Will Deal. Together they struggle to claim a Nebraska farm.

Abbie, a supremely earthy and noble woman, has five children. Although she occasionally thinks about the riches and fame she could have known in New York, she always comes back to her love for her children and knows that these children have made her life in rural Nebraska richer than anything she could have known in New York. She constantly sacrifices things that she wants for the education and opportunities of her children. When Will dies shortly after the birth of their fifth child, Abbie carries on valiantly as a widowed mother. As it did with Abbie's mother, widowhood brings out Abbie's full resourcefulness and allows her independence without calling into question her devotion to her husband. Her love for her children and her duty to them carries her through the period of mourning for Will.

The vindication of Abbie's life of sacrifice comes with the separate successes of each of her five children. But Aldrich apparently is unable to imagine this success within the farm milieu. John, the only son to settle in the rural area, travels extensively first and only later comes to settle in the small town as a prominent lawyer and legislator. Mack, another son, becomes a rich Omaha banker. Margaret, the oldest daughter, marries a Lincoln doctor and becomes an accomplished artist. The middle daughter, Isabelle, marries a musician and goes with him to Chicago, where she becomes a famous singer. The youngest daughter Grace—beautiful and surrounded by impassioned suitors—devotes her life to learning and becomes a college teacher. Not only do none of Abbie's children become farmers, but Aldrich draws an unflattering portrait of a family whose children do succeed at farming. The Deals' neighbors, the Reinmuellers, a German family, are portrayed as unclean and not very bright; but somehow they end up wealthy, owning much of the surrounding land.

As an old woman, Abbie reviews her life in a conversation with John's daughter Laura. When she was young, she says, she had dreams of being a painter or a singer, but she has been too busy. She has devoted her life to others. But even as she baked bread and patched clothes, she dreamed of vast accomplishments. She dreamed dreams and "dreamed them into children," who would do the things she had never been able to do (Aldrich 1928, 279). We are invited to conclude that Abbie, not her children, deserves the credit and honor for their successes.

In this celebration of rural motherhood, Aldrich seems to construct a sharp contrast between a feminist vision and an ideal of motherly sacrifice. Yet she gives meaning to this sacrifice by noting that Abbie had the choice of achievement in the city. The validation of her sacrifice lies with her children, who reach beyond the confines of rural life and claim their inherent nobility. In the end, Abbie's devoted granddaughter Laura speaks of the magnificent new capitol in Lincoln as the culmination of the dreams of the settlers: "They [the settlers] were like the foundation stones under the capitol. . . . They were not cultured. But they had innate refinement and courage. And they could see visions and dream dreams" (Aldrich 1928, 280). For mothers like Abbie Deal, and doubtless my grandmother as well, the culmination of their dreams was not an agrarian vision but a vision of the cities that would replace the farms. Although these women themselves could not do the things that they might have liked to do, their children would somehow be mystically inspired to live out the dreams of their mothers. Luckily, all of Abbie's children have noble aspirations that are a credit to her.

Abbie's story floats in a dream world bearing little similarity to the reality of depression life in rural Nebraska. The connection that Aldrich drew between such everyday acts as making bread and the ensuing accomplishment and fame of Abbie's children accounted for the popularity that Aldrich achieved as a writer of women's fiction.

What harm could come from making mothers feel good about what they were doing? It was only harmful when mothers and their children measured their lives against the fantasy. In that case, not only would mothers have unrealistic expectations for their children, but the children would live in the shadow of their mothers' unfulfilled dreams. None would measure up. Dreams intervened between mothers and children and could in some cases cloud and subvert what might have been a woman's closest personal relationships. The ethereal expectations of motherhood were essentially unredeemable.

Agrarian ideology was far removed from Nebraska women's daily reality. Within the agrarian framework, mothers were unable to generate a realistic image of who they and their children were in the world and what they might do with their lives. Although agrarianism had never tallied with the experiences of mothers, the crisis of the depression bared the contradictions between agricultural production and the reproduction of people. When motherhood began to be uncoupled from farm production, the mystical motherhood rhetoric dissolved at the practical level. Motherhood in itself carried little status for rural women. Nowhere was this more apparent than among the mothers who were divorced or deserted and who sought public assistance to raise their children. They received none of the respect that was given to mothers who were also middle-class wives. The effect of public assistance was to reinforce the mother's responsibility for her children without providing adequate means for her to meet this responsibility. Mothers were in dire economic and social straits if they did not have men to support them.

Mothers who stayed married to middle-class men held on to their respectability, even as their childbearing took on new economic dimensions. But motherhood was redefined for these women as well. Having a smaller number of children was coming to be associated with the values of thrift, order, and respectability. The constricted economic situation encouraged women to concentrate their resources on fewer children, who would then be more fully prepared to take their places in society.

Agricultural leaders and farm mothers were gradually converging in their beliefs that the future for rural children did not lie on the farm. The difference was that mothers were apt to see their children as professionals or entrepreneurs, whereas agricultural leaders' images of rural children's future were vague. Women who were married to middle-class men rearranged and refocused their maternal behavior; they did not reject it entirely.

The reality of Boone County women's lives during the rural depression from 1920 to 1940 demonstrates that the problems of women as mothers were not separate from the public political and economic systems. Although many women worked hard to provide what they could for their children, the hard times were not something that many could overcome with private and personal efforts. A woman's being a good mother did not save her children from suffering. If she wanted more farm income, a job, a better job, more access to schools and colleges, community childcare, or readier availability of birth control, she would have to express her motherly concerns in the political arena. The ideological privatization of basic issues of women's work as mothers precluded any public debate of the hardships that confronted them and their children.

Nor could farm mothers' problems be addressed as isolated rural oddities. Rural people were part of a larger capitalist system that would someday incorporate their children as generic labor with no regard for the mothers' experience of their children as unique beings.

Rural life offered little to most mothers and children after their cheap labor on the farm was exhausted. Mothers had little security in their old age, and very few of the children who sacrificed their young strength to the family farms could claim those farms as adults. But mothers and children were something more than victims. Some women resisted raising their children as cogs in a farm machine and encouraged them to go where they believed they would have a better chance in life. If these women misunderstood the real opportunities open to farm youths just entering city life, they clearly understood the rural alternative. The majority of young people did leave Boone County in the 1930s.

Mothers had their own instrumental reasons for having babies. Children provided various benefits for them, from help with farm work and housework, to moral support, to security in old age, to ego fulfillment. A woman's children were one of the few resources that she could claim. That she may have misunderstood and overestimated the harvest on her investment does not negate her expectations, and it does not imply an alternative. Boone County women maintained a relatively high, if somewhat reduced, level of fertility during the 1920–40 depression, thereby attesting to the continuing hope that women placed in having children. Even when a woman had difficulty raising her children, they were one of the few pleasures she could hope for in an otherwise bleak economic environment.

Yet, as much as women wanted and loved their children, the social construction of motherhood virtually guaranteed frustration and disappointment. Mothers controlled neither the society nor the households in which they raised their children. If they wanted better schools or better libraries, they could exert little power to get them. When a mother wanted to send her children to the university rather than make farm payments, she was powerless to do so unless her husband and the government agreed with her priorities. Moreover, she had little power in the society her children would enter. She could teach them the rules and show them how the world would work for them, if she understood these things, but she could not change the way the world operated by staying in the domestic world and fulfilling her role as mother. If her child had to pick corn rather than go to school, that was the way things were; if her son was drafted into military service, she had little to say about it; if her daughter was mentally slow or emotionally impaired, she had little power to shape society so that it would accept her. To affect these conditions required public political work rather than the passive acceptance of private labor and sacrifice.

The paeans glorifying motherhood had little to do with the reality experienced by most rural Nebraska women. Faced with the sacred responsibility of motherhood—the expectation that she would selflessly surrender her own needs and ambitions in order to raise the children who would transform the world—a woman was bound to fail. As ordinary, mortal human beings, mothers needed to write their own more modest agendas. All mothers fell short of the goal of perfect selflessness. Children understood this failing but lacked a more reasonable set of expectations with which to understand their mothers. More people spoke warmly of their fathers than of their mothers.

Finally, if these destructive standards fostered ambivalent feelings in children toward their mothers, they also fostered ambivalent feelings in mothers toward their life's work—their children. Only in fiction did children perfectly fulfill the dreams of a mother who had sacrificed her own opportunities for them. Even if a real mother could not directly express her disappointment in her children, she could still feel that something was wrong and that she had not fulfilled her responsibility.

AGRARIAN CONTRADICTION

Though yet in its infancy, all these agencies for the prosperity and well-being of Nebraska are steadily at work, and in fulness of time will blossom into fulfillment of its early promise.—Samuel Aughey, Sketches of the Physical Geography of Nebraska and the Northwest, *1880*

Women did not write the primary agrarian texts that shaped rural policy and formed the ideological charter for white settlement in rural Nebraska. No women's voices sounded in the state and national legislative debates on farm policy. Seldom did women themselves enlarge the dimensions of agrarian discourse in such a way that their own statements were repeated, elaborated upon, and incorporated into the stream of beliefs and knowledge about rural life. Women did not sit on the boards of directors of the railroad companies that put out the reams of glowing promotional literature on life in the West. They did not control the flow of capital that financed the development of farms.

Agrarianism, which took only secondary and derivative notice of women, identified rural women as wives and mothers on family farms. The farm woman cleaned the house, provided food for the workers, gave birth to the children who would eventually contribute to the farm, and comforted the farmer after his hard day in the fields. She was a helpmeet for her man. In bearing children she allowed for the continuity of the farm. A woman on the farm was uniquely blessed because here she was useful; she could love and serve in a special way. She did not risk the idleness and selfishness that were the lot of city women. A woman working alongside her husband on the

Substitute technology for women

farm had a unique power that grew from her close involvement in farm production, her sharing of his world.

That is the story that has filtered through the elaborations of agrarianism. The actual experience of rural women contradicted this agrarian vision, although their voices and experiences are harder to discern than are those of men. Although plains farming would have been impossible without women, their indispensability was embedded in the institution of the nuclear family, which limited and constrained any power they might have garnered through their economic activities. Life on the farm did not insulate women from the gender oppression afflicting U.S. society as a whole. On the contrary, rural women had little social protection against violence and exploitation. Their isolation on separate family farms precluded even the marginal protection and support that neighbors afforded city women. Many resisted westward migration to Nebraska. Once there, they encouraged their children to leave. Women did not receive an equitable share of the farm prosperity that accrued during the golden age of agriculture in the early years of this century.

One effect of the rural crisis that began in 1920 was to deepen the agrarian myth rather than to prompt a rethinking of it. Even as the material promise of agrarian life dissolved, the mainstream of public (male) discourse reemphasized farming as the soul of the country and identified women's sacrifices as critical to the survival of farm life. Farm wives were more indispensable than ever before. Yet nowhere did the agrarian text validate women's particular hardships on the farm, and these hardships eroded agrarian life from the interior. The loosening of social conventions in the depression years gave some women a measure of domestic power as household providers, but this power rested on male weakness and social default. Again some women resisted. As young women they left the farms and refused to marry farmers; as wives they had fewer children; as mothers they attempted to divert resources to their children rather than to the farm. But throughout, the family voice allowed to women was necessarily secondary to that of men.

Women's stories from the 1930s show patterns of resistance, but, from their position in the family environment, these women were not well positioned to trace over the patterns and become aware of what they shared as women. Restricted to the cell of the family, their primary adult relations were with men, through whom they had access to vital resources. In deference to these relationships, they muted and censored their talk with other women, thereby depriving themselves of the chance to mirror each other's wisdom, pool their knowledge, pull together common threads, and express their common condition in stories, songs, poems, speeches, paintings, and essays that would give meaning to the specificity of their experiences. Women's wisdom could not become the culture of the plains. The sister relationship among adult women, although strong in individual instances, was not consistent with the family farm structure. When it thrived, it thrived in spite of this structure.

The agrarian dream of the individual farmer working his own land and reaping his own profits contradicted the fact that farming is by its nature a collective endeavor. At no time in human history has farming been accomplished by single persons working separately and in isolation. The plan to work farms with family labor was an attempt at a solution that supplied needed labor for the individual farmer without full recognition or reimbursement of the persons providing this labor. The family bridged the contradiction between individual ownership and group effort, providing a measure of flexibility in the labor supply and production system.

Ultimately, family labor did not and could not make the majority of farms competitive in a capitalist system. The net out-migration that began in Boone County in the 1920s gathered steam over the decades. Boone County's 1980 population of 7,391 was one-half of the 1930 population; the 1990 population will be even lower (Census 1983, 165). Losses in the farm population led the overall population drop: in 1930 those living on farms represented 65 percent of the population of the county; by 1980 that number had dropped to 33 percent. Farming has consolidated into an ever-smaller population, but no other industry has replaced it locally. A number of Boone County residents now commute to jobs in other counties.

Although World War II and the policies instituted during the 1945–53 presidency of Harry S. Truman revived the flagging farm economy for a brief period in the 1940s and 1950s, the effect was only to moderate the rate of out migration. Indices of a roller-coaster land market afford an overview of a post–World War II boom-and-bust farming cycle that squeezed people out and pulled them away. Yet these composite farm economic figures obscure deepening class inequalities within the farming population. Not everyone prospered equally in the good times; not everyone suffered equally in the bad times. A clue to the continuing class polarization in the county is the fact that dividends, interest, and rent produced more income in Boone County than either farm or nonfarm earnings after 1980 (Census 1986, 131). Boone County's population does not consist primarily of capitalists; these earnings have been concentrated. Nor has the farm base of the economy provided widely distributed prosperity. In 1979, 46.4 percent of Boone County's households were living on less than a $10,000 yearly income, and 19.9 percent of the population was officially living in poverty (Census 1983, 29–283, 29–292).

Departure from the land was heartbreaking for many persons. The agrarian vision of the moral superiority and economic importance of farm people compounded the anguish of many men who lost the land that had been theirs. The city loomed as a gray proletarian hell. But an adjustment of the heady exploitative thinking that propelled the first settlement of Nebraska was inevitable. Commercial farming resulted in terrible damage to the land and to the original occupants, and this damage returned to haunt the conquerors as well. The failure to incorporate women's reality into the accepted culture of the rural plains intensified the suffering of the majority of plains people.

Unlike men, when women living in the 1980s spoke of their lives on the plains before 1940, they tended to avoid sentimental descriptions. One woman, who was born and raised on a farm and who married a farmer at age eighteen, expressed a typical position with atypical bluntness: "The farm, it's all right—as long as I don't have to live there. I would never go back to that at all. Maybe nowadays it's different, I don't know. . . . No, I would never go back." Many of the remaining farm women do not share this view and are working politically to preserve the family farm. Their voices reinforce a Jeffersonian agrarian perspective, and a few have risen to prominence in the family farm movement. These women are elite survivors, but even among them the muted voices of protest can readily be discerned.

Those women who reject the agrarian vision have continued to be peripheral to farm political movements.

Agrarian ideology remains a potent stream of political and intellectual discourse in the United States. The farm crisis of the 1980s gave rise to agrarian statements from the liberal political tradition (Harkin 1988; Schwab 1988). Conferences, scholarly journals, and books have addressed agrarianism and its modern meaning (Haynes 1985, 1990; Comstock 1987; Strange 1988).

Wendell Berry has been the most eloquent literary exponent of modern agrarian ideology. In *The Unsettling of America*, Berry laid out a compelling restatement of classical Jeffersonian agrarianism in which the return to intimate connection with the land was exalted as the best route to individual and social wholeness. Agriculture, according to Berry, was the foundation of domestic order and peace. Like Jefferson's, Berry's agrarianism was gendered, the major actors being male, and he tied his vision directly to the institution of marriage and to women's fertility. Berry (1977, 131) considered marriage the primary connection among humans and agriculture the primary connection between humans and the earth. Sexuality, he argued, should not be separated from fertility; modern birth control technology destroyed the natural order and fostered sexual amorality.

Echoing the pronouncements of Liberty Hyde Bailey sixty-five years earlier, Berry wrote that the city and the industrial age are villains that destroy vital connections: "The cities subsist in competition with the country; they live upon a one-way movement of energies out of the countryside—food and fuel, manufacturing materials, human labor, intelligence, and talent. Very little energy is ever returned. Instead of gathering these energies up into coherence, . . . the modern city dissipates and wastes them. Along with its glittering 'consumer goods,' the modern city produces an equally characteristic outpouring of garbage and pollution" (Berry 1977, 137).

Berry did not evoke marriage and fertility metaphorically; he used them as the concrete and definitive connections that give coherence to his vision of an agrarian culture. Bad or broken relationships, in this view, came from industrial development and cities. A favorable review of a recent novel by Berry did voice a reservation, immediately followed by a dismissal of that reservation: "Berry tends to objectify women as objects of worship or beauty or corporate success. Still, his impassioned commitment to the family farm and his dithyrambic prose mark this as a book worth reading" (*Progressive* 1988, 47). Once again, the treatment of women was overlooked for the good of the farm. Whatever complaints women might have had paled in the light of real issues.

Agrarianism has served as a poor charter for public policy, because its premises are false, irrelevant, or both (Peterson 1990). Farmers are not closer to nature or more moral than any other people. The same laws of nature apply in the city as in the country. Farmers on the plains removed the land cover and the wild animals that existed there naturally and substituted a refined system of livestock and crops that would serve the interests of human society. Farming represented a different kind of tampering with the environment than that which occurred in the city, but it was no more natural. Farming people have been both as moral and as immoral as nonfarmers, although their morality and immorality have been expressed in different ways. Some farming people have been kind, wise, and public spirited; some have been violent, short-sighted, and greedy. Rural claims for economic and social justice should not rest on ties to nature or moral superiority. Rural people do not carry the responsibility for the moral fiber of the nation. No logic supports this claim.

The idea that the economic life blood of the nation was carried by farmers may have been true in Jefferson's day, but it has never been true in this century. When over 90 percent of the population lived on farms, it made some sense to gauge the well-being of the nation through the well-being of farmers, although even then such a measure would have had to stretch to include African Americans, Native Americans, and women of all races. Today, when only between 2 and 3 percent of the population live on farms, it makes less sense. Food and fiber have always been necessary resources, but so have water, education, and health services. Plumbers, academics, nurses, and doctors have other ways of pressing their claims for compensation. They do not rest their political beliefs on the fear that the country would disintegrate without them, although such claims would be just as true and as misleading as those of the agrarians.

Contrary to the agrarian creed, farming has not negated class polarization. Such a polarization has occurred within the farming and the nonfarming sectors. Not everyone can succeed in farming, as both produce markets and land resources are finite. The competitiveness of the capitalist system flourished in the farm sector, and by doing so it guaranteed that losers as well as winners would emerge. Further, the structure of farming in the United States has entailed a great deal of nonowner labor. Much of this has been supplied by women and children who have never had access to farm ownership on their own. Farming regions have produced more children than they could absorb into their adult population. Cities have served as safety valves by accepting excess rural population, a condition exactly the opposite of that projected by nineteenth-century agrarians.

The position of women on the farm and in agrarian thinking has been diverse and complicated in its contradictions. Jefferson believed that women should keep house, soothe men when they came into the house, and not interfere in important male affairs. Yet this idealized subordination probably never characterized the roles of real women in middle-class households. Women forged power within the home by informal means; many controlled the family budget; many had more forceful personalities than their husbands. This is the traditional view of the domestic power of women.

According to the domestic view of women's power, women worked from within the domestic sphere to shape the lives and decisions of husbands and children. Some women express this view with a wink and a conspiratorial look, as if women enjoy a secret power that men are forever too dense to realize. Some women did dominate their husbands, but it was not something every woman could do or wanted to do. When men resented this domination and responded with violence, women had little recourse. Many sons and daughters have resented their mothers' domination and have expressed the resentment in diverse unpleasant ways. The ideal of the woman as the power behind the throne has become increasingly anachronistic as women have moved to assume responsibility for their own ambitions and beliefs.

Some agrarians have discarded the image of the traditional wife and have characterized wives as equal partners with their husbands on the farm. According to this revisionist view, women's power lies in doing the work formerly assigned to men and in having men share the work of the home. Women share ownership of the farming assets and participate equally in decisions. Represented as a unique form of feminism specifically related to the farm as a family production form, this model has been promoted by feminist agrarians (Elbert 1987). The question remains of what the family as a social form offers to the farm operation if the organic division of labor is dissolved and the farm operation does not draw on the different positions of people within the family. Dissolution of gender (and age) differences within the family farm would transform the family into a social collective operating the farm. This may be desirable, but it represents a major departure from the traditional family farm organization. Such a collective could as logically be a group of women, a group of men, or a gender-mixed collective that wished to share farm operation.

Agrarianism has been limited by its being a white male vision that has failed to consider the full human integrity of other persons. It has led rural people down a blind alley. Although agrarians would claim that farming has faltered because society has been insufficiently solicitous of agrarian concerns, such a claim is false. A more inclusive plains culture would incorporate the experience of African Americans who ventured onto the plains after the Civil War. It would incorporate the experience of the Native Americans whose past reaches back for millennia on the plains. It would incorporate the experience of Latin Americans who were on the southern plains from early years and who migrated north as laborers in the twentieth century. It would incorporate the stories of children who worked the land for their parents and fled or were pushed away to the cities. And it would incorporate the experiences of women as well as men. Perhaps a broadening of vision to include this diversity of plains experiences would create a harmony among people, other animals, and the land that is absent from a vision that remains narrowly focused on commercial farming. It could generate a new way of thinking about the plains—a new plains ideology, laying the groundwork for a more viable and democratic rural society.

APPENDIX: INTERVIEWS

When I began my fieldwork, there were not many rural Nebraska women available who were able to talk about events that happened fifty years or more in the past. Although I did some sorting and screening of interview candidates, my general procedure was to at least try to interview any woman who seemed promising. At the end of my fieldwork, I had completed successful interviews with thirty-six women and two men. Although I did not decline to interview any woman who seemed willing and able to talk with me, there were four people with whom I was unable to schedule interviews before drawing my fieldwork to a close.

I located my informants through a variety of channels. Eight of them I knew as my former teachers, mothers of my friends, or friends of my parents, and I was able to call them for interviews with no further introduction. People I met or interviewed often suggested other people to me, and I followed these networks. Sometimes I approached women at club meetings or other social events and asked if I could interview them. Three women contacted me on their own initiative and asked to be interviewed. I had known some of these women since childhood and recognized the names of others, but twenty-three of those I interviewed were total strangers to me before I began my fieldwork.

The dates of birth of my interviewees were as follows:

1890–99	2
1900–1909	13
1910–19	16
1920–29	7

They included eight women who had left rural Nebraska for a period of fifteen years or more during or after the 1930s. Four were living in cities at the time they were interviewed. Thus, the many out-migrants were represented in the study, though not in proportion to their share of the actual population.

The class breakdown of the interview group is difficult to systematize, as some owned farms for periods of time but rented or left their farms at other times. Other people repeatedly moved back and forth from farm to nonfarm jobs. Many shifted frequently between farm tenancy, farm labor, and nonfarm work. Dividing the interviewees into groups of predominantly farm owners, farm laborers or tenants, and nonfarm workers yields the following:

farm owners	18
tenants/laborers	14
nonfarm laborers	6

One group wholly missing from the interview population was that of the elite women whose husbands had been wealthy ranchers or businessmen. Although I talked with some of these women, their high visibility and general recognition throughout the area convinced me that I could not present their stories anonymously.

All of the women spoke English as a first language. At most a woman might know a prayer or a few words in another European language. Religious affiliations as they were formed before 1940 included Methodist, Lutheran, Catholic, Congregational, Presbyterian, Evangelical and Reformed, Baptist, and no church membership.

Before I began an interview, I explained my research as carefully and completely as I could and answered questions about it. I also left a typed description of the research with each informant. In this research description, I agreed not to use her or his name in any publication and promised to guard against the accidental divulging of any personal information given. I signed this statement, which included my name, address, and telephone number, and encouraged the person to contact me if there were any questions, problems, corrections, or additional information to offer.

Unless it was either impossible to tape record the interview or I was asked not to, I taped and transcribed each interview in full.

When I was unable to tape an interview I took notes, collecting as much of the interview as possible verbatim. In accordance with the American Anthropological Association's ethics code and the agreements made with those being interviewed, these interview transcripts are not open to other researchers.

More women refused to be interviewed in this research than in any I had done previously. Eleven of the women I contacted either turned me down, were constantly unavailable, or controlled the format and length of the interview so completely that it was not useful. I do not think it had anything to do with me personally, because in all but one of these cases I approached the women through close friends or often relatives. Age and poor health may explain part of their reluctance, but the personal nature of the interviews and women's disinclination to rake up the past were undoubtedly crucial factors.

Following is an outline of the topics covered in the interviews. I evolved this outline during the course of the study, discarding some questions that did not work and adding others that seemed to be of interest. I used this outline loosely. If I sensed that a question would be too intrusive, I did not ask it, and I did not press for information that the person being interviewed seemed reluctant to provide.

I. Preliminary
   A. Date of birth
   B. Family background, length of time in Nebraska, livelihood, where settled
   C. How many in family, ages
   D. Sisters and brothers
   E. Married, divorced, widowed
   F. Children: number, sex, birthdates
   G. Education
   H. How family came to rural Nebraska

II. Farm History
   A. Farm description: size, enterprises, workers, tenancy, ownership, labor
   B. Women's work: poultry, garden, dairy, animal chores, field
   C. Women's work: household workers, technology, family help

III. 1930s

    A. Enterprises, family economy, effects of depression

    B. Migration

    C. Education

    D. What were adaptive choices in 1930s: teaching school, farm enterprises, division of labor, migration, jobs

    E. Did anyone not have enough food?

    F. What did people do to relax and have fun?

    G. Did families split up because of the depression?

    H. Did you get together with just women in the 1930s? Could you sometimes spend a whole day with a friend?

    I. How did the depression affect the lives of children?

IV. Family

    A. Children: your children, siblings, cousins, nieces, nephews, you

        1. Who cared for children?

        2. What jobs were children responsible for?

        3. Education

        4. Leisure

        5. Discipline

        6. Did some children leave home at an early age? Why?

        7. Describe a good child. A bad child.

        8. Any instances of adult sexual contact with a child?

    B. Wives and husbands

        1. Division of labor

        2. Do you know of any instances in which husbands and wives didn't get along? How did they work this out?

        3. What could a wife do if she didn't like a decision her husband made?

        4. Did you ever hear of an instance in which a man struck a woman?

        5. Did any women ever talk with other women about problems with their husbands?

    C. Elderly: experiences with elderly

        1. Who assisted in care?

        2. What jobs did they do?

3. Where did they live?

4. Economic exchanges?

D. Working-age adults

1. Social contacts

2. Business arrangements

3. Work sharing

4. Help with moving, finding jobs

E. What relatives did you see the most? Did women family members and kin ever get together without men?

F. Could you go to your family if you needed help? Money? Did family members come to you for help?

G. What are some of the stories your mother told you? Did your grandmother or aunts tell you stories?

H. Do you have anything that your mother gave you that reminds you of her?

I. How did you name your children?

J. What kind of birth control was available? How did women find out about it?

K. Can you describe what a family should be? How should people in a family act toward each other?

L. What could be done if there were differences of opinion in a family?

M. Would you say that your family was typical?

N. What were some of the things that could break up a family?

V. Friends

A. Were there chances for women to get together as friends? Can you tell about a time you spent with other women?

B. What friends did you get together with most often? What did you do together? Go places? Work? Trade childcare?

C. Did you ever share living quarters with other women?

D. How did you locate jobs, find out about work?

E. Who taught you to dance? Garden? Bake bread? Play music? Sew? Change a tire? Milk a cow? Drive a tractor?

F. How did you decide on your occupation? Did you talk to friends about it?

G. What did women talk about when they got together? Problems with work? Talk about children? Gossip about each other? Personal family lives? Politics, community life? Religion? Help and advice?

H. Who helped you when you had a baby? When you were sick? Had family members who were sick?

VI. Community

A. Where did you go to school? Church? Shopping? Visiting? Can you tell any stories about Saturday night? Can you tell any stories about school parties?

B. Were you in any clubs? What other women were in clubs with you? What projects did the clubs do? Did you like clubs? How was club life different in the 1930s than today? Did your club do any relief work in the 1930s?

C. Recreation: Did you like to go fishing? Swimming? Picnics? Dances? Church events? School parties?

D. How many bars were there in your town?

   1. Did you drink? Go into bars?
   2. Did people often drink in their homes?
   3. Did you know people who drank?
   4. Did drinking cause any problems?

E. Did you ever go to Norfolk, Columbus, or Grand Island in the 1930s? Did you ever go to movies?

F. Did you have a radio? When did you get it? Do you remember the radio programs? What were the most popular programs?

NOTES

PREFACE

1. The effect of this bias may well have been to obscure my view of the worst problems in nuclear families. Correcting for this possibility would strengthen rather than negate my thesis.

CHAPTER 1

1. The ninety-eighth meridian passes through the Boone County seat of Albion at the county center. Walter Prescott Webb (1931, 34) places the line dividing the Prairie Plains and the Great Plains at this ninety-eighth meridian in central Nebraska.

2. The farming opportunities for single and divorced women are discussed in Chapters 3 and 4.

3. Historian Carl Degler (1980) has called the family universal, or nearly so. For prominent anthropological critiques of the universality of family and biological kinship reckoning, see Jane Collier, Michelle Rosaldo, and Sylvia Yanagisako (1982), David Schneider (1984), and Donald Bender (1967).

4. The *Oxford English Dictionary* gives varying definitions of family that developed under changing social conditions. Lutz Berkner (1975) has shown that census procedures and political pressures have affected historians' reconstructions of the European family. In the nineteenth century, U.S. census takers were instructed to count the inmates of a prison, hotel, asylum, or garrison as a family (Wright 1900, 151, 184).

5. Unmarried women who went to work in textile mills in the northeastern United States were among the earliest American factory workers. Typically, their employment was a short-term arrangement rather than a lifetime pattern, as was the case with most men who went into factory work at that time.

6. Bonnie Thornton Dill (1988), comparing state policies toward families of whites and those of African, Chinese, and Mexican American women in the nineteenth century, found that although such policies supported the family unit

for whites, they worked against the development of family relations among African, Chinese, and Mexican Americans. Government policies that supported warfare against Native Americans, removed them from their land, removed children from their homes, and reorganized their economies were among the measures that subverted kinship relations among Native Americans.

CHAPTER 2

1. Locke, Taylor, and Jefferson meant men; it would be misleading to recast their arguments in gender-inclusive language.

2. Historian Julie Roy Jeffrey cites an instance in which one Alliance woman brought up the question of marriage, declaring that women should be independent so they could marry for love rather than financial support. Yet the overall position proposed for an Alliance woman was one of commitment to the improvement of life on the farm, where she would be a housewife (Jeffrey 1975, 81–83).

3. The only extant record of the survey replies is the brief summary published in *Good Housekeeping*.

4. Rural sociologist George Beal (1947) dates a possible first use of the term *family farm* to 1914. Farms based on capitalist production prospered on the Illinois frontier in the 1860s and 1870s and in parts of the Dakotas and Minnesota in the 1880s and were later replaced by household production units (Friedmann 1978, 572–73).

CHAPTER 3

1. Melody Graulich (1989) and Annette Kolodny (1975, 1984) have discussed sexual symbolism in the idea of the virgin land and in western adventure stories. Men and women reacted to the symbolism of the West in different ways.

2. Lillian Schlissel (1982) and Susan Armitage (1982) discuss women as reluctant migrants to the West. For a contrary view, see Sandra Myres (1982).

3. Details on sod houses are found in a 1957–58 *Nebraska Farmer* series consisting of letters from people, mostly women, who had lived in such structures. Luna Kellie (1926) also described her sod houses in detail. Everett Dick (1975) discusses the technology of sod houses.

4. Edith Eudora Kohl, who homesteaded in western South Dakota in 1908, stated that most of those who were homesteading there at the time wanted the land as an investment; few wanted to farm it. These homesteaders would file their claims and, instead of living on the land for five years, they would use the commutation clause, which allowed them to buy the land for $1.25 per acre after six months. Kohl estimated the costs of homesteading at $300 and the sale price

of the land at $1,000 to $1,500. Two-thirds of the homesteaders, she said, would leave the land after they had bought it (Kohl 1986, 8, 31). A similar pattern held true in other western regions. Only 51 percent of the persons who homesteaded in Montana were farmers before homesteading (Hargreaves 1976, 186).

5. Federal census schedules, which are opened to researchers after seventy-two years, are the census takers' papers that enumerate household composition and selected characteristics of each person. The 1890 census schedules were destroyed in a fire, so the 1900 and 1910 schedules are the first to define a settled ten-year period in Boone County.

6. Indications are that a substantial number of farmers were being squeezed out, even in this boom period. Richard Bremer (1976, 130), examining land tenure in a region west of Boone County, found that the lowest level of persistence during the first half of the twentieth century occurred in 1915, in the midst of the farm boom.

7. Net out-migration was computed as initial population, plus births, minus deaths, minus final population.

8. For purposes of class analysis, ownership of the means of production refers, not to legal title to the land, but to *control* of the production. Although the legal system usually coincides with and buttresses de facto control, under certain circumstances this control may lie outside of the formally recognized channels. Insofar as land titles confer the illusion of control by farmers themselves, the farming population may not be unified, articulate, and effective in its efforts to contest the actual transfer of control of the production process (Davis 1980; de Janvry 1980). Wide dispersal of land titles cannot be taken as conclusive proof of dispersed control of production. On the other hand, increasing concentration of land ownership, in which some individuals come to own significantly more land than can be worked by one household, can be used as an indicator of concentrated production control. Susan Mann (1990) disputes this distinction between formal ownership and production control. She finds that the staying power of the petty commodity production form stems from the material logic of the farm production process, not from the advantage of this production form to capitalists.

9. Information on estates comes from an analysis of records in probate books 41–43 at the Boone County Courthouse and a comparison of the number of estates probated with the total number of deaths occurring in Boone County over the period 1933 to 1935. Unfortunately, it has been impossible to obtain a comparable reading from the probate records of the early years of Boone County settlement. Registration of deaths was not mandatory in Nebraska until 1920, so it is impossible to know what percentage of the deceased left estates for probate. Further, before 1920 it seems to have been common to probate an estate at the time the property was subsequently transferred rather than at the time of death. Some earlier probates involved the estates of persons who had been dead for over twenty years. My guess is that probate records from the early years give a fairly

complete picture of the estates of those people who had substantial amounts of property to be dispersed, but it is difficult to know what percentage of the estates of all deceased persons this represented. The heirs of deceased persons who owned 160-acre farms could save court costs and lawyers' fees by remaining on the land and postponing the probates, an action that seems to have caused no long-term legal problems. In sum, for the years before 1920 it is impossible, from reading estate probates and death records, to know what percentage of the population owned productive property at their deaths.

10. This suggests a contrast between women's experiences on the prairies and the plains. Glenda Riley does not find this contrast. She discovers, instead, a female frontier that transcends geographic divisions. According to Riley, women's focus on female tasks—such as domestic production, childcare, and family relationships—meant that the resources of an area affected them only secondarily (Riley 1988, 2, 195). My work suggests that the level of poverty, the proximity of neighbors, and the availability of services *did* affect the women's work and their social lives.

CHAPTER 4

1. The concept of organic solidarity derives from sociologist Émile Durkheim's (1947) analysis of the division of labor. Organic solidarity is based on a division of labor that makes individuals dependent on one another for survival. It contrasts with mechanical solidarity, which is based on everyone's doing the same work.

2. Carole Larson, a lawyer practicing in rural Saunders County, Nebraska, is my authority on legal issues. Jule Sandoz, son of "Old Jules," relates an exceptional incident in which his mother successfully stood in the way of a land transfer by refusing to sign her name to the sale of the Nebraska property she and Jules owned together. Jules attacked his wife—either to persuade her to change her mind or maybe, failing that, to kill her and gain sole ownership of the property. According to son Jule, only his interference saved his mother's life. She did not sign, and the property was not sold (Pifer and Sandoz 1987, 82).

3. Luna Kellie (1926, 77) gives an account of a married woman in central Nebraska who declared herself the head of the family and recorded a homestead entry in her name. Kellie notes this as an oddity, however, explaining that the husband had had a major business failure from which he had never recovered and was, therefore, unable to transact business. The role reversal was exceptional enough to require an explanation and was apparently the only such case of which Kellie knew.

4. Outside of the Boone County vicinity there were isolated instances of single European American women who farmed, usually for short periods of time (Miller 1896b; Lambrigger 1897). Homesteading without actually farming was

not unusual for single women. Edith Eudora Kohl's account of homesteading with her sister in South Dakota is about nonfarming women. In fact, Kohl (1986, 8) specifically mentions that homesteading was more expensive for women than for men because women had to hire labor to get things done. Similarly, the letters of Elizabeth Corey (1990), who homesteaded in South Dakota in 1909, made clear that Corey did none of the physical farm labor of proving up her homestead. Historian Paula Nelson (1986, 47) found that single women homesteaders rarely took more then a minimal part in the actual farm work. Usually they supported themselves with "women's" jobs such as teaching, cooking, and maid work. Some research on women's homesteading—particularly that based on homesteading records—combines information on women who were operating farms and those who were not (Webb 1989).

5. The number of eggs sold in Boone County increased from 247,439 dozen in 1909 to 334,884 dozen in 1919, and then to 703,330 dozen in 1929 (Census 1913b, 39; 1932a, 1223). In 1909, 162,422 pounds of butterfat (in cream) were sold in Boone County, compared with 680,969 pounds in 1929 and 575,050 pounds in 1939. Most of the intermediate increase occurred because women had shifted from the selling of butter to the selling of butterfat in cream. The amount of butter sold decreased from 471,698 pounds in 1909 to 20,764 pounds in 1929 to 2,703 pounds in 1939 (Census 1913b, 39; 1932a, 1265; 1942, 602). This shift coincided with the adoption of the centrifugal cream separator.

6. Data are from the 1900 manuscript census for Boone County.

7. A moving five-year average of the number of divorces in Boone County from 1889 to 1904 shows a 50 percent increase during that time (Census 1908, 727):

1889	4.4	1897	5.6
1890	5.0	1898	5.8
1891	5.6	1899	6.8
1892	4.4	1900	7.0
1893	4.2	1901	6.4
1894	5.4	1902	6.6
1895	5.0	1903	7.0
1896	5.4	1904	6.6

There are no county statistics available on divorces between 1906 and 1940, but the overall state level showed an increase (Stouffer and Spencer 1938–39, 553).

8. Data are from the 1910 manuscript census.

9. These trends can be seen in the 1900 and 1910 manuscript censuses of Oakland Precinct and Albion.

10. "Family," as used in this account of dividing an estate, could not have referred to the nuclear family of husband, wife, and children. For purposes of property ownership, people tended to think in terms of the extended family.

CHAPTER 5

1. Computed from National Office of Vital Statistics (1946, 209); USDHEW (1973, 31); and Census (1975, 64).

2. Data on estates are from volumes 41–43 of the Probate Record in the Boone County Courthouse. These three volumes include 161 probated estates, of which 58 involved wills.

3. In contrast, only four married women wrote wills in this period, two of them naming their husbands as executors. The other two women left their husbands minimal property and named third parties as executors.

CHAPTER 6

1. Claudia Koonz (1987) has described the parallel ways in which Nazi women's softness and otherworldliness enabled Nazi men to carry out their plans without holding themselves morally culpable. Although the removal of Native Americans from the plains was not as well coordinated as was the Third Reich's genocide, its effects were even more devastating for the people involved.

2. In contrast, Elizabeth Hampsten (1982, 9) found discussions of sexuality to be "consistently present" in the writings of working-class women in North Dakota. The question hinges, in part, on the definition of sexuality and on how transparent and direct a sexual remark must be. Hampsten (1982, 127–29) gave an example of a mother's sentimentalizing her daughter's sexuality when she wrote about the daughter not having a beau. This is both more general and more indirect than what I consider to be a discussion of sexuality.

3. This situation is similar to that described for women in Michigan, where a father, even though he had legal custody, would frequently disperse his small children among his wife's female kin at her death (Motz 1983, 85).

4. Data on households are taken from the 1900 and 1910 U.S. census schedules for Boone County.

5. For a more detailed examination of household composition and number of children, see Fink and Carriquiry (1990).

6. I have taken thirty-five to forty-four as my age range for purposes of comparison even though most of these women would still have been fertile. This afforded a control for differing fertility by age. Had women who were past childbearing age by 1900 (those aged forty-five to fifty-four, for instance) been used for comparison, a larger percentage of the fertility rate would reflect their behavior preceding their recent arrival in Boone County. In addition, more women in an older age range could conceivably have retired from farming within the ten years studied because of age or death rather than farm failure, particularly as the majority of wives were younger than their husbands.

7. A possible alternative hypothesis is that more prosperous farming families

would have more children, regardless of their utility as farm workers. Relative prosperity of the farm operation represents a third variable that might independently affect both the likelihood of a family's remaining on the farm and the number of children. It was impossible to test this variable using census data.

8. The 1900 and 1910 census counts of Oakland Precinct each show that approximately 5 percent of the households included grown children and their parents.

CHAPTER 7

1. Mimi Abramovitz (1988, 191, 203) relates the Progressive period child welfare reforms to a concern with children as a natural resource. The capitalist system was not paying wages that would enable the working class to reproduce itself, and the state stepped in to meet the shortfall without challenging the capitalist economy (Zaretsky 1986, 104).

2. It was not until 1953, after post–World War II mechanization relieved the labor needs of farms, that the Nebraska legislature omitted the exception for necessary labor and stated that fourteen- and fifteen-year-olds had to be in school rather than working.

3. This exception did not apply to children of migrant laborers, who were not required to attend school (Trattner 1970, 204).

4. George Stewart of Albion, the Boone County welfare director in the late 1930s, compiled a complete record of the number of cases (without listing names of recipients) and the amount of money given out each month in 1939. Information on Boone County welfare in the 1930s comes from his personal records.

REFERENCES

Abramovitz, Mimi
1988   *Regulating the Lives of Women: Social Welfare Policy from Colonial Times to the Present*. Boston: South End Press.

Albion Argus
1935   14 March.
1938   13 January.

Albion News
1936   9 January.
1937   14 January.
1939   12 October.

Alcott, Alice
1906   Letter. *Nebraska Farmer* 38:412.

Aldrich, Bess Streeter
1928   *A Lantern in Her Hand*. New York: D. Appleton.

Anthan, George
1987   "Poll Shows Public Likes Farmers, Farm Subsidies." *Des Moines Register* (18 January): 2C.

Appleby, Joyce
1984   *Capitalism and a New Social Order: The Republican Vision of the 1790s*. New York: New York University Press.

Armitage, Susan H.
1982   "Reluctant Pioneers." In *Women and Western American Literature*, edited by Helen Winter Stauffer and Susan J. Rosowski, 40–51. Troy, N.Y.: Whitson Publishing Company.

Atkeson, Mary Meek
1929   "Women in Farm Life and Rural Economy." *Annals of the American Academy of Political and Social Science* 143:188–94.

Baier, Hazel
1935   "Sheep Are Her Hobby." *Nebraska Farmer* 77 (27 April): 6.

Bailey, Liberty Hyde
1911   *The Country-Life Movement in the United States*. New York: Macmillan.

1915   *The Holy Earth*. New York: Charles Scribner's Sons.

Bailey, Liberty Hyde, Henry Wallace, Kenyon L. Butterfield, Walter H. Page,
Gifford Pinchot, C. S. Barrett, and W. A. Beard

1909   *Report of the Country Life Commissioner: Special Message from the
            President of the United States Transmitting the Report of the
            Country Life Commission*. Washington, D.C.: Government Printing
            Office.

Ball, F. (Mrs.)

1896   "Absoluteness of the Marriage Tie." *Nebraska Farmer* 20:216.

Baltensperger, Bradley H.

1985   *Nebraska: A Geography*. Boulder, Colo.: Westview Press.

Barns, Cass

1970   *The Sod House*. Lincoln: University of Nebraska Press.
[1930]

BCDC. *See* Boone County District Court

Beal, George M.

1947   "Economic Aspects of the Family Farm Unit." Master's thesis,
            Iowa State College.

Bean, Lee L., Geraldine P. Mineau, and Douglas L. Anderton

1990   *Fertility Change on the American Frontier: Adaptation and
            Innovation*. Berkeley: University of California Press.

Bender, Donald R.

1967   "A Redefinement of the Concept of Household: Families, Co-
            resident and Domestic Functions." *American Anthropologist*
            69:493–504.

Berkner, Lutz K.

1975   "The Use and Misuse of Census Data for the Historical Analysis
            of Family Structure." *Journal of Interdisciplinary History* 5:721–
            38.

Berry, Wendell

1977   *The Unsettling of America: Culture and Agriculture*. San Francisco:
            Sierra Club Books.

Biedermann, Henry W.

1930   "Hens Pay for Home Conveniences." *Nebraska Farmer* 72:801.

Bloch, Ruth H.

1978   "American Feminine Ideals in Transition: The Rise of the Moral
            Mother, 1785–1815." *Feminist Studies* 4:100–120.

Blood-Patterson, Peter, ed.

1988   *Rise Up Singing*. Bethlehem, Pa.: Sing Out Corporation.

Boone County

1933   Probate Record No. 1963. Boone County Courthouse, Albion,
            Nebraska.

Boone County District Court (BCDC), Boone County Courthouse, Albion,
Nebraska

1930   Case no. 3671.

1931   Case nos. 3810, 3811.

1935   Case no. 4385.

1937   Case no. 4664.

1938   Case no. 4838.

Boone County Extension Service, Boone County Courthouse, Albion, Nebraska

1938   Annual Report (manuscript).

1939   Annual Report (manuscript).

Boone County Historical Society

1986   *Boone County History, 1871–1985.* Dallas, Tex.: Curtis Media Corporation.

Bowers, William L.

1974   *The Country Life Movement in America, 1900–1920.* Port Washington, N.Y.: Kennikat Press.

Bradford, M. E.

1977   Introduction to *Arator: Being a Series of Agricultural Essays, Practical and Political, in Sixty-four Numbers,* by John Taylor. Indianapolis, Ind.: Liberty Classics.

Bremer, Richard G.

1976   *Agricultural Change in an Urban Age: The Loup Country of Nebraska, 1910–1970.* Lincoln: University of Nebraska Press.

Brown, Judith K.

1985   Introduction to *In Her Prime: A New View of Middle-aged Women,* edited by Judith K. Brown and Virginia Kern, 1–11. South Hadley, Mass.: Bergin and Garvey.

Bryan, William Jennings

1966   "Cross of Gold" Speech. In *A Populist Reader: Selections from the*
[1896]   *Works of American Populist Leaders,* edited by George Brown Tindall, 203–11. New York: Harper and Row.

Burma, John Harmon

1941   "A Study of Migration from a Nebraska County during the Drouth-Depression." Ph.D. diss., University of Nebraska.

Byfield, Hattie

1896   "The Farmer's Children." *Nebraska Farmer* 20:504.

1906   "Some Things to Think About." *Nebraska Farmer* 38:1005.

Cape, Mrs.

1931   "Letter to Walter Gifford." President's Organization of Unemployment Relief. RG 78, box 185, 620.1, Nebraska. National Archives, Washington, D.C.

Cather, Willa

1918   *My Ántonia.* Boston: Houghton Mifflin.

1967   *Not Under Forty.* New York: Knopf.
[1936]

Census. *See* U.S. Bureau of the Census

Chodorow, Nancy

1978   *The Reproduction of Mothering: Psychoanalysis and the Sociology of Gender.* Berkeley: University of California Press.

Clark, M. Ruth

1931   *The Contribution of Nebraska Farm Women to Family Income through Poultry and Dairy Products.* Bulletin no. 258. Lincoln: University of Nebraska, Agricultural Experiment Station.

Collier, Jane, Michelle Z. Rosaldo, and Sylvia Yanagisako

1982   "Is There a Family?: New Anthropological Views." In *Rethinking the Family: Some Feminist Questions,* edited by Barrie Thorne, 25–39. New York: Longman.

Comstock, Gary, ed.

1987   *Is There a Moral Obligation to Save the Family Farm?* Ames: Iowa State University Press.

Corey, Elizabeth

1990   *Bachelor Bess: The Homesteading Letters of Elizabeth Corey, 1909–1919,* edited by Philip L. Gerber. Iowa City: University of Iowa Press.

Cott, Nancy F.

1977   *The Bonds of Womanhood: "Woman's Sphere" in New England, 1780–1835.* New Haven, Conn.: Yale University Press.

"Country Girl"

1896   Letter. *Nebraska Farmer* 20:216.

Cowan, Ruth Schwartz

1983   "Two Washes in the Morning and a Bridge Party at Night: The American Housewife between the Wars." In *Decades of Discontent: The Women's Movement, 1920–1940,* edited by Lois Scharf and Joan M. Jensen, 177–96. Westport, Conn.: Greenwood Press.

Creigh, Dorothy Weyer

1977   *Nebraska: A Bicentennial History.* New York: W. W. Norton.

Danbom, David B.

1979   *The Resisted Revolution: Urban America and the Industrialization of Agriculture, 1900–1930.* Ames: Iowa State University Press.

Davis, John Emmeus

1980   "Capitalist Agricultural Development and the Exploitation of the Propertied Laborer." In *The Rural Sociology of the Advanced Societies: Critical Perspectives,* edited by Frederick H. Buttel and Howard Newby, 133–53. Montclair, N.J.: Allanheld, Osmun.

Day, Barbara, and Karlie Koinzan

1977   "The Saga of Billy Mills." In *Wheeler County History Book,* 173–74.

Degler, Carl N.
1980   *At Odds: Women and the Family from the Revolution to the Present.*
           New York: Oxford University Press.
de Janvry, Alain
1980   "Social Differentiation in Agriculture and the Ideology of
           Neopopulism." In *The Rural Sociology of the Advanced Societies:
           Critical Perspectives*, edited by Frederick H. Buttel and Howard
           Newby, 155–68. Montclair, N.J.: Allanheld, Osmun.
Dick, Everett
1975   *Conquering the Great American Desert: Nebraska.* Publication no.
           27. Lincoln: Nebraska State Historical Society.
Diggs, Annie L. (Mrs.)
1892   "The Women in the Alliance Movement." *Arena* 6:161–79.
Dill, Bonnie Thornton
1988   "Our Mothers' Grief: Racial Ethnic Women and the Maintenance
           of Families." *Journal of Family History* 13:415–31.
Dinnerstein, Dorothy
1976   *The Mermaid and the Minotaur: Sexual Arrangements and Human
           Malaise.* New York: Harper and Row.
Dobry, George
1938   "She Switched to Turkeys." *Nebraska Farmer* 80 (16 July):
           18.
Drummond, Lee
1978   "The Transatlantic Nanny: Notes on a Comparative Semiotics of
           the Family in English-Speaking Societies." *American Ethnologist*
           5:30–43.
Durkheim, Émile
1947   *The Division of Labor in Society.* Translated by George Simpson.
[1893]   Glencoe, Ill.: Free Press.
Durland, Mrs. A. J.
1902   "The Mutual Benefits of Rest Rooms." *Nebraska Farmer* 30:369.
Easterlin, Richard A.
1976   "Factors in the Decline of Farm Family Fertility in the United
           States: Some Preliminary Research Results." *Journal of American
           History* 63:600–614.
Eblen, Jack
1965   "An Analysis of the Nineteenth-Century Frontier Population."
           Demography 2:399–413.
Edwards, Mrs. J. F.
1902   "Rest Rooms." *Nebraska Farmer* 30:473.
Einstadter, Werner J.
1978   "Robbery-Outlawry on the U.S. Frontier, 1863–1890: A
           Reexamination." In *Violent Crime: Historical and Contemporary*

Issues, edited by James A. Inciardi and Anne E. Pottieger, 21–35. Beverly Hills, Calif.: Sage.

Elbert, Sarah

1987   "The Farmer Takes a Wife: Women in America's Farming Families." In *Women, Households, and the Economy*, edited by Lourdes Benería and Catharine R. Stimpson, 173–97. New Brunswick, N.J.: Rutgers University Press.

1988   "Women and Farming: Changing Structures, Changing Roles." In *Women and Farming: Changing Roles, Changing Structures*, edited by Wava G. Haney and Jane B. Knowles, 245–64. Boulder, Colo.: Westview Press.

Elder, Glen H., Jr.

1974   *Children of the Great Depression*. Chicago: University of Chicago Press.

Fairbanks, Carol, and Sara Brooks Sundberg

1983   *Farm Women on the Prairie Frontier: A Sourcebook for Canada and the United States*. Metuchen, N.J.: Scarecrow Press.

Faragher, John Mack

1979   *Women and Men on the Overland Trail*. New Haven, Conn.: Yale University Press.

1981   "History from the Inside-Out: Writing the History of Women in Rural America." *American Quarterly* 33:537–57.

Farm Security Administration. *See* FSA

Fedde, Margaret, and Ruth Lindquist

1935   *A Study of Farm Families and Their Standards of Living in Selected Districts of Nebraska, 1931–1933*. Research Bulletin no. 78. Lincoln: University of Nebraska, Agricultural Experiment Station.

Fink, Deborah

1986   *Open Country, Iowa: Rural Women, Tradition, and Change*. Albany: State University of New York Press.

1987a   "Farming in Open Country, Iowa: Women and the Changing Farm Economy." In *Farm Work and Field Work: Anthropological Studies of North American Agriculture*, edited by Michael Chibnik, 121–44. Ithaca, N.Y.: Cornell University Press.

1987b   "Rediscovering Small Town Violence." *Plainswoman* 11 (3): 5–7.

1988   "Sidelines and Moral Capital: Women on Nebraska Farms in the 1930s." In *Women and Farming: Changing Roles, Changing Structures*, edited by Wava G. Haney and Jane B. Knowles, 55–72. Boulder, Colo.: Westview Press.

1990   "Farm Wives and Agrarianism in the United States." In *Key Papers Number 1: Rural Women*, edited by Margaret Alston, 1–7. Wagga Wagga, New South Wales, Australia: Centre for Rural Welfare Research.

1991   "Separate and Not Equal: Agrarian Ideology and Gender in Rural
            Nebraska." Paper presented at annual meeting of the Society for
            Applied Anthropology, Charleston, S.C., March.
Fink, Deborah, and Alicia Carriquiry
1990   "Who Had Lots of Babies and Who Didn't: Household
            Composition and Fertility Levels in Rural Iowa and Rural
            Nebraska, 1900–1910." Paper presented at Social Science
            and History Association meeting, Minneapolis, Minn.,
            October.
Fink, Deborah, and Mikel Johnson
1988   "The Land Owns Itself: An Historical Approach to a Feminist
            Land Ethic." Paper presented at conference, Explorations in
            Feminist Ethics. Duluth, Minn., October.
Fite, Gilbert C.
1959   "Flight from the Farm." *Nebraska History* 40:159–76.
1966   *The Farmers' Frontier, 1865–1900.* Albuquerque: University of
            New Mexico Press.
1985   "'The Only Thing Worth Working For': Land and Its Meaning for
            Pioneer Dakotans." *South Dakota History* 15:2–25.
Flora, Cornelia Butler
1986   "Values and the Agricultural Crisis: Differential Problems,
            Solutions, and Value Constraints." *Agriculture and Human Values*
            3 (4): 16–23.
1988   "Public Policy and Women in Agricultural Production: A
            Comparative and Historical Analysis." In *Women and Farming:
            Changing Roles, Changing Structure,* edited by Wava G. Haney and
            Jane B. Knowles, 265–80. Boulder, Colo.: Westview Press.
Flora, Cornelia Butler, and John Stitz
1988   "Female Subsistence Production and Commercial Farm Survival
            among Settlement Kansas Wheat Farmers." *Human Organization*
            47:64–69.
Folbre, Nancy
1983   "Of Patriarchy Born: The Political Economy of Fertility
            Decisions." *Feminist Studies* 9:261–84.
Friedmann, Harriet
1978   "World Market, State and Family Farm: Social Bases of
            Household Production in the Era of Wage Labour." *Comparative
            Studies in Society and History* 20:545–86.
FSA (Farm Security Administration)
✓ 1938   "Home Supervisor Narrative." Case 505-32-14-139664, RG 96,
            FSA Lin, Farm Ownership Cases, 1938–46, Axt-Bec. National
            Archives Repository, Kansas City.
1939   Instruction 611.1, "Farm Tenancy Family Selection," RG 96, FSA

Lin, General Correspondence, 1935–42, 505, "Relocation, General." National Archives Repository, Kansas City.

1940   Report (February). Papers of Governor Robert LeRoy Cochran, Box 33, Folder 656. State Archives, Nebraska State Historical Society, Lincoln.

1941   Letter. Case 505-32-39-133110, RG 96, RSA Lin, Farm Ownership Cases, 1938–46, Bur-Butt. National Archives Repository, Kansas City.

Fuller, Raymond G.

1923   *Child Labor and the Constitution.* New York: Thomas Y. Crowell.

G.S.H.

1906   "The Mother's Joy." *Nebraska Farmer* 38:128.

Galpin, Charles Josiah

1923   *Rural Life.* New York: The Century Company.

Garland, Hamlin

1962   "A Day's Pleasure." In *Main Travelled Roads,* 173–81. New York:
[1899]   Signet.

1969   "Under the Lion's Paw." In *Agrarianism in American Literature,*
[1891]   edited by M. Thomas Inge, 154–65. New York: Odyssey Press.

Gilman, Charlotte Perkins. *See also* Stetson, Charlotte Perkins

✓ 1909   "That Rural Home Inquiry." *Good Housekeeping* 48 (1): 120–22.

Good Housekeeping

1909   "A *Good Housekeeping* Commission." 48 (1): 122.

Goody, Jack

1976   *Production and Reproduction: A Comprehensive Study of the Domestic Domain.* Cambridge: Cambridge University Press.

Gordon, Linda

1976   *Woman's Body, Woman's Right: A Social History of Birth Control in America.* New York: Grossman/Viking.

1982   "Why Nineteenth-Century Feminists Did Not Support 'Birth Control' and Twentieth-Century Feminists Do: Feminism, Reproduction, and the Family." In *Rethinking the Family: Some Feminist Questions,* edited by Barrie Thorne, 40–53. New York: Longman.

1986   "Family Violence, Feminism, and Social Control." *Feminist Studies* 12:452–78.

1988   *Heroes of Their Own Lives: The Politics and History of Family Violence, Boston 1880–1960.* New York: Viking.

Graulich, Melody

1983   "Every Husband's Right: Sex Roles in Mari Sandoz's *Old Jules.*" *Western American Literature* 18:3–20.

1984   "Violence against Women in Literature of the Western Family." *Frontiers* 8 (3): 14–20.

1989   "'O Beautiful for Spacious Guys': An Essay on the 'Legitimate
              Inclinations of the Sexes.'" In The Frontier and the American
              Dream: Essays on American Literature, edited by David Mogen,
              Mark Busby, and Paul Bryant, 31–49. College Station: Texas
              A&M University Press.

Griswold, A. Whitney
1946   "The Agrarian Democracy of Thomas Jefferson." American
              Political Science Review 40:657–81.
1971   "Jefferson's Agrarian Democracy." In Thomas Jefferson and
[1948]   American Democracy, edited by Henry C. Dethloff, 39–58.
              Lexington, Mass.: D. C. Heath.

Hammel, E. A., Sheila R. Johansson, and Caren A. Ginsberg
1983   "The Value of Children during Industrialization: Sex Ratios in
              Childhood in Nineteenth-Century America." Journal of Family
              History 8:346–66.

Hampsten, Elizabeth
1982   Read This Only to Yourself: The Private Writings of Midwestern
              Women. Bloomington: Indiana University Press.
1989   "The Nehers and the Martins in North Dakota." In Far from
              Home: Families of the Westward Journey, edited by Lillian
              Schlissel, Byrd Gibbons, and Elizabeth Hampsten, 175–229. New
              York: Schocken.

Hargreaves, Mary W. M.
1976   "Women of the Agricultural Settlement of the Northern Plains."
              Agricultural History 50:179–89.

Harkin, Tom
1988   Foreword to Raising Less Corn and More Hell, by Jim Schwab.
              Urbana: University of Illinois Press.

Harris, Katherine
1984   "Sex Roles and Work Patterns among Homesteading Families in
              Northeastern Colorado, 1873–1920." Frontiers 7 (3): 43–49.

Harris, Olivia
1981   "Households as Natural Units." In Of Marriage and the Market:
              Women's Subordination Internationally and Its Lessons, edited by
              Kate Young, Carol Wolkowitz, and Roslyn McCullagh, 136–55.
              London: Routledge and Kegan Paul.

Hartman, Heidi I.
1981   "The Family as the Locus of Gender, Class, and Political Struggle:
              The Example of Housework." Signs 6:366–94.

Hawks, Nellie
1892a   "One of Our Afternoon Visits." Nebraska Farmer 16:40.
1892b   "Swinging in the Hammock in the Shade." Nebraska Farmer
              16:520.

1896a   "How Women May Make Money." *Nebraska Farmer* 20:312.

1896b   "Maternity." *Nebraska Farmer* 20:489.

1896c   "Reply to Penticost." *Nebraska Farmer* 20:329.

Haynes, Richard P., ed.

1985   "The Land, the Agrarian Tradition, and the Common Good."
         Agriculture and Human Values 4 (2). Special issue.

1990   "Agrarianism and the American Philosophical Tradition."
         Agriculture and Human Values 7 (1). Special issue.

Helmbold, Lois Rita

1987   "Beyond the Family Economy: Black and White Working-Class
         Women during the Great Depression." *Feminist Studies* 13:629–
         55.

"Hired Girl"

1896   "Hired Girl Seeks Advice." *Nebraska Farmer* 20:648.

Hodgkin, Carlyle

1935a   "First Homesteader." *Nebraska Farmer* 77 (14 September): 1, 18.

1935b   "Resident Number One." *Nebraska Farmer* 77 (16 February): 1,
         27.

Hofstadter, Richard

1955   *The Age of Reform: From Bryan to F.D.R.* New York: Knopf.

1956   "The Myth of the Happy Yeoman." *American Heritage* 7 (April):
         42–53.

Holder, Preston

1970   *The Hoe and the Horse on the Plains: A Study of Cultural
         Development among North American Indians.* Lincoln: University of
         Nebraska Press.

Hoy, Nancy Jo

1987   "One Orange for Christmas: An Interview with Meridel LeSueur."
         Iowa Woman 7 (1): 14–22.

Ise, John

1936   *Sod and Stubble: The Story of a Kansas Homestead.* Lincoln:
         University of Nebraska Press.

Jefferson, Thomas

1784   "Notes on Virginia," 185–288.

1785a   Letter to John Jay, 377–78.

1785b   Letter to Reverend James Madison, 388–90.

1787a   Journal entry, 135. ✔

1787b   Letter to Martha Jefferson, 417–20.

1816   Letter to John Taylor, 668–73.

1818   Letter to Nathaniel Burwell, 687–89.

         All in *The Life and Selected Writings of Thomas Jefferson*, edited by
         Adrienne Koch and William Peden. New York: Modern Library,
         1944.

1788   Letter. In *Writings*, 922–23. New York: Library of
          America/Viking, 1984.
1829   *Autobiography*. Introduction by Dumas Malone. New York:
          Capricorn Books, 1959.
Jeffrey, Julie Roy
1975   "Women in the Southern Farmers' Alliance: A Reconsideration of
          the Role and Status of Women in the Late Nineteenth-Century
          South." *Feminist Sudies* 3:72–91.
Jensen, Joan M.
1981   *With These Hands: Women Working on the Land*. Old Westbury,
          N.Y.: Feminist Press.
1986   *Loosening the Bonds: Mid-Atlantic Farm Women, 1750–1850*. New
          Haven, Conn.: Yale University Press.
Johnson, Alvin
1952   *Pioneer's Progress*. New York: Viking.
Johnson, Hannah Priscilla Patterson
1880–84   Diary (manuscript copy in D. Fink's possession).
Juster, Norman
1979   *So Sweet to Labor: Rural Women in America, 1865–1895*. New
          York: Viking.
Kearney, Fannie H.
1895   Letter. *Nebraska Farmer* 19:152.
Kellie, Luna E.
1920   "The Farmers' Alliance in Nebraska." Manuscript no. 2623, State
          Archives, Nebraska State Historical Society, Lincoln.
1926   "Memoirs." Manuscript no. 3914, State Archives, Nebraska State
          Historical Society, Lincoln.
Kerber, Linda K.
1980   *Women of the Republic: Intellect and Ideology in Revolutionary
          America*. Chapel Hill: University of North Carolina Press.
Kirk, Eleanor
1891   "Household." *Nebraska Farmer* 15:283.
Kohl, Edith Eudora
1986   *Land of the Burnt Thigh*. Introduction by Glenda Riley. St. Paul:
[1938]   Minnesota Historical Society Press.
Kohl, Seena
1976   *Working Together: Women and Family in Southwestern
          Saskatchewan*. Toronto: Holt, Rinehart and Winston of Canada.
Kolodny, Annette
1975   *The Lay of the Land: Metaphor as Experience and History in
          American Life and Letters*. Chapel Hill: University of North
          Carolina Press.
1984   *The Land Before Her: Fantasy and Experience of the American*

Frontiers, 1630–1860. Chapel Hill: University of North Carolina Press.

Koonz, Claudia

1987   Mothers in the Fatherland: Women, the Family, and Nazi Politics. New York: St. Martin's Press.

Lambrigger, L. E. R. (Mrs.)

1896   "Let the Whole Truth Be Told." Nebraska Farmer 20:610.

1897   "Pioneering in Nebraska." Nebraska Farmer 21:118.

Lappé, Frances Moore

1989   "Saving the Family Farm Can Benefit Us All." Utne Reader 34:86.

Lawrence, Elizabeth Atwood

1982   Rodeo: An Anthropologist Looks at the Wild and the Tame. Chicago: University of Chicago Press.

Leadley, Thomas A.

1935   "Shall Congress Control Our Children?" Nebraska Farmer 77 (2 February): 1, 24.

Lebsock, Suzanne

1984   The Free Women of Petersburg: Status and Culture in a Southern Town, 1784–1860. New York: W. W. Norton.

Lederer, Louis

1944   "My First 70 Years, 1874–1944" (manuscript copy in D. Fink's possession).

Lee, L. L., and Merrill Lewis, eds.

1979   Women, Women Writers, and the West. Troy, N.Y.: Whitson Publishing Company.

Lee, Richard

1979   The !Kung San. Cambridge: Cambridge University Press.

Lewis, Faye C.

1971   Nothing to Make a Shadow. Ames: Iowa State University Press.

Literary Digest

1920   "Why Young Women Are Leaving Our Farms." 67:56–58.

Long, Francis A.

1937   A Prairie Doctor of the Eighties: Some Personal Recollections and Some Early Medical and Social History of the Prairie State. Norfolk, Nebr.: Huse Publishing Company.

Long, Maggie E.

1937   "The Prairie Doctor's Wife." In A Prairie Doctor of the Eighties, by Francis A. Long. Norfolk, Nebr.: Huse Publishing Company.

McKenney, Ellen

1935   "Outlook and Inlook." Nebraska Farmer 77 (16 February): 6–7.

MacLeod, Duncan

1980   "The Political Economy of John Taylor of Caroline." Journal of American Studies 14:387–405.

Malone, Dumas
1962   *Jefferson and His Time*. Vol. 3, *Jefferson and the Ordeal of Liberty*.
            Boston: Little, Brown.
Mann, Susan Archer
1990   *Agrarian Capitalism in Theory and Practice*. Chapel Hill:
            University of North Carolina Press.
Mead, Margaret
1935   *Sex and Temperament in Three Primitive Societies*. New York:
            William Morrow.
Miller, Rose Seelye
1896a   "Maternity." *Nebraska Farmer* 20:232.
1896b   "Women Farmers of Dakota." *Nebraska Farmer* 20:568–69 (pt. 1),
            588–89 (pt. 2).
Mohr, James C.
1982   "Abortion in America." In *Women's America: Refocusing the Past*,
            edited by Linda K. Kerber and Jane DeHart Mathews, 179–89.
            New York: Oxford University Press.
Mooney, Patrick H.
1983   "Toward a Class Analysis of Midwestern Agriculture." *Rural
            Sociology* 48:563–84.
1986   *My Own Boss? Class, Rationality, and the Family Farm*. Boulder,
            Colo.: Westview Press.
Motz, Marilyn Ferris
1983   *True Sisterhood: Michigan Women and Their Kin, 1820–1920*.
            Albany: State University of New York Press.
Mundschenk, William K.
1986   "Boone County." In *Boone County History, 1871–1985*, 1–38.
            Dallas, Tex.: Curtis Media Corporation for the Boone County
            Historical Society.
Myres, Sandra L.
1982   *Westering Women and the Frontier Experience, 1800–1925*.
            Albuquerque: University of New Mexico Press.
National Office of Vital Statistics, U.S. Public Health Service, Federal Security
Agency
1946   *Marriage and Divorce in the United States, 1937 to 1945*. Vol. 23,
            no. 9. Washington, D.C.: Government Printing Office.
Nebraska
1887   *Laws of Nebraska*, Act of 19 February 1875, 79–80. The
            Legislature of the State of Nebraska at the 11th Session.
1907   *Laws of Nebraska*, chap. 50, 198–99. The Legislature of the State
            of Nebraska at the 30th Session.
Nebraska Farmer
1892   Advertisement. 16:463.

1896   "Her Sod Home." 20:313.
1903a   Advertisement. 35:494.
1903b   Advertisement. 35:1022.
1915   "Home Circle." 40:960.
1930   "Home Circle." 72:708.
1932a   Editorial. 74 (26 November): 4.
1932b   "How We Earn Extra Money." 74 (2 April): 10.
1932c   "Poultry Paid 1931 Bills." 74 (6 February): 3, 19.
1935a   "Day by Day." 77 (26 October): 12.
1935b   Editorial. 77 (16 February): 36.
1935c   "Young Love Laughs at If's." 77 (6 July): 8.
1936   "Diary of a Farm Woman." 78 (1 August): 10.
1937a   Letter. 79 (8 May): 12.
1937b   "Oratory Champion." 79 (22 May): 11.
1938a   "Let's Talk It Over." 80 (26 March): 6.
1938b   "Let's Talk It Over." 80 (7 May): 14.

Nelsen, Jane Taylor
1989   "History from 'The Inside-Out': Luna Kellie and the Mid-Road
            Populist Movement in Nebraska." Undergraduate Honor Thesis,
            American Studies, University of Iowa.

Nelson, Paula M.
1986   *After the West Was Won: Homesteaders and Town Builders in
            Western South Dakota, 1900–1917.* Iowa City: University of Iowa
            Press.

Neth, Mary
1988   "Building the Base: Farm Women, the Rural Community, and
            Farm Organizations in the Midwest, 1900–1940." In *Women and
            Farming: Changing Roles, Changing Structures*, edited by Wava G.
            Haney and Jane B. Knowles, 339–55. Boulder, Colo.: Westview
            Press.

Newton, Isaac
1863   *Report of the Commissioner of Agriculture, 1862.* U.S. Department
            of Agriculture. Washington, D.C.: Government Printing Office.

Okun, Bernard
1958   *Trends in Birth Rates in the United States since 1870.* Johns
            Hopkins University Studies in Historical and Political Science,
            ser. 76, no. 1. Baltimore, Md.: Johns Hopkins University Press.

Olsen, Tillie
1981   "Tell Me a Riddle." In *Tell Me a Riddle*, 72–125. New York: Dell.
[1961]

Olson, James C.
1966   *History of Nebraska.* 2d ed. Lincoln: University of Nebraska Press.

Opie, John
1987   *The Law of the Land: Two Hundred Years of American Farmland
            Policy.* Lincoln: University of Nebraska Press.
Osterud, Nancy, and John Fulton
1976   "Family Limitation and Age at Marriage: Fertility Decline in
            Sturbridge, Massachusetts, 1730–1850." *Population Studies*
            30:481–94.
Papanek, Hanna
1979   "Family Status Production: The 'Work' and 'Non-Work' of
            Women." *Signs* 4:775–81.
Pateman, Carole
1988   *The Sexual Contract.* Stanford, Calif.: Stanford University Press.
Pease, Blanche
1940   "Moving Time." *Nebraska Farmer* 82 (23 March): 10.
Pease, R. L. (Mrs.)
1937   Letter. *Nebraska Farmer* 79 (5 June): 16.
"Penticost"
1896a   "Household, Another Side to the Picture." *Nebraska Farmer*
            20:328–29.
1896b   Letter. *Nebraska Farmer* 20:458.
Petchesky, Rosalind P.
1984   *Abortion and Woman's Choice: The State, Sexuality, and
            Reproductive Freedom.* Boston: Northeastern University Press.
Peterson, Tarla Rai
1990   "Jefferson's Yeoman Farmer as Frontier Hero: A Self-Defeating
            Mythic Structure." *Agriculture and Human Values* 7 (1): 9–19.
Pifer, Caroline Sandoz, and Jules Sandoz, Jr.
1987   *Son of Old Jules: Memoirs of Jules Sandoz, Jr.* Lincoln: University
            of Nebraska Press.
Potter, Minnie P.
1902   "Rest Rooms." *Nebraska Farmer* 30:445.
Progressive
1988   Review of *Remembering,* by Wendell Berry. 52 (December): 46–
            47.
Pyne, Stephen J.
1982   *Fire in America: A Cultural History of Wildland and Rural Fire.*
            Princeton, N.J.: Princeton University Press.
Quick, Herbert
1913   "The Women on the Farms." *Good Housekeeping* 57:426–
            36.
Quinowski, John
1935   Letter. *Nebraska Farmer* 77 (16 February): 36.

Rasmussen, L., L. Rasmussen, C. Savage, and A. Wheeler
1976   *A Harvest Yet to Reap: A History of Prairie Women.* Toronto: The
          Women's Press.
Rice, Frank
1970   "Growing Up in Mid-Nebraska, 1908–1970" (manuscript). State
          Archives, Nebraska State Historical Society, Lincoln.
Rich, Adrienne
1976   *Of Woman Born: Motherhood as Experience and Institution.* New
          York: W. W. Norton.
Riley, Glenda
1988   *The Female Frontier: A Comparative View of Women on the Prairie
          and the Plains.* Lawrence: University Press of Kansas.
Ritter, Darlene
1982   "Marie Louise Ritter: The Pioneer Woman in Fact and Fiction."
          In *Women and Western American Literature*, edited by Helen
          Winter Stauffer and Susan J. Rosowski, 17–27. Troy, N.Y.:
          Whitson Publishing Company.
Robbins, Roy Marvin
1935   "Horace Greeley: Land Reform and Unemployment, 1837–1862."
          Agricultural History 7:13–41.
Roosevelt, Theodore
1909   "Special Message to the Senate and House of Representatives, 9
          February." In *Report of the Country Life Commission.* U.S. Senate,
          60th Cong., 2d sess., S. Doc. 705. Washington, D.C.: Government
          Printing Office.
Ross, Joseph B.
1909   "The Agrarian Revolution in the Middle West." *North American
          Review* 190:376–91.
Ryan, Mary P.
1981   *Cradle of the Middle Class: The Family in Oneida County,
          New York, 1790–1865.* New York: Cambridge University
          Press.
1982   *The Empire of the Mother: American Writing about Domesticity,
          1830–1860.* New York: Haworth Press.
1983   *Womanhood in America: From Colonial Times to the Present.* 3d ed.
          New York: Franklin Watts.
Rynkiewich, Michael A., and James P. Spradley
1976   *Ethics and Anthropology: Dilemmas in Fieldwork.* New York: John
          Wiley.
Sachs, Carolyn E.
1983   *The Invisible Farmers: Women in Agricultural Production.* Totowa,
          N.J.: Rowman and Allanheld.

Sanday, Peggy Reeves
1981   "The Socio-Cultural Context of Rape." *Journal of Social Issues* 37
            (4): 5–27.
Sandoz, Mari
1935   *Old Jules*. Boston: Little, Brown.
1970   *Sandhill Sundays and Other Recollections*. Lincoln: University of
            Nebraska Press.
Sanford, Mollie Dorsey
1959   *Mollie: The Journal of Mollie Dorsey Sanford in Nebraska and
            Colorado Territories, 1857–1866*. Introduction and notes by
            Donald F. Danker. Lincoln: University of Nebraska Press.
Scharf, Lois
1980   *To Work and to Wed: Female Employment, Feminism, and the Great
            Depression*. Westport, Conn.: Greenwood Press.
Schlissel, Lillian
1982   *Women's Diaries of the Westward Journey*. New York: Schocken.
Schneider, David M.
1968   *American Kinship: A Cultural Account*. Englewood Cliffs, N.J.:
            Prentice-Hall.
1984   *A Critique of the Study of Kinship*. Ann Arbor: University of
            Michigan Press.
Schwab, Jim
1988   *Raising Less Corn and More Hell: Midwestern Farmers Speak Out*.
            Urbana: University of Illinois Press.
Schwieder, Dorothy, and Deborah Fink
√ 1988   "Plains Women: Rural Life in the 1930s." *Great Plains Quarterly*
            8:79–88.
Sheldon, Addison E.
1936   *Land Systems and Land Policies in Nebraska*. Publications of the
            Nebraska State Historical Society, vol. 22. Lincoln: Nebraska State
            Historical Society.
Smets, Laura Mae
1957   "I Lived in a Soddy." *Nebraska Farmer* 99 (18 May): 32.
Smith, Daniel Scott
1974   "Family Limitation, Sexual Control, and Domestic Feminism
            in Victorian America." In *Clio's Consciousness Raised: New
            Perspectives on the History of Women*, edited by Mary S.
            Hartman and Lois Banner, 119–36. New York: Harper
            Torchbooks.
Smith, Henry Nash
1950   *Virgin Land: The American West as Symbol and Myth*. Cambridge,
            Mass.: Harvard University Press.

Smith, J.

1892   "From Red Willow County." *Nebraska Farmer* 16:523.

Smith, Thurman A.

1939   "Settlers Come to the North Loup." *Nebraska Farmer* 81 (25 February): 3 (pt. 1), 81 (11 March): 22, 27 (pt. 2).

Smith-Rosenberg, Carroll

1982   "The Female World of Love and Ritual: Relations between Women
[1975]   in Nineteenth-Century America." In *Women's America: Refocusing the Past*, edited by Linda Kerber and Jane DeHart Mathews, 156–78. New York: Oxford University Press.

Snyder, Grace (as told to Nellie Snyder Yost)

1963   *No Time on My Hands*. Caldwell, Idaho: Caxton Printers.

Sparks, M. E. (Mrs.)

1903   "The Large Family." *Nebraska Farmer* 35:779.

Stauffer, Helen Winter, and Susan J. Rosowski, eds.

1982   *Women and Western American Literature*. Troy, N.Y.: Whitson Publishing Company.

Stetson, Charlotte Perkins

1896   "The Voting Mother." *Nebraska Farmer* 20:964.

Stewart, Elinore Pruitt (Mrs.)

1914   *Letters of a Woman Homesteader*. Boston: Houghton Mifflin.

Storer, Horatio Robinson

1974   *A Proper Bostonian on Sex and Birth Control*. New York: Arno
[1868]   Press.

Stouffer, Samuel A., and Lyle M. Spencer

1938–39   "Recent Increases in Marriage and Divorce." *American Journal of Sociology* 44:551–54.

Strange, Marty

1988   *Family Farming: A New Economic Vision*. Lincoln: University of Nebraska Press.

Stratton, Joanna L.

1981   *Pioneer Women: Voices from the Kansas Frontier*. New York: Simon and Schuster.

Sturdevant, C. D.

1935   Letter. *Nebraska Farmer* 77 (16 February): 36.

Suckow, Ruth

1926   "Renters." In *Iowa Interiors*, 37–49. New York: Knopf.

Swierenga, Robert P.

1968   *Pioneers and Profits: Land Speculation on the Iowa Frontier*. Ames: Iowa State University Press.

Sykes, Mrs. Hope Williams

1935   *The Second Hoeing*. New York: G. P. Putnam's Sons.

Tanner, Nancy
1974   "Matrifocality in Indonesia and Africa and among Black
          Americans." In *Woman, Culture, and Society*, edited by Michelle
          Zimbalist Rosaldo and Louise Lamphere, 129–56. Stanford, Calif.:
          Stanford University Press.

Taylor, John
1977   *Arator: Being a Series of Agricultural Essays, Practical and Political,*
[1818]   *in Sixty-four Numbers.* Edited and with an introduction by M. E.
          Bradford. Indianapolis, Ind.: Liberty Classics.

Taylor, Phebe J. (Mrs.)
1896a   Letter. *Nebraska Farmer* 20:569.

1896b   "Some Questions Answered." *Nebraska Farmer* 20:680.

Trattner, Walter I.
1970   *Crusade for the Children: The History of the National Child Labor
          Committee and Child Labor Reform in America.* Chicago:
          Quadrangle.

Turner, John
1903   *Pioneers of the West: A True Narrative.* Cincinnati, Ohio: Jennings
          and Pye.

U.S. Bureau of the Census
1895   *Report on the Population of the United States at the Eleventh
          Census, 1890: Part 1.* Washington, D.C.: Government Printing
          Office.

1900   *Twelfth Census of the United States, June 1, 1900: Instructions to
          Enumerators.* Washington, D.C.: Government Printing Office.

1901   *Twelfth Census of the United States, 1900.* Part 1, *Population.*
          Washington, D.C.: Government Printing Office.

1902   *Twelfth Census of the United States, 1900.* Vol. 2, *Population, Part
          2.* Washington, D.C.: Government Printing Office.

1908   *Special Reports: Marriage and Divorce, 1867–1906.* Washington,
          D.C.: Government Printing Office.

1913a   *Thirteenth Census of the United States, 1910.* Vol. 3, *Population,
          1910: Nebraska–Wyoming.* Washington, D.C.: Government
          Printing Office.

1913b   *Thirteenth Census of the United States, 1910.* Vol. 7, *Agriculture,
          1909 and 1910: Nebraska–Wyoming.* Washington, D.C.:
          Government Printing Office.

1922a   *Fourteenth Census of the United States, 1920.* Vol. 3, *Population,
          1920: Composition and Characteristics of the Population by States.*
          Washington, D.C.: Government Printing Office.

1922b   *Fourteenth Census of the United States, 1920.* Vol. 6, pt. 1,
          Agriculture. Washington, D.C.: Government Printing Office.

1924   *Fourteenth Census of the United States.* Vol. 2, *Population: General Report and Analytical Tables.* Washington, D.C.: Government Printing Office.

1932a   *Fifteenth Census of the United States, 1930.* Vol. 2, pt. 1, *Agriculture: The Northern States.* Washington, D.C.: Government Printing Office.

1932b   *Fifteenth Census of the United States, 1930.* Vol 3, pt. 2, *Population: Montana–Wyoming.* Washington, D.C.: Government Printing Office.

1942   *Sixteenth Census of the United States, 1940.* Vol. 1, pt. 2, *Agriculture: State Reports.* Washington, D.C.: Government Printing Office.

1943   *Sixteenth Census of the United States, 1940. Population. Internal Migration, 1935 to 1940: Color and Sex of Migrants.* Washington, D.C.: Government Printing Office.

1946   *Sixteenth Census of the United States, 1940. Population. Internal Migration, 1935 to 1940: Social Characteristics of the Migrants.* Washington, D.C.: Government Printing Office.

1952   *Census of the Population, 1950.* Vol. 2, pt. 27, *Characteristics of the Population: Nebraska.* Washington, D.C.: Government Printing Office.

1975   *Historical Statistics of the United States, Colonial Times to 1970.* Bicentennial Edition, pt. 2. Washington, D.C.: Government Printing Office.

1983   *Census of the Population, 1980.* Vol. 1, *Characteristics of the Population,* chap. C, pt. 29, "General Social and Economic Characteristics: Nebraska." Washington, D.C.: Government Printing Office.

1986   *Local Area Personal Income.* Vol. 1, *Summary, 1978–84.* Washington, D.C.: Government Printing Office.

USDA (U.S. Department of Agriculture)

1863   "Health of Farmers' Families, Part 2: Hardships of Farmers' Wives." In *Report of the Commissioner of Agriculture for the Year 1862,* 362–70. Washington, D.C.: Government Printing Office.

1872   "Industrial Education of Women." In *Report of the Commissioner of Agriculture for the Year 1871,* 336–46. Washington, D.C.: Government Printing Office.

√ 1915   Report 103, *Social and Labor Needs of Farm Women;* Report 104, *Domestic Needs of Farm Women;* Report 105, *Educational Needs of Farm Women;* Report 106, *Economic Needs of Farm Women.* Washington, D.C.: Government Printing Office.

USDHEW (U.S. Department of Health, Education, and Welfare)

1973   *One Hundred Years of Marriage and Divorce Statistics, United*

States, 1867–1967. Department of Health, Education, and Welfare
Publication No. 74-1902. Vital and Health Statistics, ser. 21 (Data
from National Vital Statistics System), no. 24. Washington, D.C.:
Government Printing Office.

Vach, Mrs. Jim

1930   "Biddy Pays the Bills." *Nebraska Farmer* 72:395.

Vanek, Joann

1980   "Work, Leisure, and Family Roles in Farm Households in the
United States, 1920–1955." *Journal of Family History* 5:422–31.

Wagner, MaryJo

1984   "Prairie Populists: Luna Kellie and Mary Elizabeth Lease." In
Northwest Women's Heritage, edited by Karen Blair, 200–210.
Seattle, Wash.: Northwest Center for Research on Women.

1988   "'Helping Papa and Mama Sing the People's Songs': Children in
the Populist Party." In *Women and Farming: Changing Roles,
Changing Structures*, edited by Wava G. Haney and Jane B.
Knowles, 319–37. Boulder, Colo.: Westview Press.

Wallace, Henry C.

1925   *Our Debt and Duty to the Farmer*. New York: The Century Company.

Ward, Florence E.

1920   *The Farm Woman's Problem*. Cooperative Extension Work in
Agriculture and Home Economics. U.S. Department of
Agriculture Circular 148. Washington, D.C.: Government Printing
Office.

Weaver, Anna Dee

1941   "Looking In on a Topnotch Cattle Sale." *Nebraska Farmer* 83 (18
October): 12–13.

Webb, Anne B.

1989   "Minnesota Women Homesteaders: 1863–1889." *Journal of Social
History* 23:115–36.

Webb, Walter Prescott

1931   *The Great Plains*. New York: Grosset and Dunlap.

Wells, Rev. Charles Wesley

1902   *A Frontier Life*. Cincinnati, Ohio: Jennings and Pye.

Weltfish, Gene

1965   *The Lost Universe: Pawnee Life and Culture*. Lincoln: University of
Nebraska Press.

White, Richard

1983   *The Roots of Dependency: Subsistence, Environment, and Social
Change among the Choctaws, Pawnees, and Navajos*. Lincoln:
University of Nebraska Press.

Wilcox, Ella Wheeler

1896   "The Farmer's Wife." *Nebraska Farmer* 20:424.

Wilder, Laura Ingalls

1932   *Little House in the Big Woods*. Tibaron, Calif.: Cadmus.

1933   *Farmer Boy*. Tibaron, Calif.: Cadmus.

1935   *Little House on the Prairie*. New York: Harper and Row.

1937   *On the Banks of Plum Creek*. Tibaron, Calif.: Cadmus.

1939   *By the Shores of Silver Lake*. Tibaron, Calif.: Cadmus.

1940   *The Long Winter*. New York: Harper and Row.

1941   *Little Town on the Prairie*. New York: Harper and Row.

1971   *The First Four Years*. New York: Harper and Row.

1988a   "My Work." In *A Little House Sampler*, edited by William T.
[1937?]   Anderson, 176–80. Lincoln: University of Nebraska Press.

1988b   "Speech at J. L. Hudson Department Store, Detroit." In *A Little*
[1937]   *House Sampler*, edited by William T. Anderson, 216–24. Lincoln:
          University of Nebraska Press.

Winther, Sophus

1976   *Take All to Nebraska*. Lincoln: University of Nebraska Press.
[1936]

1979   *Mortgage Your Heart*. New York: Arno Press.
[1937]

Worster, Donald

1979   *Dust Bowl: The Southern Plains in the 1930s*. New York: Oxford
          University Press.

Wright, Carroll D., comp.

1900   *History and Growth of the United States Census*. Prepared for the
          Senate Committee on the Census. Washington, D.C.: Government
          Printing Office.

Wyman, Katharine

√ 1909   "Inspiring Examples of Rural Uplift." *Good Housekeeping* 48:289–
          93.

Yanagisako, Sylvia Junko

1985   *Transforming the Past: Tradition and Kinship among Japanese*
          Americans. Stanford, Calif.: Stanford University Press.

√ Zaretsky, Eli

1986   "Rethinking the Welfare State: Dependence, Economic
          Individualism and the Family." In *Family, Economy and State: The*
          Social Reproduction Process under Capitalism, edited by James
          Dickinson and Bob Russell, 85–109. London: Croom Helm.

INDEX